W9-AHR-596

Yugoslavia

The New Class in Crisis

About the Author

Until his defection to the West in 1961, Nenad D. Popovic was a Minister Plenipotentiary in the Yugoslav Ministry of Foreign Affairs and, prior to that, an executive director of the International Monetary Fund (1950–52). As vice-governor of Yugoslavia's National Bank, he participated in and planned negotiations and consultations on international finance, foreign aid, trade, investments, and loans.

From 1956 to 1960 the author was a representative to the General Agreement on Tariffs and Trade, and during the same period was assistant state secretary in the Yugoslav Ministry for Foreign Trade. In the 1950's he represented his country at the International Chamber of Commerce in Paris, the UN Economic Commission for Europe, and the UN Economic and Social Council, both in Geneva. In 1955 he was appointed by UN Secretary-General Dag Hammarskjold to the Scheyven Group on the International Development Association.

Popovic is presently Visiting Professor, Maxwell Graduate School of Citizenship and Public Affairs, Syracuse University.

Yugoslavia
The New Class in Crisis

Nenad D. Popovic

SYRACUSE UNIVERSITY PRESS

FIRST EDITION

Library of Congress Catalog Card No.: 68-26995

Manufactured in the United States of America

To My Friend

Huntington Harris

Acknowledgments

Now, as this book is published, I pay due homage to those invaluable friends who made my work possible, who helped, encouraged, and assisted me with their advice, guidance, and good words. My primary debt is to Rita and Tom Beale, who substituted their *protocolaire* courtesy of diplomats with the profound sincerity of dear friends. Without their moral support this manuscript, which encompasses my thirty years of experience with communism, could never have been written.

I wish also to offer tribute to the memory of my kind friend, the late Elim O'Shaughnessy, whose sophisticated but superbly human understanding meant much to me.

Huntington Harris, to whom this book is dedicated, extended decisive assistance patiently, quietly, and sincerely. Inspiring, impartial, generous, tactful, and above all modest, he sets for me the example of noble achievement.

My friend, the late Professor Albert George, a colleague at Syracuse University, read the first drafts of the manuscript, and he invested his interest, friendship, and love into my work.

It would be an important omission if I failed to emphasize the fact that the Yugoslav newspapers were every bit as helpful to my work as their editors or rather publishers would have liked them not to be. The same is true of those prominent Yugoslavs who, in their present capacities as politicians or theorists, enabled me to use their statements, thoughts, and writings, though perhaps not exactly in the way and sense they were intended.

Finally, primarily, the person whom I feel is as involved in this book as I am: my wife Tatyana. Interested, motivated, informed, experienced, tempered in our past common sufferings, reasonable, uninhibited in her frank criticism, she was always both taxing my patience and improving the manuscript. When readers find anything in the book that remains inconclusive, they may be sure that it is because I succeeded in having my own way.

Foreword

In this turbulent world of contending political ideologies, one cannot escape the fact that one-third of mankind lives under the dictatorship of communism. Whether that status is voluntary or the result of coercion, the global dimensions of communism remain a stark reality. It is a fact, moreover, that one of the basic Marxist-Leninist objectives is a world system of communism, and that Communist efforts to establish that system in the present century have been characterized by impatience and aggression.

Given these conditions, Yugoslavia is a good illustration of the processes and adaptations of Marxism that evolve within and between all Communist countries and parties. This book takes the stand that Yugoslavia, rather than separating itself from the world Communist movement, as many well-wishers believed, has in fact developed an internal power shift from the body of the Communist Party to its exclusive realm, the nucleus of Party command.

Although that process has been spontaneous and in some ways unique to Yugoslavia, it is closely related to the natural tendency of a Communist or any totalitarian regime to develop and preserve its power at any price; in so doing, Yugoslavia's regime has created a "new class" in direct opposition to the tenets of orthodox Marxism which deny the possibility of the evolution of classes in socialism. Marxist ideology, which sees history as a dialectic—the inevitability of the class struggle and its ultimate resolution in a dictatorship of the proletariat—asserts that only communism can ultimately create a classless society. At the outset, a hierarchical power structure in Communist countries facilitates the management of the Party and the ruling of the state; later, however, structural control becomes concentrated in a relatively small number of people who in many respects acquire the earmarks of a distinct social class.

Milovan Djilas, a former vice-prime minister of Yugoslavia, exposed this phenomenon in his book, *The New Class,* published in 1957. Although the term *new class* has been popular only since Djilas, it was used by Nikolai Bukharin in a public speech delivered in Leningrad in 1923. It was Georgi Valentinovich Plekhanov, Lenin's mentor and one of the first Communist theoreticians, who analyzed the new class, using the term *socialist caste,* as long ago as 1883. Although three quarters of a century later the concept that a Communist society could develop separate classes was still rejected resolutely by Party ideologists, Djilas' discovery dealt a crushing blow to Communist theory. For this reason, Djilas was stripped of his rank and imprisoned in 1957. He was conditionally released in 1967.

Even though history has not yet given it a definite name and it differs in form and substance from all previous classes, the new class is now so firmly entrenched in Yugoslavia that it warrants a comprehensive study. In tracing the genesis of the new class, I have reviewed the appropriation of the spoils of war and "temporary" privileges by the Yugoslav Partisan victors. From these seemingly harmless beginnings—the age-old practice of victorious armies—there was a slow but persistent accrual of power by one specific group and a blurring of national objectives which resulted in the strengthening of that particular stratum of society. The postwar confusion and disruption, plus the pressure of Stalin after 1948, provided the basis for the consolidation of power by Tito and collaborating Party leaders around him.

Although the maintenance of a controlled power base would seem to be a unifying element, the Yugoslav new class cannot allow its power to become diluted in large-scale relegations of responsibility. The fact of new-class power is no less real because of the difficulty in defining it; it manifests itself in many ways. Those who established Yugoslav communism in the name of equality achieved a ruling status which actually sustains inequality. This means that every member of the new class would point to another member as being equal within their own ranks. But the general deviations from proclaimed Marxist ideals, along with the specific adaptations peculiar to the Yugoslav Communist Party, continually force the new class to maneuver for better positions. On the one hand it takes in new personnel, who are needed for pervasive control, and on the other hand it constantly purges those who resist or fail to participate satisfactorily. As it regroups its ranks, Yugoslavia's new class forestalls the attempts of middle- and lower-echelon Party bureaucrats who, in imitation of those at the top, try to preserve power in their own increasingly restricted spheres of influence.

Thus the new class is a study in contradictions and paradoxes which are difficult to unravel. There is no doubting the existence of this ruling elite, but because of Party idiosyncrasies and the opinion of other Communist regimes, it does not yet dare come out into the open and identify itself officially. The new class tries, therefore, to blend itself into Yugoslav society which also, apart from the Party, is shaken with conflict and change.

Presented here against such a background is a view of Yugoslav foreign policy, the principal aim of which is to protect the new class in a world setting. Following the discussion of foreign relations is a breakdown of the internal, administrative, and political reorganizations which are geared to reinforce domestic political security. The next chapter describes the economic theory of "Yugoslav socialism" and its terminology, and Marx's formula is used to show the *de facto* existence of the exploiting class. Similarly, I have used the speeches and writings of Yugoslav Marxist theoreticians who have designed dialectical and materialistic models to justify contemporary Yugoslav reality but have failed to recognize the conclusions which are pointed out in the present study. My analyses required interpretations based on Marxist logic—not to affirm the reasoning, but to confront the new class with its own ideological and theoretical criteria. In the last chapters I have not attempted a comprehensive analysis of the Yugoslav economic crisis but have endeavored, rather, to show how the new class seeks to subordinate economic laws to its needs, thus pushing the national economy into successively deeper crises.

Under the social conditions which the new class has helped to create in Yugoslavia, there is not much freedom for dissent there today, notwithstanding the apparent trend toward liberalization after 1948. The economic crises of the sixties, in addition, demonstrate that the regime is incapable of achieving concrete economic and social gains. In other words, the present or indicated developments in Yugoslavia do not justify an expectation that the Communist system could go so far in its liberalization as to democratize itself in an internal evolution.

Only the future can reveal the patterns of development of this unique new class and communism. So far Tito has shown definite evidence of efforts to create a means whereby the regrouped Party, controlled by the new class, should resolve the issue of succession of its future chief. In this respect Tito's recent maneuvers are remarkable in discouraging and even eliminating any potential dictator—after himself. That is the reason why, in March of 1967, the vice-presidency of Yugoslavia—held by Alexandar Rankovic, the official No. 2 man and automatic heir to Tito's supreme power—was abolished. The treatment of both Djilas and Rankovic, however, has compromised the regime both at home and abroad, the former by exposing the undemocratic character of the regime and the latter by fanning internal nationalistic and intra-Party frictions.

The consequences of the two moves—exposure and conflict—were the price paid by Tito for a pool of new-class leaders from which a collective rule could one day be formed.

From all appearances the regime of Yugoslavia's new class represents both a process of maturation and a definite phase in the "negating of communism itself," as Marx might have phrased it. Simply stated, the system, in its dialectical transformations, unavoidably develops those forces that will eventually bury both the new class and communism.

Nenad D. Popovic

Syracuse, New York
December, 1967

Contents

Introduction, Karl L. Rankin xiii

1 *Metamorphosis of a Dictatorship* 1

2 *Characteristics of the New Class* 13

3 *Mentality of the New Class* 41

4 *The New Class and the Communist Party* 61

5 *Foreign Relations* 91

6 *Administrative Structure* 111

7 *Yugoslav Economics* 135

8 *Background to the Crisis* 149

9 *A New Economic Reform* 169

10 *The Golden Coach* 193

Appendix 215

- A. *Selected Biographical Notes* 215
- B. *Statistical Notes* 218

Notes 221

Bibliography 233

Index 235

Tables

1 *Changes in Yugoslav Counties and Communities* 131

2 *Counties and Communities in Serbia* 131

3 *Comparisons of Yugoslav Production* 156

4 *Average Earnings, August, 1964* 164

5 *Geographic Distribution of Wages and Per Capita Income, 1964–65* 165

Introduction

Nenad Dushan Popovic is uniquely qualified to analyze the postwar political and economic history of his native Yugoslavia. Already in the 1930's, he occupied a position in banking, and after 1945 he held official posts of increasing importance at home and abroad—as executive director of the International Monetary Fund's Executive Board and as alternate executive director of the World Bank. During my service as American Ambassador to Yugoslavia, from 1958 to 1961, Popovic occupied a position approximately equivalent to Assistant Secretary of Commerce. He then became Minister Plenipotentiary in the Foreign Office, with duties which took him to various parts of the world to negotiate economic agreements. In the latter part of 1961, he and his wife determined to make their home in the United States, and now, after seven years of mature reflection and study, he has given us this book about his native country.

Complete objectivity is impossible for anyone who has been so intimately involved in Yugoslavia's postwar history as Nenad Popovic. Moreover, I cannot confirm from personal experience many of the developments which he describes. But from acquaintance with him in Belgrade, and from other observation during that period and my two earlier tours of duty in Yugoslavia (1940–41 and briefly in 1945), I believe that he has written an honest book, critical but without rancor.

The author traces the metamorphosis of the Yugoslav Communist regime from a patriotic resistance movement against the Nazi invaders in 1941, to a copy of Stalinism after liberation in 1945, and subsequently to rule by a self-perpetuating "new class." Throughout, however, socialism or communism (the terms are used more or less interchangeably in Yugoslavia, although the former is heard more often) remained first an instrument to maintain the power of the ruling regime, and only secondarily a socio-economic system. Probably this was unavoidable. Communism as developed to date is undoubtedly the most effective vehicle of power ever devised. Yet no Communist regime, once in power, has ever ventured to tolerate either an organized and substantial political opposition or any meaningful competition by free enterprise with socialized economic operations.

Monopoly, therefore, remains the keystone of the Communist structure, and the palliatives of decentralization have not been permitted to weaken ultimate control at the top. A political monopoly is maintained by the ruling group to insure against undermining or overthrow by an organized opposition. This is accomplished by well-established methods dating back to the Communist takeover in Russia half a century ago. Only the details have been refined. Economic monopoly has undergone a more complex development, but in essentials the present system in Yugoslavia is that envisaged by Marx and Lenin. Private capital is effectively nonexistent. A majority of the population are dependent on the state for their livelihood, while the remainder exist on sufferance.

Probably the most significant feature of Popovic's book is his detailed analysis of Yugoslavia's ruling "new class." He credits President Tito with its conception early in the postwar years, and its subsequent development into a group large enough to fill the key positions in all fields yet small enough to be controlled by the inner circle around the President. Leaving aside anyone willing to lead a Spartan and strictly nonpolitical existence as an "intellectual," technician ("expert"), or peasant, only membership in the new class offers opportunity for the ambitious. While political reliability doubtless is the first qualification for selection and preferment, ability and personality are by no means neglected in the personnel system of the ruling elite. Abroad, Yugoslavia is represented by a diplomatic service which compares with the best. At home, important posts generally are filled by able men. That the country runs as well as it does is a tribute to their ability; without the albatross of communism around their necks, they could do far better.

The author describes the continuing efforts of the regime to make itself more acceptable to the Yugoslav public without relinquishing ultimate control. The new "delegate" system in elections gives the voter some choice among officially approved candidates without the risk of electing an undesirable. Ostensible decentralization of government among the country's six republics or states, with their five or more nationalities, does not prevent reserving final decisions of importance for Belgrade. "Self-management" of economic enterprises by workers' councils has evolved into a vehicle calculated to keep the workers' representatives largely absorbed with trivia, and perhaps available as whipping boys when something goes wrong. Effective control is exercised by behind-the-scenes selection of managers and by the manipulation of taxes, credit, and foreign trade. The degree of freedom permitted in quoting prices to consumers and the amount of net profit which may be shared by the workers are also judiciously influenced from above.

The author's remarks on Yugoslavia's foreign relations illustrate the complete consistency of Communist policy with materialistic philosophy. Except by occasional coincidence, a Communist state does not take a position based on the intrinsic merits of an international question, but purely on the supposed advantage to itself. Also with a materialistic approach, a statement of purpose accompanying the position normally has little relation to the true motivation. The latter may involve such considerations as a private quid pro quo, or no more than an opportunity to curry favor with another Communist state and to embarrass the West. Such conduct is common enough among other countries, of course, but only the Communists appear to have established it as doctrine.

Popovic has written a book which contributes importantly to our understanding of the internal workings of a Communist state. He deals specifically with Yugoslavia, but what he says also applies in large if varying degree to the Communist world as a whole. Moreover, Western influences probably are stronger in Yugoslavia than elsewhere in Eastern Europe. Evolution can be somewhat more rapid in consequence, and may give us a preview of developments in other countries. There is also the personality of Tito. However one may disagree with his policies and actions, the author of the present book and the rest of us will agree that Tito is unique. The people of Yugoslavia do not love him, but he is widely respected for his ability, courage, and astuteness.

The author suggests that hope for the future lies largely with the intellectuals. Probably so; the human resources of Yugoslavia are very great. Given time, the intelligent and industrious people of that country will surmount the troubles which war and communism have brought upon them.

Karl L. Rankin

Athens, Greece
December, 1967

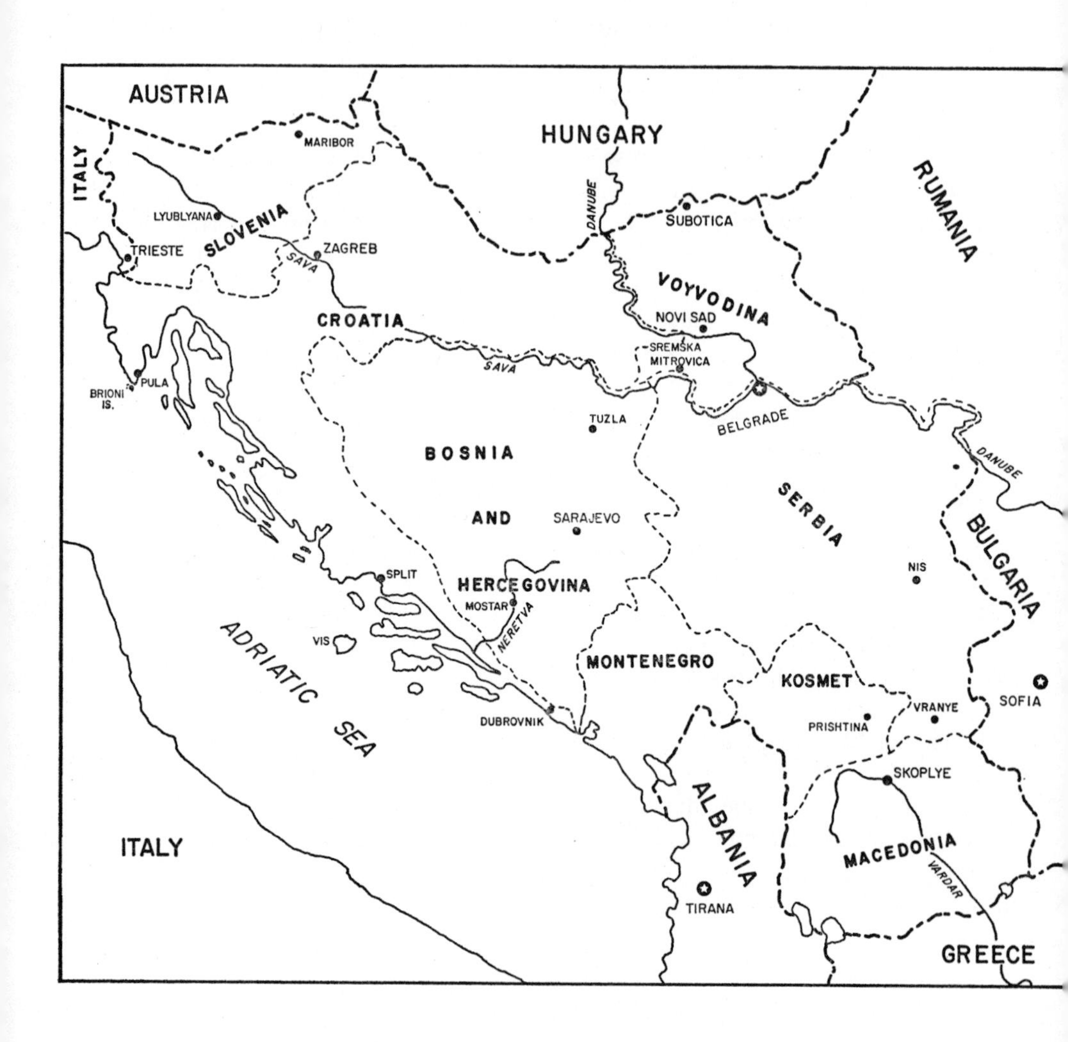

SOCIALIST FEDERAL REPUBLIC OF YUGOSLAVIA

1 *Metamorphosis of a Dictatorship*

To understand the evolution of the new class, one must look to the Communist revolution in Yugoslavia after World War II. This war, a weird one for Yugoslavia, was fought not only against Nazi Germany, a strong and aggressive power intent on annihilating the very substance of the Yugoslav nations, and against Fascist Italy, a country with territorial aspirations. Not merely a war of national liberation and many-cornered civil struggle between Communists and Nationalists, as well as among embittered Yugoslav nationalities, it was interwoven simultaneously with inflamed mutual religious crusades of Moslems, Roman Catholics, and members of Eastern Orthodoxy. Also inherent in these conflicts was a social revolution in which those stricken by poverty asserted themselves successfully against those holding wealth. The war reflected the bitterness of people who had suffered for centuries. Victory was expected. It was welcomed partly as justice and partly as revenge for accumulated humiliations, and the enemy was seen as a villain to be deprived of all rights when defeated.

The victors—mostly peasants and some workers and intellectuals—had promised prosperity, freedom, and happiness to all. The only condition was that socialism had to be achieved first. The war brought sweeping moral, material, and political victory to the Communist Party of Yugoslavia, but as the Party received the accolades of the populace, it sought a firm grip on the power structure. The victorious Partisans, with few exceptions well-tested Communists, asserted their authority and distributed the war booty.

History has shown that acquiring booty is easier than dividing it. In Yugoslavia, to add to the problem, there were more people who wished to share than there was loot to divide; furthermore, the destruction of war was so extensive, the injustices and losses so great, and the misery and poverty so ubiquitous that all the usual criteria of compensation were irrelevant. It was decided to honor the victors. They already controlled the spoils of war, and because of their distinguished war records they were the rightful claimants. The desires of the Communist Party, whose ranks were filled with Partisan victors, were decisive in the division of booty. In fact one might describe the size and value of allocations as being in direct proportion to the individual's activities and position in the Party. This was unassailable logic because every war right (and Yugoslavs have warred for centuries), moral right, suffering, and contribution to victory only justified the claims of the Communists for preferential treatment.

The spoils of war consisted in large part of the offices of the former rulers, but there was also the question of properties. A huge expropriation of capitalists, landowners, and all those who cooperated with either the Yugoslav or Partisan enemy was carried out. Collaborators deprived of their civil rights were imprisoned or even executed. According to a legal theory created for the occasion, even when the owner had not cooperated with the enemy of his own volition, e.g., the enemy had imprisoned him and had used the property or factory, the property was nevertheless confiscated. While general capital, such as plants and banks, was nationalized, personal possessions and commodities for individual use, such as shops, apartments, or furniture were given to those in the echelons of power. Positions of command, naturally, were held by Party members, functionaries, and Communist collaborators. Material expropriations were understandable, especially after the hardships of war, but the division of spoils soon proved to be a compromise of the Party's moral integrity. An elaborate system of privileges gradually developed among the favored, with the utilization of privileges growing, in time, to proportions so far exceeding the limits of modesty and justifiability that no one in the Party dreamed of denying himself convenient privileges. It was felt in the circles of the new regime that, after all, the entire population had profited greatly too.

Namely, the Yugoslav people had obtained peace and victory and achieved basic republican political goals; a federal structure had been established in a multinational state, and for the most part the minimum food needs of the population had somehow been met. Wartime inflation had wiped out old debts, thus pleasing the peasantry who had labored under excessive burdens before the war. Since a thorough agrarian reform meant the complete abolition of large private landholdings, many poor and landless peasants gratefully approved of this measure. A mass relocation of peasants from overpopulated, underdeveloped, and war-ravaged areas to wealthy northeastern Yugoslavia was undertaken successfully.

As a result of wartime destruction in urban areas, housing was scarce;

thus the freezing of rents at prewar levels pleased the city dwellers. Measures were enacted to prevent inordinate rises in the price of basic commodities, and staples were made available to consumers in quantities which, if not abundant, were at least sufficient for survival. A dwelling, or rather a space under a roof, was guaranteed, as were bread, sugar, and lard. The roughly $500 million in commodities provided by the United States and distributed by the United Nations Relief and Rehabilitation Agency helped greatly to meet the needs of mass consumers. It is true that these achievements were sufficient to sustain the minimum needs of the population, but they did not create a climate conducive to self-denial on the part of the new rulers—although the new rulers themselves had fought the war mindful of the ideals of equality.

The key positions in Yugoslavia's postwar ruling bureaucracy were staffed by former Partisan warriors, who, it should be remembered, were primarily Communists who had received the lion's share of the spoils of war. Taking power slowly but resolutely, the Party finally encompassed every aspect of the life of the Yugoslav citizen. The period between 1945 and 1948 marked the growth and strengthening of the Party and was the first phase in the metamorphosis of that dictatorship in which the Party members and apparatus formed a power monopoly—their own adaptation of Marxism, but still a monopoly. Yet, the fact of the matter was that Party cadres, particularly those at the top, had managed prematurely to seize a piece of the Communist cornucopia promised to one and all. In the meantime the privileged groups understood that there would be shortages in Yugoslavia indefinitely because of indigenous political and economic difficulties and increasing pressures from Stalin to join the Soviet satellites. The ruling Yugoslav Communist functionaries did not want to relinquish their independence to Stalin or their privileges to the people, but the need to reduce spending was of vital importance. The normal course of rescinding privileges was considered too radical a move. Rather, a reappraisal was needed, not to eliminate privileges but to reduce them by determining which persons should be eligible for them.

Early privileges were clear cut and relatively minor: Should a disabled war veteran stand in a packed streetcar while a healthy young man sat down? Should the veteran use the rear entrance of a trolley or bus along with the crowd, or could he enter through the front door, usually reserved only for exit, to avoid inconvenience? Should the worker awarded the title "Socialist Shock Worker" or "Hero of Socialist Work" be permitted to go to the movies? Certainly! But how could the man cope with restive youngsters besieging a ticket office? He ought simply to be given the privilege of walking past the waiting line straight to the window.

These and similar rationalizations helped settle such questions and others of a slightly different nature. If foreign diplomats in Yugoslavia could buy what they needed without standing in lines, why should high Yugoslav officials not be similarly privileged? Then, if one official had been given certain privileges, why not another? If someone in Belgrade could profit, then too should his counterpart in Zagreb. Obviously, too many could have wormed their way into the lists of the privileged or tried to attain a higher privilege level than that to which they were entitled. For example, a person who had lost ministerial rank might still continue to patronize a ministerial level "special shop." It was difficult to secure an objective solution to this problem since it could be solved only by clearly indicating the difference between those in the leadership ranks and those who did not belong there. Thus the defining structures of an emerging elite group can be seen. The members of this group, however, were of particular importance to Tito for two reasons: Tito was moving Yugoslavia out from under the heavy hand of Soviet communism, but he was also in the process of consolidating his personal dictatorship.

A Communist pattern already established in the Soviet Union repeated itself in part in Yugoslavia. Although Tito's role was very important during the Party dictatorship, it was definitely set within certain bounds. At that time (1945–53) he was not even formally the head of the state but functioned as the commander in chief of the armed forces and secretary general of the Party. It is true that Tito governed the Party, but he was also dependent on it. Much as the collective rule of Lenin's Bolsheviks became Stalin's personal dictatorship, Tito's personal dictatorship supplanted that of the Party, as a consequence of the internal development of the Party control which was unable to avoid the progressive concentration of power, culminating in the supreme rule of a single person. Stalin's pressure on Yugoslavia—a stimulus from abroad—tightened the ranks around Tito even more. One must note, however, that during these transformations Tito's power was not only essentially Communist but was exercised with an even greater intensity.

Sincere in its commitment to Leninism, the Party emulated every move of the Soviet Union with adoration, admiration, and slavish dedication. The Yugoslav pupil applied himself so assiduously that he caught up with his teacher. Although the natures of Yugoslav and Soviet communism were strikingly similar, differences of opinion regarding their respective roles of authority in world communism made a head-on Soviet-Yugoslav collision unavoidable. This collision occurred in 1948. The Cominform and the Soviet Union accused Tito of being hostile to the U.S.S.R., of deviating from the Communist program, of being a militaristic and nationalistic dictator, and of suppressing criticism by terroristic means.

At the beginning of the conflict, the Party leadership in Belgrade considered the 1948 encounter a deep tragedy of misunderstandings and injustices. Speaking at the Tenth Belgrade Party conference on April 19, 1967, Tito said, "This was at once the gravest and at the same time the most unjust attack on our Party."[1] Attempts at reconciliation with the Soviet Union continued for nearly a year, but failed.

Those Party members who had vacillated or sided with Stalin were weeded out without ceremony. Excessive bloodshedding was not deemed necessary, but any individual thought traitorous was unsurreptitiously eliminated. Thus Arsa Yovanovic, at the time chief of the general staff of the Yugoslav armed forces, was killed on the Rumanian border when he tried to defect to the Russians. Although the rank-and-file cadres had withstood the purge of the Party, they were nevertheless under suspicion as potential sympathizers of the Soviet Union. Consequently, the Yugoslav Party had to be reshaped from its very roots. A portion of the cadre was to be reeducated, the rest was to be replaced. This also meant that the Party was rejuvenated with young men and women who had not yet been exposed to foreign, albeit Communist, influences. In the interim before a "new" Party could be created the "old" Party was to be sterilized.*

Changes were effected by Tito and a relatively small number of top Party members, mainly war-hardened and closely allied people. Even before the Stalinist conflict this nucleus had a firm hold on all key Party and state positions, including the two essential instruments of power—the secret police (including all security organs) and the armed forces. The members composing that group, with Tito at their head, never intended to relinquish their power position; indeed the organization of power, a preliminary of which was the Party purge, finally established Tito's personal dictatorship as the second stage in the metamorphosis of power.

In contrast to the Soviet Union, where during Stalin's dictatorship the influence of the Communist Party apparatus was balanced by the political police, state hierarchy, and armed forces, the Yugoslav situation called for supplementing and partly replacing the Party apparatus with a new force. In resisting Stalin, Tito relied upon Party collaborators and the population as a whole, but his personal power could not survive without an adequate social and institutional character and resource. The paradox is that the dictatorship of one man, in the long run, seems unsound and unreliable from the point of view of the dictator himself. Consequently, a loyal, compact, and united social unit had first to be

* According to official data in 1964, the total number of Party members was 1,030,041; of them, only 268,127, or about 26 per cent, were enrolled in the Party before 1948.

established as the backbone of that power; secondly, specific institutions designed to implement that power had to be created. The dictatorship, already in full control by 1949, was not based on the supremacy of a mere clique (as, for example, a military junta might assume at least nominal control of a government apparatus). Rather than the figurehead of a superstructure, the dictatorship held complete power. It was Tito's power which radiated through and permeated Yugoslav life in its entirety. For this reason his personal dictatorship could not limit itself to such individual administrative tools as the police, the armed forces, or the bureaucracy of state since each of these instruments would tend inherently to become independent and exclusive of Tito and certainly would create new receptacles of power. Both Tito and his cohorts recognized this threat to their nearly autonomous holds on power, and they labeled the threat a "bureaucratic deviation within socialism."

On the other hand, while Tito needed the support of the people until his dictatorship became stable, under no condition was there to be a sharing of power with the people. Such a move, in effect, would have introduced democratic elements which by evolution or revolution would eventually change the dictatorship into a democracy. This possibility had to be suppressed as a threat to the power monopoly. It, too, was immediately recognized as a danger and carefully labeled the "reactionary bourgeois" distortion.

Faced with the dilemma of retaining and further strengthening absolute authority, and concomitantly providing that authority with a specific and recognizable social identity, Tito set out on a definite course. He intensified the Communist nature of his dictatorship by condensing power within a smaller area rather than allowing it to remain as the vague dictatorship of the proletariat or within the broad Communist Party apparatus. That area was composed specifically of those associates who shared power with Tito and who are known today as the new class.

That such a new class was created first in Yugoslavia was the result of particular conditions, one of which was the confrontation between Stalin and Tito in 1948. Favorable circumstances did not then exist in the Soviet Union or in other Communist lands for the shaping of ruling elites into new classes. Thus Yugoslavia set a precedent in developing new patterns of authority and class structure that are becoming peculiar to communism. Today when one encounters certain phenomena in other Communist lands, phenomena already noted in Yugoslavia, one should remember that this is due less to imitation than to similar and parallel developments which have come about after a certain time lag.

Since 1948, especially between 1949 and 1952, the Party nucleus has faced the task of making changes and reforms, drastic if need be, to reinforce its position. This political problem was complicated by a number of specific economic and social conditions; namely, the weakening of the Party's apparatus called for compensatory political support through greater reliance on the broad masses who, though non-Communist at that time, still were not yet anti-Communist. On the other hand, cohesiveness with the nucleus of control required that ancillary organs, such as the secret police and the army, be strengthened. The Party remained the most suitable instrument available for this purpose, since it was essentially a generalized version of the new class and was imbued with the same ideology and social theory. In other words, it was convenient for the new class to nestle in the hierarchy of the Party, comprising both its summit and core, the quintessence of the Communist Party of Yugoslavia.

The initial design of the new class resembled a pyramid with Tito at the pinnacle; below were those who held power, stratified in accordance with their degree of actual participation in the rule; further down, finally, were those subordinated to that power. The top group surrounding Tito rules because its members are reliable and personally involved, not solely on the basis of their Party affiliation or position. In other words, function no longer defines one's position; instead, one's position in the new class determines one's function in society. It was of paramount importance to belong to that social group which, as far as outsiders were concerned, was exclusive, closely knit, harmonious, and compact. Marx and Engels had defined a social class in much the same manner:

> . . . the community into which the individuals of a class entered, and which was determined by their common interest against a third party, was always a community to which these individuals belonged only as average individuals, only insofar as they lived within the conditions of existence of their class—a relationship in which they participated not as individuals, but as members of a class.[2]

Still, the sudden emergence of the new class in Yugoslavia was more than even dialecticians, normally accustomed to many surprises and somersaults, had bargained for. Now there appeared in fact a superclass, right in the middle of a political system and ideology which proclaimed the lofty goal of abolishing all classes forever. Such a social phenomenon had never before existed, since intrinsically it contains not one but a whole set of characteristics over and above those of the earlier exploiting classes, particularly as defined by Marx. Indeed, the existence of the new class supports those very notions challenged by Marxist theory and unmasks the myth that Communist rule leads to a "classless" society in which everyone will be free with every need satisfied. Ironically, a new form of class society has been established: rather than a society in which slaves, serfs, or capital is owned, there is now a class which owns nothing but takes what it wants because it controls power in a social structure.

If one continued the analysis from a Marxist standpoint, one could aver that the metamorphosis of the Communist dictatorship in Yugoslavia was a significant breakthrough affecting the entire structure of modern communism's eschatological dialectics: Although the dictatorship of the new class means that the Communist Party has rationalized its rule in changing conditions and cemented its hold on Yugoslavia, it also means that the existence of that new class has prompted another chain of developments leading ultimately, by the same dialectical logic, to the rejection and overthrow of both the new class and communism.

The new class was not created by any complex strategy. Instead, it resulted from the interaction of the dialectical forces of society which indeed do bring about change when conditions are ripe and when that society is directed by strong men with workable social schemes. Yet, though the coming of the new class was spontaneous, it was in no way chaotic. At its beginning the new social group remained fully within the structure of a militantly disciplined Leninist party whose authority emanated from one center. The change in the dictatorship, in fact, was the process by which a personal, autocratic, and Communist regime assumed the concrete structure of a smaller, stronger, reconstructed, and somewhat modified Party based on and run by the trustworthy new class with its materialistic interests. In this manner the Communist system had reached a new—Lenin perhaps would have called it higher—stage of development by overcoming dialectical contradictions. Instead of a potentially unbalanced personal dictatorship supported by a bureaucracy, a united leadership based on Tito's authority had been established, and the Party had come under the control of a relatively small social group.

Just as Marx pointed to the best interests of the proletariat in the fight against capitalism, so Tito founded the new class as the social group with the deepest vested interests in support of the power which he had seized. With reference to the consolidation of power by a smaller group, Lenin said, "The movement must be led by the smallest possible number of the most homogeneous group."[3] A thesis, the Communist Party, and its antithesis, a personal dictatorship, had found a dialectical synthesis in the new class. In this way, the Yugoslav new class effectively fused a structure of political power within a social context. Analyzed from a Marxist viewpoint, one might assert that this solution was both possible, since Tito and the Party were not mutually antagonistic, and necessary, since it was useful to the further promotion of the power monopoly.

This synthesis followed an internal logic inherent to Communist regimes and now represents a significant rationalization of the social and political, even of the economic, mechanism of Communist rule in Yugoslavia. There is no doubt that the Yugoslav regime profited by change. It weathered two political storms—Stalin in the late forties and Djilas in the early fifties—and emerged stronger after each one. However, the Communist revolution in Yugoslavia (1941–45) was unable to solve social, political, and economic contradictions because it was a vehicle of the Party to maintain control. Similarly, the present regime is unable to attain the social and economic goals of socialism because it is foremost a tool for maintaining and expanding the power of the ruling class. While the revolution was the weapon of the Party to assume control, the Yugoslav Party now is the means by which the new class retains power.

The evolution of the new class was complex and obscure, but two men were clearly involved in its beginnings. One of them, Tito, actually created it, while the other, Milovan Djilas, discovered it. Neither man played his role by chance. Tito maneuvered to strengthen his power and concurrently assert his command of the new class. Nor did Djilas stumble across the new class accidentally, since when he defended the Communist Party of Yugoslavia against Stalin in 1949, he was also defending the ideals of his youth. For though Djilas might not have known what he would encounter in the Party when he joined it before the war, he certainly knew what he sought there. His experiences were probably filled with questions, vacillations, doubts, and dialectical clashes. Surely he was disappointed by much of what he witnessed and in many with whom he labored, but Djilas, it seems, had also been convinced that the results would more than justify the losses, the price paid, and the bitterness suffered. It was only when he was forced to focus his doubts on Stalin and the Soviet Party, and then on communism itself, that he had to balance the weight of the sacrifices against the elusive achievements of the Communist system.

Tito fought the "old" Yugoslav Party because he saw Stalin's supporters arrayed within it against him. As the purge of the Party gradually formed an essentially new organism—with the new class as its center—Tito's alignment with the "new" party increased. Djilas, however, steadily and more resolutely concluded that the very principles of the Party, as well as its nascent new class, were both immoral and dangerous. Despite their differences in motives and ultimate goals, Tito and Djilas used identical terminology at the time, and the immediate targets of their attacks were the same. Concerning the Party's course, Tito and Djilas appeared as allies in more than words, and they apparently cooperated effectively, perhaps cordially. Although it cannot be determined how far-reaching was Tito's conception of the organizational structure of the emerging new class, there appears to be no question that at the time he fully appreciated its place and role within the Yugoslav Communist Party machinery.

In their respective positions, Tito and Djilas seemed to be moving in parallel directions; there existed, for instance, an apparent identity between Tito's and Djilas' approaches to the issue of whether the workings of the Party should be overt or covert. Djilas fought secrecy because he wanted to expose the activities of the Party functionaries who were protected by the conspiratorial cloak of the organization. Even more, Djilas wanted the Party to be an institution subject to public approval or censure. For Djilas, a policy of openness meant the first move in the evolution of democracy—or the unmasking of the Party's totalitarianism. Tito, on the other hand, agreed to the Party's uncovering but for opposite reasons. With deep concern Tito recognized the decreasing importance of conspiratorial work which had been so essential in the days of the Party's prewar illegality and during the revolution, and which was so useful just after the war when the new state was organized. Moreover, Tito resented Stalin's derisive remarks that the Yugoslav Party was unpopular and afraid to face the people. Tito also realized that it was technically impractical to keep secret a growing organization whose membership would come to embrace more than 5 per cent of the total Yugoslav population. He faced a dialectical puzzle: How could he condense power while expanding his influence, and hide while moving into the spotlight?

Tito solved the problem brought about by an enlarged Party membership by depriving the rank and file of the chance to make decisions, thus strengthening the authority of the Party apparatus. These deprivations, among others, were accomplished by transforming the cell meetings into open formal public gatherings, deftly led by functionaries (secretaries of cells and committees). Actual decision making became the responsibility of the upper echelon so that effective authority within the Party was narrowed to a controlling core now recognized as the new class. Similarly, it was the "surfacing" of the Party which enabled the new class to submerge itself, hiding not only from the average man but also from the Party's rank-and-file members. In both operations, manifested outwardly in the transformation of the Party into a public organization, the Party as a whole began to lose its earlier sovereign grip on power, eventually becoming a useful but hardly contrite instrument of the new class.

The events which followed the changes enacted at the Party's Sixth Congress (Zagreb, November, 1952) indicated the imminent birth of the new class. In January, 1953, another state constitution was established. Under this constitution Tito was elected president of the republic in addition to his functions of prime minister, commander in chief of the armed forces, and secretary general of the Communist Party. Thus all power was concentrated in Tito. His position was further enhanced when Stalin died in March, 1953. That summer the Central Committee met at Tito's resort on the Brioni Islands to reaffirm "democratic centralism"* as the fundamental principle of the Party. This reaffirmation revealed a decisive shift of intra-Party power to that commanding corps which became the new class. In light of this decision the tack taken by Djilas to expose the group appeared incomprehensible because he was still chief Party ideologist and propaganda head. His high position lent authority to his pronouncements and partially explains the confusion which took place in Yugoslavia during the autumn of 1953. In general, people assumed that Djilas was acting with the blessings of Tito and his colleagues. Djilas' fiery words made the broad Party membership feel that great changes were coming in the direction of liberalization. Tito secluded himself on the Brioni Islands (from there visiting India), and Vice-Prime Ministers Kardelj and Rankovic became taciturn and noncommittal. Such a silence could have signaled a gathering storm or the Party's disintegration. This situation lasted until the end of December, 1953, when the newspaper *Borba,* then the Party's official political organ, started to print a new and more violent series of Djilas' attacks on the Party. Nothing happened, though at that time Party life was relatively free. It appeared, in fact, that Yugoslavia had simply to take a small, perhaps only formal, step to become a democracy. No one guessed, and only a few feared, that contrary decisions had just been made.

The whole matter exploded in public early in January, 1954, when Djilas published a short story entitled "The Anatomy of a Moral," which concerned the refusal of new-class society to accept the bride, a former actress, of a high official, who was also a known Party leader. The implications of the story were clear, and the new class, still without a name, faceless, and outwardly formless, reacted quickly and decisively. The Central Committee immediately convened into full extraordinary session, and the agenda's very wording on the official notification made

* Democratic centralism means that lower-echelon members of the Party elect functionaries who must then unconditionally carry out the directives of higher Party divisions and functionaries. The democratic election of functionaries is actually bypassed by having the lower organs and members vote only for candidates nominated officially from above. Or in other words, while elective procedures are pure formality, the backbone of democratic centralism is obedience to higher ranks of the Party.

it clear there was nothing to be decided, only Djilas' guilt to be made public. The Central Committee members were forced to prove their loyalty to something that lacked definition but was nonetheless real. They showered condemnations and insults on Djilas, and all proclaimed unity with, and above all their loyalty to, Tito. No one knew exactly what that unity was all about until Djilas described it later in his book *The New Class,* which was published in New York in 1957.

At the beginning of 1954 Yugoslavia's new class existed in fact. It is true that it hardly knew its own name, had little idea in what direction it was moving, and had no conception of how it was going to develop. Nor did the new class know what it was, who comprised its membership, or what positions the members held. Still in its infancy, it cautiously followed Tito's lead. During this period Tito was essential to the new class, and Tito, in turn, needed that group as the foundation and backbone of his dictatorship. This was the great dialectical synthesis of which Marx and Engels had spoke:

> . . . every class which is struggling for mastery . . . must first conquer for itself political power in order to represent its interest, in turn, as the general interest.[4]

2 Characteristics of the New Class

Nature

Individuals belonging to the new class have various and even mutually conflicting interests. Nevertheless, each is dependent on the group as a whole in order to achieve his respective degree of authority. As Marx explained it, "Separate individuals form a class only insofar as they have to carry on a common battle . . . otherwise they are on hostile terms with each other as competitors."[1] Although united by common goals and enemies, new-class members differ in that some are deeply committed to the new class, others less deeply committed. All, however, are frightened of losing whatever authority they possess.

As the power of the new class grew stronger, members of the elite stressed common participation in the war and the revolution, all the while becoming more aware of their mutual interdependence and interests, and since they were concerned with one objective, persons in the new class formed a monolithic unity of unequals. Eduard Kardelj conceptualized the objective in an interview with *Nova Makedoniya* in 1965: "Unity is untenable if it is an aim in itself. Unity will constitute a real force only if it becomes a function of genuinely common needs and interests."[2]

This curious mixture of identity and inequality is completely natural to the new class because each member thinks of himself in terms of a hierarchic relationship to his supervisors and subordinates. One could view such an individual as a sunflower: One side, which always faces the most important person present, is sunny and radiates joy and devotion; in contrast, the other side is directed toward persons of lower rank. This side is not quite unfriendly, but it is somehow aloof and remote from the person of lower position. Members of the new class fully appreciate the fact that their strength lies not just among themselves but in a monolithic structure under Tito. While unity under their leader is that of obedience, cohesion among themselves is the determination to maintain power. The maintenance of power, of course, calls for a fusion of organizations, ideals, actions, and conduct.

Yugoslavia's new class had cautiously adopted Party unity in ideology and organization and had no need, therefore, to establish specialized new structures or organs which already existed in the state and Party administration. According to its needs and desires, the elite can manipulate both the Party and state, a clear revelation of the undemocratic nature of its authority. Manipulation is essentially the molding of the organs of government so that the elite can devise for itself an adequate state-political form. This continually exposes Yugoslavia to waves of reorganization and reform, while the ruling elite seeks more suitable public images and nesting places. Thus, since the new class avoids becoming an officially separate political body, it must create the mechanisms necessary for political action—one of these was an organ of information telling members exactly what they can or cannot do. If new-class members do not behave properly, they soon become casualties; simple obedience to Party and state directives means respecting the new class itself. In this manner the new class marshals the tools and methods for executing its plans. On the one hand its laws are identical to those of the state, and whoever breaks them is criminally responsible; on the other hand the Party is also a projection of the new class, and whoever violates Party discipline becomes politically responsible. In obedience to state laws and Party directives a citizen serves the new class and perpetuates it throughout society.

But Communist discipline is not just obedience. The wording of relevant Party directives is usually vague, and one must do more than read an instruction in order to carry it out. More important is that kind of Party discipline which calls for the "creative" implementation of directives. The new class refuses to accept passive obedience even from the mass of non-Party members. For example, though one can vote only for officially approved candidates, every citizen is expected to vote of his own free will, and to be in a festive mood while doing so. In Yugoslavia one votes in his Sunday clothes, and as flags pass by and music plays, children decorate the voters with flowers—not necessarily red after the liberalization of political life—congratulate them on the "happy occasion," and wish them a pleasant holiday.

Members of the new class, too, are expected to fulfill directives with total dedication and commitment of their own creative abilities. This suggests that the elite must be able to command the highest kind of conformity, which is more complicated and sophisticated than stiff, compulsory discipline. This does not mean that discipline is not necessary, rather that mere discipline does not suffice. Coercion is used only when all other methods have failed. In fact, the use of force in political situations is regarded by the upper echelons as a sign of inefficiency or negligence in having allowed matters to develop so far that force is unavoidable.

Conformity, therefore, is based on more than the unity of authority, goals, and Yugoslav Marxist ideology. In addition, one must consider emulation, a sensitive political "nose," and very often good luck. It is generally safe to imitate higher-level persons, and as one moves up in the ranks of the new class the probability of mistakes diminishes; to avoid errors, however, one learns whose example to follow. Perhaps the new class could rule itself informally, but in such rule it must stay relatively small, compact, and, above all, continually united. Power, the strongest rallying point for unity, is raised far above everything else, and no personal, national, international, or other consideration can be allowed to crack the monolithic structure of the identity of interests.

The manipulation of power was the main consideration in the establishment and evolution of the new class. Those in leadership positions were well aware of the enormous possibilities offered by their rank: Power was the magic potion that could change poverty to wealth, failure to success, crime to virtue, and ignorance to brilliance. The point was not only to acquire political advantage—that was done by the revolution and the dictatorship of the Party—but to create a system for exercising political advantage in a way that would benefit a particular social group. Bolshevik functionaries after the Russian Revolution of 1917 had also commanded immense power, but no new class of the Yugoslav type appeared in the Soviet Union because power remained concentrated within the Bolshevik Party. Only when power was channeled systematically through institutions for a well-defined social group did the new class emerge in Yugoslavia.

The first great Yugoslav political and economic reorganization of 1949–53, just prior to the Djilas affair, completed the process by which Party and state functionaries surrounding Tito were transformed into a distinct social group. Although its cardinal asset was its proximity to authority, the group was characterized by its flexibility in breaking away from old social ties and loyalties and shaping itself into a distinct new entity. Its members severed ties with peasant relatives, old friends with whom they had played on the streets of industrial suburbs, and colleagues from schools and universities, and formed a separate social organism. Although not yet fully aware of the change in themselves, Milovan Djilas told them of it. Some of the more erudite could recall that Marx had already analyzed the whole process of change in detail and defined it as *Verbuergerlichung,* or *embourgeoisement,* which can be translated into English as "becoming bourgeois."

During the process of becoming bourgeois, the recipients of privileges responded to criticism with varying degrees of sensitivity. In the summer of 1948, the Belgrade weekly *Literary News* printed an article critical of "ministers' stores," restricted hotels and beaches, exclusive summer resorts, and the like. The official reaction was mildly in favor of the new class, claiming that the criticism was correct in principle, but pointing out that such criticism could be used by the enemies of socialism to unjustifiably embarrass those who contributed the most in the creation of the "new Yugoslavia." As a result, only a few stores were closed, and those that remained open operated with great discretion.

In January of 1954, however, when Djilas attacked the conduct of the new class in his story[3] which did not even mention the important material privileges (as did the article of 1948), he was instantly removed from high office. The new class indeed existed and reacted vigorously, but it was still not prepared to admit publicly its own existence. This fact was the first significant political defeat of the new class and revealed its two main characteristics—conspiratorial nature and conservative spirit.

In the same way that the Communist Party of Yugoslavia hid from the law and public eye as a conspiracy before the war, so today the new class has mottled its identity within the Union of Yugoslav Communists.[4] It is hard, therefore, for outsiders to discuss the new class, while members neither want nor dare to say anything. The new class considers itself secure in its authority and privileges if it remains well camouflaged.* Nevertheless, as the group becomes increasingly noticeable, comments concerning it are based more on facts than on guesswork. Projecting itself as a political, social, and economic force upon the whole of Yugoslav society, the new class cannot avoid self-exposure, especially because of its growth, which has been so rapid that it must be channeled in an efficient system. Disregarding public reaction, the new class spares no effort to organize its instruments of authority thoroughly—be they the Party, the army, the police, or other areas of society and cultural life in general.

Its complex social group is smaller than that of the Communist Party,

* "But every exploiting class, whatever its achievements, has always to find some way of *disguising* its real position and aims, both from itself and from the exploited, and of making out that its rule is just and permanent." C. M. Cornforth, *Materialism and the Dialectical Method* (New York, 1960), p. 10.

but it permeates the country effectively through control of political, economic, and social institutions. It is easy to delineate the new class by studying its top echelon; it is more difficult, however, to examine the middle, lower, and provincial sections because of constant ferment in the peripheral regions where recruits are always being added or discarded. The center of the federal administration of the group is Belgrade, with branches in the diplomatic, security, and military posts in Yugoslavia and abroad; provincial organizations convene mainly in the capitals of the republics, and local levels are found in the county and community seats.

Owing to its conspiratorial nature, it is often difficult to state the exact difference between actual members of the new class and those who serve national or new-class interests. For instance, armed and security forces, almost separate defense organisms, are as much a part of the new class as they are its obedient and efficient instruments. A detached category, the armed forces are organized basically like other armies, but military leaders form an integral part of the new class. Military personnel are better paid than corresponding personnel in civilian service (for example, at the end of 1966, when one policy of the economic reform was frozen wages, salaries of army personnel were lineally increased by 10.7 per cent[5]), and they also enjoy certain material privileges which are not great enough to categorize them within the structure of the new class but are sufficient to create the belief that there is no difference between the defense of the fatherland and the defense of its regime.

The administrative organization of the police presents a somewhat different problem. Like the armed forces, the police (and all related security personnel) comprise a closed and privileged circle of the various service branches permeated and controlled by high-level secret police. Although not identical with the new class, members of the secret police make up one of the most important instruments of its authority. At the outset of the new regime the secret police often seemed to embody rather than channel dictatorial authority, and such an allocation of power only aroused the suspicion and enmity of the new class. The problem was solved in 1967 by full subordination of the secret police to the new class, thus avoiding, too, a power struggle.

Yet, the time has long passed when the emergence of the new class could be ignored or emphatically denied. Notwithstanding the strenuous efforts of the regime to keep Djilas' book under the cloak of oblivion, the Yugoslav people have heard its message—a battle cry to which its leaders, willy nilly, had to react. The regime took the ingenious course of telling the public that a certain new class does indeed exist, but it disclaimed any connection with it. To establish a foolproof alibi, in 1967 the new class applied Djilas' concept of a new class to Yugoslavia's state and Party bureaucracy. In other words, the group sought to hide its identity by shifting attention to another "new class." This maneuver of Tito's frightened elite was confirmed by Vladimir Bakaric, a prominent new-class leader, in his address to the Zagreb, Croatia, garrison, as reported in *Politika,* November 5, 1967, "*We have new classes*—bureaucracy and direct producers. As you know, Djilas arrived at this conclusion when he wrote the book, *The New Class,** quasi in accordance with Marx's concept of social contradictions. They have changed: the contradiction between the working class and the *bourgeoisie* has turned now into the contradiction between democracy and the new-class bureaucracy."

Going along with the wave of popular resentment against itself, the new class did not even think about changing its basic attitudes, much less giving up its right to rule. It has only changed the direction of its attacks, constructing a paper effigy in order to burn publicly the "new class of bureaucracy."

Thus disguise is one of the essential qualities of the conduct of the new class. Internal affairs are never discussed publicly and are mentioned in private only with the greatest caution. Silence is preferred as a tacit principle in itself since it is not politically advisable to discuss even everyday routine. This caution has its roots in the conspiratorial practices of earlier underground life when any detail carelessly revealed could have had unhealthy consequences. There are still many high-level Yugoslav officials who prefer to be called by an odd nickname rather than their own. They do not like to see their names and addresses in the telephone book and stare angrily at their secretaries if they are asked where they can be reached if urgently needed. One official who never permitted his secretary to enter his office or to call him on the intercom, unless for something very urgent, would sneak out through another exit. She would sit for hours assuming that he was in his office, daring neither to leave nor to call. Then, too, since widespread poverty in Yugoslavia makes people sensitive to the fact that material privileges are enjoyed by others, the new class knows that the ostentatious use of privilege, or mere public talk of it, could do more damage to the political stability of the regime than well-organized counterrevolutionary propaganda.

All members of the elite are vaguely included in the common designation "comrade." This form of address was earlier used only for members of the Party who in this manner expressed their allegiance to a common

* Even now in Yugoslavia it is a crime to possess this book, heretical to read it, and dangerous to mention it.

ideology and political movement. From its original sense of belonging to the Party, then of sharing wartime combat and sacrifices, the term gradually came to mean something else. It appears outwardly as a formal, even officially necessary, mode of address. In another sense *comrade* refers to nationals of other Communist countries, or members of the Yugoslav or any other Communist Party. Finally, in its narrowest meaning, *comrade* indicates someone belonging to the ruling elite, but in this case the word is pronounced with a particular intonation, as if in capital letters.

Those constantly in touch with the new class, however, have of necessity developed their own vocabulary. When a chauffeur wants to point out that someone belongs to the new class, he refers to such a member as "comrade," in a lower voice, or will simply say "high official," or even "very high official." The new class apparently does not wish these conversational habits to become ingrained; official propaganda and even pressure is brought to bear on everyone to use *comrade* as the general form of address. The most interesting title for this top group comes from the peasants, who call the new class simply *them.* This word, however has a broader meaning which includes the Party and all who serve the Communist regime. Consequently, when the peasants want to specify the new class they speak of the "new masters" (*nova gospoda*).

In extraordinary cases, when the new class does want to impress people, it refers to its members as the "best sons and daughters of our nation," "distinguished Partisans," "old socialist fighters," "revolutionaries," "humanitarians," or simply, "patriots."

Only two decades old, the new class is still dynamic, in continual evolution toward a more rational form, organization, and scope of influence. Its development is in full swing, progressing by flexible adaptations to given situations, searching for optimum solutions, and trying to examine all possibilities without dogmatic prejudices. Communist theory is not essential as a guide or reason for the existence of the elite, but it does justify power politics to the masses. Although young, the new class has already been corrupted by its power objective—the accumulation of material and political favors—by its exploitative nature, and by its methods based on the principle that the end justifies the means.

As already seen, the origin and existence of this group are closely connected with sharp internal contradictions within communism. In keeping with dialectical Marxist thinking, the revolutionary qualities of communism have been transformed into reactionary practices with the main purpose of preserving power. Created in violence and international conflict, the new class remains revolutionary and militant in behavior but grows conservative in spirit. This paradox is easily explained by the fact that the new aristocracy is a condensation of those Communist elements which preserve themselves unconditionally and destroy anyone who opposes them, and since the new class exploits all other social groups in Yugoslavia, it is increasingly set both intuitively and consciously against any change in the present relationships among classes.

Much more polishing must be done, however, before the new class attains full stature. It must be institutionalized; it must determine the criteria of membership; it must fortify its political power mechanism; and, finally, it must solve the questions of replacement and rejuvenation. While initiating unavoidable changes, the new class must also adjust to deep transformations in Yugoslav society. Consequently, even though the new class grows increasingly conservative in its goals, it must use revolutionary methods for continued development. In contrast to the old classes, the new one does not dare consider the complacent tranquility of maturity.

But from the point of view of the new class there is no apparent paradox in the relationship of its conservative spirit and revolutionary methods; there is only a shifting of the objectives of the "revolution." The first goal of the revolution was to acquire and organize power, and later the goal was to change Yugoslavia's political, economic, and social system; now, however, the goal of the new class is to dominate the minds of the people in order to condition them to its permanent rule. In this way the present Yugoslav system cannot avoid dehumanizing both those in its own ranks and the average citizen.

PRACTICES

Before considering the criteria for admission into the inner ring, several factors which determine ineligibility must be recognized. Among those excluded from the new class are capitalists, the *bourgeoisie* (occasional exceptions), wartime collaborators, postwar emigrants, defectors, Yugoslav Germans, White Russians, and persons condemned by postwar courts for political offences. Also excluded are all who, even if they are the firmest of Communists, have at any time insulted, slighted, overtly doubted, or opposed Tito. Finally, those who attend church, mosque, or synagogue, as well as those not registered as members of the Socialist Alliance,[6] are excluded.

Requisites for admission to the new class are less objective than the grounds for exclusion, but they are more numerous. Of first priority is membership in the Party, now called the Union of Yugoslav Communists, which formally indicates that one does not belong to any of the ineligible groups. Party membership does not automatically qualify one for participation in the new class, however, because each case must be investigated anew for admission, promotion, and advancement. The red tape is less cumbersome for Party members, since they are constantly investigated, but no one's reliability is assumed in the Party, and there are never two people of equal rank.

Dependent upon fluctuating and often imperceptible political variations, members are also formally differentiated according to their "Party service," or seniority. Those members of long service theoretically and practically have priority, all other conditions being equal. Short service has validity only for a young person; for an older person a short term of service means disqualification from the new class—Why did he not become a member of the Party earlier? Higher priority goes to those whose membership antedates 1948, in other words, to those who survived the purges after the struggle with Stalin. Anyone who became a party member before 1945, the time of the Communist takeover in Yugoslavia, is not in as good favor as one who joined before September 9, 1943, when Italy surrendered and a Partisan victory seemed almost certain. The most favored of all are those who were Party members before the end of 1941, when the outcome of the revolutionary struggle was highly uncertain. Great respect is also shown to persons who became members around 1937, when Tito took control of the Party. There is an ambivalent attitude, however, toward Party membership which predates 1937: if the person had always been unconditionally loyal to Tito, membership in the Party was symbolic of the highest rank in the new class, but the period before 1937 is so confusing to new-class ideologists that Party members who joined at that time are somewhat suspect and at a disadvantage. Distinctions listed here for Party members can apply to nonmembers who effectively supported the Partisans, but this rarely happens; the few exceptions merely confirm the rule that the new class recruits members exclusively from the Party. In other words, just as the Socialist Alliance offers a wide circle or an antechamber to the Party, so the Party constitutes a wide circle or reservoir from which the new class is replenished.

It was stated earlier that function does not define position, but his new-class position does determine a man's function. Acceptance into the group is not a formal act, as is becoming a member of the Party; rather, one first gains admittance by promotion to a high position earmarked for members of the elite. A person appointed to such a job may not realize that he has actually changed status until he suddenly finds himself surrounded by completely different colleagues. Then privileges—the tangible proof of acceptance—are promptly made accessible to him. Such privileges do not come all at once, and they are not always the same for each new member. Incredibly complex gradations and nuances of participation in the ranks of the elite are created by the allocation of privileges, a practice with which the neophyte member of the new class soon becomes acquainted.

Experience reveals that it is possible to join the group on a temporary basis. Thus, for instance, every ambassadorial position automatically includes a high-ranking member of the new class. Minor ambassadors, as well as subordinate officials, return to former echelons when they are transferred back to Belgrade, where they can advance only as their over-all status in the new class improves. But experience also demonstrates that some remain safely in the new class regardless of position or function, if any. Those holding power in the nucleus surrounding Tito keep their status primarily because of their relationship to Tito or to a few very important leaders.

One indication of new-class membership is the award, *Partisan Memorial of 1941,* and even better, the *National Hero* medal, both of which carry a series of privileges. The *Memorial of 1941* apparently, but not actually, has the objective of recognizing one who joined the Partisans before the end of 1941 and participated in the war. The number of those awarded the *Memorial of 1941* became too great as the qualifications expanded. Was it necessary, for instance, to have been a Partisan in public, or was conspiratorial work sufficient? Both grounds were eventually accepted. Some have been awarded the *Memorial of 1941* though they were not in Yugoslavia during the entire war but worked, for example, for the Communist Party in the United States or Canada.

Tito personally awards the *National Hero* medal, and in this instance the top leadership of the new class is not dependent on any objective criteria. In contrast to the *Memorial of 1941,* no one may request the *National Hero.* Award of the *National Hero* is thus a convenient formal ceremony for new-class initiation or advance in position. National Heroes are not considered ordinary people[7] but are called "the best sons of our nation." In addition to the diploma and medal, worn suspended around the neck on a silk ribbon, National Heroes have many other rights. Like those for the *Memorial of 1941,* these rights are not systematized but were instituted by many special decrees and regulations. Benefits include a cash payment each month; thirty days of paid vacation,[8] regardless of work rank; special facilities in medical services;

retirement advantages and benefits; reduced prices at summer and winter resorts; convalescent homes; hotels, etc. All privileges are valid until death, when the government pays for the funeral—including military music and the burial salute of a military detachment.

As stated in *Politika,* March 2, 1965, a National Hero has the right to "free travel twice a year on railroads, ships (first class), buses, and airplanes twice a year; authorized passage at 75 per cent discount of the regular fare for an unlimited number of trips by railroad, ship, and bus; and a payment in cash of 12,000 dinars each year." Further, members of the family (wife, children, and parents) of a National Hero who dies, or was posthumously awarded the medal, receive a grant of 12,000 dinars each year. After the inflationary crisis of 1965–66, the payments were presumably increased.

Although Yugoslavia has a voluminous and detailed system of awards and medals—forty-one different groups[9]—it is interesting to note that these decorations are presented after entry into the new class, whereas anyone already in the new class almost automatically receives decorations corresponding to his position. Besides the normal but subtle signposts of new-class membership, advancement also comes discreetly because the group is not a formal institution. The issue of institutionalized rank arose from a nascent conflict within the new class, the choice between right and might. Members of the group subconsciously tend to deny the authority of their superiors when they feel manipulated, though upper-echelon authority is the very essence of the power scheme. The trend to create vested rights grows stronger as the new class becomes more openly settled as a social entity.

One could view the new class as a circle of old fighters. Though compact, it is steadily shrinking through attrition—deaths, political casualties, and defections—thereby becoming smaller. This is partially true because the processes of concentration and condensation of political power which created the new class simultaneously reduced the number of its members; yet the complexities of growth require a constant infusion of fresh blood. The leading cadres that participated in the war and the revolution have not been renewed on a large scale, and the new class remained basically the same. If the elite wanted to protect the interests of each of its members, the existing standards of individual admission would suffice. But the fact is that the new class is aware of itself primarily in terms of the pervasiveness of its power; when old members consider a new candidate, their major concern is their own narrow and personal interests. Each feels that the group should continue as the locus of power, but each also wants his children included in the group. Formerly, no attention was given to emotional matters in discussions of power, and thoughts of the family were viewed as mere sentiment. To secure a pleasant and easy life for children and to forgive them if they were unruly was thought earlier to be sufficient parental duty; children were not to be given authority, but today the new class finds itself in quest of a method whereby its children can be awarded the right to remain in the elite, though not necessarily with the same position as their parents. In this way children can be cared for and parental instincts satisfied. Dr. Radomir Lukic, professor of the Law School at Belgrade University, stated that "The high stratum tends to reproduce itself, as evidenced by the fact that a small percentage of officials' children become workers, and even fewer workers' children go to college."[10] The new class has not yet solved this problem, and there is no evidence that any attempt has actively been made to do so.

In practice, the problem of recruitment is resolved in a roundabout but nonetheless efficient manner. The essential condition for admission into the new class is reliability, and who could be more reliable than one's own children! Children are not yet a part of the new class, but they realize that their well-being and social status depend upon the perpetuation of the power elite. For this reason the family background of a candidate is a decisive condition in his acceptance or rejection. Although one born during or just after the war cannot submit evidence of war participation, he can point to a father who fought bravely. Since the main political upheavals occurred in 1948 (Stalin) and 1954 (Djilas), a boy could not have taken any political stand, but he could profit by the position taken by his father. Family background as a condition for admission has a somewhat synthetic character and tends to replace the numerous earlier prerequisites. Family status is restrictive because it limits the new recruits to a narrow group already objectively defined as the new class. This, of course, is exactly the point. Nevertheless, new-class parents often become concerned because their children, who can receive a good education, perhaps abroad, frequently become so enlightened that they begin to rebel against their fathers and communism in general, frequently motivated by the very ideals for which their fathers began a revolutionary struggle a generation ago.

Besides giving priority to young people from Partisan families,[11] new-class selections are actually made by fathers, uncles, in-laws, and intimate comrades. Naturally they favor their own children. For the present, the new class has chosen this method to perpetuate itself because the procedure is discreet, efficient, and flexible, yet eludes confirmation that it is anything but honest and open to everybody. In fact, new-class nepotism is imitated on all levels of Yugoslav society. The extent of its development in business, for example, can be seen from the caption of a cartoon published in 1967 which read, "My dear nephew, tell uncle-director and brother-in-law–secretary that our firm will open bids for a position for a cousin-bookkeeper."[12]

The problem of succession did not exist a few years ago, but in the not too-distant future it will inevitably become acute. Most children of the new class are still in school, just reaching college age. Their elders, however, are not yet tired of ruling and, in fact, will accept the inevitable change reluctantly, even from their own children.

Closely connected with the worries of succession are the problems of retirement and pensions. In the first postwar days, Yugoslav Communists thought that every pensioner was a potential enemy and in any case an expendable parasite. This attitude toward pensioners outside the new class has not changed—it is difficult to find a fate as miserable as that of the ordinary Yugoslav pensioner. But twenty years have passed since the war; young men are now middle-aged, and the middle-aged are old. Builders of the new class are approaching retirement age, allowing a change in viewpoints and modification of retirement laws for new-class members. Upon retirement, separate legal provisions are made for those "who made special contributions and tirelessly worked for the revolution."[13] For such people, retirement becomes something exalted and honorable, as well as remunerative, and deserves the highest and most elaborate ceremonies. According to Tito, retirement is only a new beginning: "In fact, there ought not to be a single retired office-bearer who is not a political activist."[14]

Although the new class seized power not by excellence in education or ethical integrity, but by political scheming—and luck—it has discovered that the complex task of organizing and running an entire society requires a certain kind of knowledge. A smattering of intellectuals and experts was insufficient to balance the great bulk of the new class who had only an elementary-school education. This group includes Tito and many around him; in the top echelon of the new class are several who attended college before the war, but few received degrees.

After the war, the desire for education became intensive and sincere in the ranks of Communists, but formal education was not in keeping with the dignity of those who ruled. After all, mature and distinguished men could not sit in schoolrooms on benches. Then, too, studies are time consuming, difficult, and, at that time, inadequate for immediate needs. This is why comrades soon sought more facile methods of learning and more practical course materials. For a while there mushroomed many "evening courses," "Partisan schools," and so on, which, if they did not impart vital knowledge, at least dispensed diplomas. But comrades who in the meantime formed the new class wanted practical experience, and they gradually lost interest in formal education in the belief that they could learn more on the job. So they introduced the method of rotating functions, chumming together, and traveling abroad. One example of the system of rotating functions is the following case. Rato Dugonyic was a political commissar during the war and became secretary general of Communist Youth on the federal level; then he was the coordinator of Local Business; for several years he was an ambassador (to Poland and the United Arab Republic); later he was "elected" chairman of the Socialist Alliance for Bosnia and Hercegovina; recently he was made chairman of the Assembly for Bosnia and Hercegovina, and finally, in 1967, he was promoted to the position of chairman of the Socialist Alliance of Yugoslavia. By rotating his function, Dugonyic gained more knowledge from a variety of practical experiences than would have been possible from a mere study of theory.

No one really dares become highly qualified in any area because it would label him an "expert." For new-class members there can be drawbacks from too much formal education. Cases are not rare in which successful comrades study assiduously in college but quit just before graduation so that they can remain without a diploma. The formal degree would place them among the experts, and that is exactly what they fear as a threat to their new-class position. If a member embarks on a serious course of study, he does so with the approval of the upper echelons, since the new class knows that it cannot rule with ignorance and that its cadres must be aware of changes in the political, economic, and social climates of their country and the world. The new class believes that its members, as politicians, should know as much as necessary for effective control. Otherwise they are rarely expected to work hard, and they hope to work even less in the future. Experts, however, form a different category of people who usually are not accepted into the new class—unless they are of outstanding ability or merit. An expert is dangerous in principle because in mastering his professional field he discovers that the objective logic of scientific reasoning is more effective than the subjective empiricism of the new class.

The initial tendency of the new class to educate and edify itself was, from its point of view, healthy and necessary. Throughout history other classes followed the same reasoning. The Yugoslav regime, however, reacted earlier than its predecessors against profound scientific objectivity, and thus the quality of its education tends to be superficial. The new class does not deliberately stand against learning; instead, it suspects the independent objectivity of scientific truth while at the same time firmly believing that it possesses another type of all-inclusive knowledge. Marxist theory, particularly of the dialectic, allows such self-confidence to develop. Almost any member of the elite comes to feel that his Marxist-dialectical-materialistic knowledge is in direct proportion to the height of his political position: the higher he stands, the more he is permitted to know. The opinion also prevails that Yugoslav Communists, i.e., the new class, capable of an expanded interpretation of Marx, Engels, and Lenin in their country, have achieved the highest level of applied Marxism. Concluding, therefore, that they automatically possess the right amount and kind of knowledge, those in the new class do not see any need for tiresome learning.

The analysis of Marxist theory is becoming the specialty of outstanding "ideologists," almost exclusively politicians, led by Milentiye Popovic and Eduard Kardelj. New-class and Party membership is slowly coming to identify knowledge with Marxism, transformed in practice into well-organized and slogan-ridden systems of prejudices.* This process parallels a facet of the transformation of the group's ideology and theory with the result that any possible vestiges of scholarship are degraded to serve as instruments of power. The new class does not see the point of becoming proficient in science and technology because it considers political acumen more important, seeing it as the final crystallization of ultimate, supreme knowledge which, in turn, makes possible the attainment of power. The new elite unequivocally seeks to be not creators or producers, but rather rulers and exploiters.

The essential function of Communist power is handling the people. For this purpose the new class utilizes personnel services—a broad range of agencies and channels from education, scholarships, studies abroad, transfers, and demotions, to full control over the people and their private lives (often, for example, deciding who is not allowed to marry or divorce whom). Nevertheless, the decision on the fundamental issue of who will or will not join the new class is, as has been shown, reserved for the leaders. Since the top echelon cannot always devote its complete attention to this question, a certain division of labor has evolved. While all leaders participate in making or modifying decisions, only a few are

* After the war in Yugoslavia, special Marxist political schools were compulsory for Communists; at present, such schools continue to exist not so much for the new class as for the secondary and specialized apparatus strata of the Party.

entrusted with the preparation and formulation of proposals or the implementation of final decisions. These men are *kadroviks*,[15] cadremen, or, in Serbo-Croatian, *personalci,* meaning "personnel men." Separate departments of the personnel service exist in the administration, the Party, the Army, business bureaus, sciences, and elsewhere. They are nominally headed by the Federal Authority for Personnel Affairs, but all agencies are actually a part of and administered by the Cadre Department of the Party's Central Committee. Personnel services affect all citizens, but those in the new class, as well as those with functions of any consequence, receive special treatment and investigation.

Personnel departments have complete information on all individuals; everyone admitted to the Party must submit his autobiography, which is considered more acceptable if it contains a report in the nature of a confession that can be used against him later, if necessary. Personnel services gather all pertinent information on each person from his superiors, subordinates, peers, the police—data which may consist of gossip, references, exhibits, evaluations, opinions, recommendations, accusations, denunciations, and newspaper clippings. Information accumulated in each file must present a brief, up-to-date but comprehensive picture of each individual. The central organization of the personnel service maintains a unity of function, which was embodied for fifteen years in the one man (Veljko Zekovic) who held the key position in personnel matters both in the government and the Party. Similar fusion of government and Party personnel services exists on corresponding federal, republic, and local levels, as well as in businesses and all other basic institutions of society.

Officials in the personnel services have enormous control over the people. Their main function is to implement all personnel decisions, i.e., entry into and movement within the new class, and to manipulate the career of each individual. Thus the department became a bastion of supreme authority, equaling and increasingly overshadowing the secret police, which also falls within the network of personnel services. Personnel men evaluate people, adding, subtracting, or substituting just that bit of decisive information necessary for the purpose of the moment. Thus friends of *kadroviks* and those with mutual interests can be rated highly and be recommended for new positions; on the other hand those who suffer may never find out why, how, or because of whom their fate changed.

So long as the personnel services functioned as an apparatus which prepared materials for decisions, it existed only as an instrument of its chiefs. The situation changed, however, when the new class emerged after 1953 and strengthened the authority of that department. The paradoxical feature of the whole matter was that the authority of personnel services became stronger and more influential at exactly that time when they were publicly denounced as inefficient and unnecessary; they were even formally disbanded. Actually, the personnel service moved underground, becoming secret and subject to no control but that of its chiefs.

As a separate part of the new class, the personnel service supports and even leads those forces which want that group to became internally institutionalized. Some want as soon as possible to introduce a more objective new-class status which would help solve the question of entry, advancement, and coordination of membership, so that exclusion would be less arbitrary. These tendencies are inevitable in the still-young new class in which present vested interests seek to become formal vested rights.

The protocol division of the personnel services performs a most important and delicate function for the new class. The original scope of protocol's duty was purely formal: it merely certified a man's rank, which was decided elsewhere, so that he could assume his assigned role. Earlier, members of the elite would be seated at a dinner in proper order or led to the group to which they belonged at a reception, but the original technical duties of protocol evolved and changed, creating a specific "palace etiquette" and also establishing the rank of everyone but a few at the top to whom no rules apply. Protocol, for instance, is responsible for organizing state receptions, held at the President's White Palace, which are a current review of the new class where one can see who is in favor among the several hundred of the elite. Upon entering the White Palace, one is conducted by protocol officials to the particular salon or seat at table denoting one's rank.

A protocol service is now found in separate organizations of all government branches from the federal to the local level. In this way it long ago ceased to be a mere function of diplomatic procedure and became, instead, a factor which regulates relations within the new class. Protocol, together with and as a part of the personnel services, represents an influential complex of authority on which the entire new class structure depends. Exact knowledge of the status of an individual in the elite is known to the personnel services but displayed by the protocol division. Many in the new class do not know where they stand since the rank list changes daily—belonging to the elite actually brings constant anxiety, rather like speculation on the stock market. Protocol will answer his hopes or confirm his suspicions by inviting him to or excluding him from activities of different levels of importance. The sign of highest favor is a private dinner with the President, an honor reserved for a very restricted circle, but one could also be asked to go hunting with him or be invited to an important reception. The seat assigned by protocol at table or the place allotted at a theater opening night attended by Tito are important clues to the rank of members of the new class.

As protocol informs an individual of his advancements, it also signals his fall from favor; oddly, however, protocol rarely announces exclusion from the new class. If the exclusion is without political overtones, the man simply does not receive any more invitations. He does not notice that invitations have stopped coming because those who do receive invitations are silent about them, and afterwards he finds out by chance and slowly realizes that he has outlived his usefulness.

If political implications are involved in the exclusion, then the secret police or other similar organs are concerned. The new class has succeeded, nevertheless, in avoiding discontent among the many persons who, for various reasons, are ejected from it. Exclusion is usually unexpected and final. A technique has been perfected whereby the fall from grace stops at a very low point from which, after a short time and by the mercy of the new class, a slight increase in status takes place. When the disgraced person is shown the seriousness of his mistake, he also learns that compassionate comrades might grant him a more lenient punishment. It is specifically pointed out that there are greater depths to which he will inevitably descend unless he can see his guilt completely and sincerely and gladly cooperate with comrades who wish to "heal" him. If he honestly atones and unreservedly rededicates himself to those in authority, his punishment may be lightened. The punished man, who usually knows all this, experiences a psychological reversal often employed now throughout Eastern Europe: He does not miss what was taken away as much as he appreciates those crumbs beneficently returned or later accorded to him.

The new class exploits society by an elaborate system of privileges. The word *privilege* is not exactly appropriate because, theoretically, no privileges exist in Yugoslavia. One speaks of functions, or rather of facilities, benefits, awards, and sometimes rights which are granted on merit. On the surface, a benefit appears only as the attribute of a work arrangement, but in other cases benefits are an expression of a separate and deserved recognition of excellence, perhaps in war or revolutionary work. At first glance the system of privileges gives the impression of objective simplicity, but in reality it is extremely complex and arbitrary.

Privileges do not depend on one's true merit but on the attitude of those who grant or merely tolerate them. Whoever wants to retain a privilege must constantly requalify for it every day and almost every hour. Consequently, new-class members use and dispense privileges in a hasty manner—a privilege that exists today may be gone tomorrow. There is never a pause in the struggle to obtain advantages. Members of the elite are caught up in a breakneck race to grasp the prize, which somehow eludes them as they draw near to it. When the race seems to be finished, it has only started anew under more difficult conditions. Even a a functionary of the regime who retires with high honors under "special rules" must still participate in public (political) life and consistently requalify himself.*

The situation is even worse for those with distinguished war and work records who never qualified for the new class. Sometimes such cases are corrected, but only at a politically opportune moment. For example, in 1964 the Yugoslav press reported the case of miner Edhem Shkoric,[16] whose photograph appeared repeatedly on the front pages of Yugoslav newspapers and was even printed in the textbooks prescribed for obligatory eight-year schools in 1949. Shkoric was declared a "shock worker" forty-five times; he had been awarded the "Medal of Work," first and second degree; he had received three laudatory commendations from the Mining Union; he had been awarded the "Commendation of Merit" of the National Committee of Yugoslav Unions; and he had received the *Oblast* (district) award on September 12, 1949. President Tito personally presented a pocket watch to Shkoric. From the Ministry of Internal Security he received a revolver with the inscription: "To Edhem Shkoric—a fighter for high work productivity." He was a Partisan during the war, and in January, 1947, was made a member of the Communist Party. He had never been punished by the Party. Shkoric was the president of the Mining Union Committee, vice-president of the mine's Board of Directors, several times a member of central and shop Workers' Councils, and furthermore was a member of the Republic Economic Council for Bosnia and Hercegovina. He was a member of the General Directorate for Coal, the Central Committee of the Yugoslav Council of Trade Unions, and the Tuzla Municipal Council of Producers; he was a director of Civil Defense Services. Shkoric was a Party member of many achievements, but in the end his record proved to be of little consequence since he never moved into the new class. In 1963 he injured his spine at work and was retired. In the middle of inflation he was given a pension of 20,800 dinars, 1,800 dinars in addition as an invalid, which made a month's total of 22,600 dinars, or, at the official rate of the

* Because of the inflation in Yugoslavia a pension will become fairly meaningless in a few years, and if the man fades from sight there will be no political necessity to help him.

time, $30.13. Only then did Shkoric protest, weeping at the editorial office of *Borba,* because he thought that he had more rights than the average worker. A public scandal arose. The matter was corrected when Shkoric received compensation of 1.2 million dinars and a higher pension, and social insurance assumed the expenses of his medical treatment.

As a matter of fact, even for those who are firmly entrenched in the new class there is always a lever (usually a privilege, personal information, and such) that can be used to coerce a member to be more active. Perhaps this should not be called blackmail, but the fact remains that each benefit can be withdrawn at any moment without notification or explanation. The decision to withdraw or increase benefits is made by a superior body; thus, as a person becomes more firmly established in the new class, his personal independence decreases.

Salaries for a given position are in no way commensurate with the other advantages afforded by that position. Salary is but the first rung of an intricate ladder of fringe benefits that make up the system of privileges. The entire scheme is so designed that one's function (position) may reflect one's rank in the new class, but there are many high-salaried and high-ranking employees in important positions who are barely on the periphery of the new class. Yet, salaries can have an important supplementary dimension in the case of those high officials who hold several functions concurrently. A man may be a member of the Cabinet (minister's salary), a member of the Central Committee (special salary), a member of the Parliament (salary and per diem), with additional functions in the Party, the Socialist Alliance, and elsewhere.

In addition to regular salaries, certain functions carry with them many separate rights, benefits, facilities, and discounts. Some are based on the letter of the law, but the majority, which "make matters easier," are found in an unusual twilight zone of legality.[17] Subterfuge is necessary because equality is the official principle on which the system is based, so any departure from it must be represented as compensation for past achievements or present function or else must be covert. Even if the law forbids an action, it is possible to find and tolerate a loophole, a convenient legal interpretation, or a legal technicality or simply to look the other way when certain persons are involved.

The official interpretation, in the early stages of Yugoslavia's privilege system, was that privileges did not exist or, so far as they did, were explained or justified as facilities and fringe benefits accompanying certain functions. But as the new class grew in strength, it increasingly dismantled the structure of state and Party bureaucracy, simultaneously eliminating and denouncing the privileges of the bureaucracy. Even more, as the new class appropriated privileges for itself, it actually separated them from functions and openly asked for a "systematic solution, instead of privileges."[18]

In the practice of self-management,* established in the early 1960's as the form by which the state and society is governed, the elite succeeded in dislodging bureaucratic competitors and in eliminating, by personnel rotation, the job permanency of functionaries. Yet, to retain its privileged position, the new class decided, though unwillingly, to regulate by federal laws[19] the status of "old revolutionaries who had dedicated their entire life to the struggle for the building of our country and socialist society."[20] It is not difficult to recognize the new class itself in this reference. Republics and other "social organizations" have also enacted their corresponding laws, by-laws, and regulations. In this way the new class has, in a somewhat roundabout manner, identified itself with the federal and republic levels at the top and the provincial levels at the bottom.

The rights established by these laws include that beneficiaries, i.e., members of the new class retain a "personal income" after their functions expire, although they have no real function. These rights are honored for periods ranging from one to six years. A one-year guaranteed personal income is foreseen for those with total employment (new-class seniority) of less than twelve years; for employment between twelve and twenty years the period is three years, while "old revolutionaries" with an employment record of longer than twenty years are entitled to a six-year guaranteed income.[21]

Notwithstanding the obvious advantages of an expanded privilege system, it was a hard decision for the new class to make. Evidence for this conclusion is found in the deliberately ambiguous wording used in legal documents and public explanations. To analyze the real meaning of these laws, one must study not only the texts of the laws but also the parliamentary minutes, uncoordinated statements, press reports, and above all, the practical implementation of such regulations.

The attitudes of the privileged have come full circle in the last twenty years. In 1967 the new class openly requested that "the responsibility of society *toward functionaries*"[22] be fixed, thus elevating privileges to the level of legal principles. Yet, in 1946, "shops for special provisions" were discreetly established to serve a select register of authorized,

* "Self-management," in new-class terminology, is a subtle propaganda phrase applied to nearly every area of Yugoslav life—the Party, business firms, economics, etc. It is used to create the illusion of autonomous decision-making, but in reality, it is a formal camouflage for the new class. Various "self-management" organs can be blamed for making their own mistakes, while the new class, behind the scenes, absolves itself of responsibility.

well-placed customers. The prices at first were considered "not overly high," but in reality they soon became very low, often only nominal. Some shops catered to ministers (federal or republic), others to diplomats, and still others to the military and the police. Privileged persons believed that these shops provided favorable and just compensation for the hardships of their positions, but it was not long before the average citizen's attitude toward them turned sour. In a time of scarcity, even staples or modest goods are considered luxuries. Because of popular unrest, officials ordered the shops camouflaged and their windows painted to mask the merchandise and hide the customers within.

Explanations put forth to justify these shops were apologetic and stressed their temporary nature; the government intended to abolish them as soon as there were no more shortages. But the shortages did not disappear, and the patrons of these shops increased. The number and variety of shops also grew; some had better, even luxurious, goods at reasonable and often very low prices; others had a narrower selection of goods. Association with such shops solved the important problem of material provisions and also indicated a man's specific standing within the ranks of the privileged. Association with a shop gradually became an indication of rank; shops became a status symbol of members of the new class. As special shops became less important, the symbols of status themselves changed. *Politika,* August 5, 1966, stated in a humorous report that military rank could be spotted easily by the number of stars on a man's uniform; civilian rank is determined by the number of medals acquired, bears killed, ceremonial ribbons cut, or the make and year of a man's car, or even, finally, how poor a man's parents were; but the latest distinction, after protests against the secret police in 1966, appeared as "how many microphones a man had planted in his house."

Privileges did not end with special shops. Allocation of dwellings was another example, because a housing shortage of incredible proportions existed in all cities of Yugoslavia, particularly at the key administrative centers of Belgrade, Zagreb, Lyublyana, Sarajevo, and Skoplye, the nesting places of the new class. One could hardly find a single room, not to speak of a whole apartment. But at the same time luxurious residences which had previously belonged to wealthy people were now available. These residences had survived the war largely intact, complete with furniture and even the personal belongings of the former owners, most of whom had left in haste or disappeared unexpectedly. If a functionary liked the residence of a private citizen, the owner would simply be evicted by a procedure which violated the law. There are examples that courts at all levels, including the Supreme Court of Yugoslavia, decreed several times in vain that an illegally occupied house be returned to its lawful owner. It should be kept in mind that it is not easy for a Yugoslav court to decide against anyone in or connected with the new class, the Party, or the state authority because the courts are considered just another political instrument in the class struggle.

Naturally only a small number of the top echelon of the new regime received the most desirable residences and apartments. To be granted such a dwelling clearly indicated that one stood on a high rung of the ladder of authority. Comrades nearest the top were given or allowed to build residences of an appropriate type—with a private park, playground, orchard, and recreation area. Maintenance costs of such buildings and often even current operating expenses were transferred in various ways to the government's Building Directorate of the Federal Executive Council.

At the height of the severe housing shortage, some members of the new class, however, could not restrain themselves. They extravagantly built new residences or had the existing ones rebuilt or renovated. Often when a remodeling job was finished, the comrade, rather his wife, would change his mind, move to another house, and thereby open a new series of remodeling.

The new class either could not accommodate its needs comfortably in the available housing space or simply needed more modern facilities. Consequently, the apartment question created discord within the ranks of the group itself. In addition, the general housing shortage became so acute that new-class residences and apartments could no longer be hidden from the despairing eyes of the average citizen. It was then clear that apartments were not only material benefits but also potential kegs of political dynamite. Thus, when the government, around 1959, decided to begin large-scale construction of apartments, easing the housing shortage, however, was not primarily geared to help the neediest. Instead, the government introduced a merit system which allows new-class members to take what they want almost unobserved and to reward those whose support is expected. In offices and other units for which housing is arranged, waiting lists of the neediest are compiled, but usually at the last moment "meritorious persons" are given priority. These persons are usually of the rank and file who had participated in the war for national liberation, and who currently happen to be in good political standing.

Extensive new housing projects have begun in all cities. Apartments are usually utilitarian, in modest but large blocks. Luxury apartments are assigned to specially selected persons, "leaders," whose earlier apartments pass on to their relatives, friends, or those next in line in the new class. The political decision regarding housing created an upsurge in employment and morale in Yugoslav towns whose appearance today is a great improvement over five years ago. The new construction programs satisfied an immediate need and also created a substantial rise in employment which was considered economically useful and politically advantageous. It also showed the world that Yugoslavia's growing cities were proof of a successful and sound socialist economic system.

While the shops were masked and dwellings hidden behind fences and hedgerows, some privileges like automobiles could not escape public notice. It seemed only natural that high officials should have state automobiles at their disposal. Besides, automobiles permitted the elite to flaunt its status symbols in public. Nobody could prevent the still-green new class from showing off, and cars served as an indication of rank—the type, make, year of manufacture, with or without chauffeur. The number of government automobiles—at first no private cars were tolerated at all in Communist Yugoslavia—"for personal use" increased yearly. As abuses grew, public opinion turned against the government and the Party, and "strict" measures were taken to limit the use of government automobiles. The leaders of the new class attempted to set a trend in the use of smaller, more modest cars, and anyway they had other limousines. Also, private ownership of cars was allowed. Since there are more private automobiles today, the use of government-owned cars is less conspicuous, but automobiles became an issue of public dissent every few years with crusades launched against those who were extravagant. Some members were censured, but the elite persistently uses and misuses expensive American and German cars, while those in the lower ranks must struggle along in various "official use only" car pools.

Protests regarding the use of automobiles can be heard today even in the generally docile parliaments.* Yet, the automobile issue taught the new class an important lesson: Privileges which threaten to bring public resentment into open debate must be reexamined for their relative value. The abuse of automobile privileges has entered the delicate zone of

* In Montenegro, where the use of government cars was extensive, pedestrian outrage has also been widespread. There was a heated debate in the Montenegrin parliament about the *paushal,* a lump sum paid to functionaries as compensation for not having the use of government automobiles. The Montenegrin government requested parliamentary approval of the budget in which *paushals* were inserted. The parliament balked. One representative suggested reducing the number of compensated officials since they would use the cars anyway. When the government opposed the change and tried to halt further discussion, the parliament refused to discontinue debate, and an amendment was submitted by fifty representatives who had insisted on reductions. Only one day later, and by a majority vote, the government proposal was passed. Thus the automobile question led to one of the first parliamentary mutinies in Yugoslavia. *Politika,* July 17 and 18, 1964.

scandal, and a new course has been taken, with automobiles more available, thus weakening public discussion. As a result, it is difficult today to rely on the automobile as a yardstick of social and political rank because clear lines of stratification have been blurred.* It seems most probable, however, that neither the new class nor the Yugoslav public will be able to rid themselves easily of the automobile problem. The attraction of cars is too great, and even though the new class as a whole may accept definite restrictions, individual members will always find devious ways to elude regulations.

Important and expensive privileges are not the only desires of the new class. No one neglects the minor privileges—to do so would seem the violation of a sacred duty. Even telephones, for instance, are used free of charge and thus are a privilege. But hard-core members of the new class have another special telephone because they always imagine that someone is eavesdropping. Therefore, the secret police built a separate network of special underground cables and ultra-shortwave radio beams. These telephones move with the new class from offices and homes to clubs and "special" sea beaches. Directories of such telephones are strictly confidential, while receivers must be locked in steel boxes and rooms guarded. It is easy to see how such practices could lead to popular resentment, especially when it is almost impossible for the average citizen to obtain a home telephone. Those who apply for telephones are put on a waiting list of five or more years. It was reported that before the end of 1966, a few of the more ostentatious privileges—telephone bills paid by the state, for instance—were rescinded.

Among other privileges are prompt medical attention and hospitals or wards reserved for comrades. When specialized treatment is needed, the patient recuperates at leisure at mineral spas and mountain or sea resorts. If his illness is complicated, the comrade goes to distinguished foreign physicians for consultation and treatment, while expenses are paid by social insurance or the state.

Furthermore, privileges include free or reduced passage on public transportation, newly printed books from publishing houses, and free home delivery of daily papers. Appropriate and seasonal gifts come from government farms—fruit, meat, dressed young pigs for the New Year's

* It seems that in the summer of 1965 the new class sounded full retreat. The *paushal* was abolished first for the lower top-level functionaries; a little later under-secretaries, deputy-secretaries, and "other functionaries" received the same treatment. Thus, "it can be said that for federal officials this kind of compensation is fully eliminated." Still, however, certain officials such as ministers are authorized to use government cars. Also, "those using their own automobiles for official purposes will be refunded an amount equal to a first-class express return rail ticket, plus sleeping accommodations, covering the same distance for which the car was used." *Politika,* August 19, 1965.

Eve roast, and so on. Often new appliances are distributed—vacuum cleaners, television sets, refrigerators, washers, and dryers. Then there are the New Year's gifts, mostly of the bottled type, to comrades from business firms. A foreign language can be learned without charge; the instructor may even come to the home or more often to the office during working hours (when comrade minister has a lesson in French or English, nothing can justify interruption of the lesson). A person can even go abroad for a few months to practice the language, too.

New-class members are often patrons of soccer or basketball clubs. Other favorite sports are hunting, fishing, and water skiing. Professional sports were therefore introduced in Yugoslavia, usually paid for by local governments or firms and prey to corruption, waste of public money, and accompanying scandals. Considerable sums are invested to preserve wildlife, and certain types of game are imported from abroad for modern hunting grounds with blinds and other accessories. Very indicative of privilege is a network of luxurious "closed" hunting lodges. Desiring to satisfy the elite, the obsolete Yugoslav railways, which are operating on a deficit,[23] have obtained a dozen or so rail coaches which are half sleeping compartments, half lounge bars. Upon questioning, a railroad official shrugged his shoulders and told the author that during the winter season it is more convenient to travel to distant hunting grounds in these trains.

At the beginning, "facilities" were used to satisfy important and justifiable needs. The distinctions between importance and luxury seems indefinable, however. In time, originally justifiable "facilities" became exclusive benefits, and benefits became privileges. Traveling is one such instance. Persons once travelled for official purposes only, but today, at home and abroad, journeys have become one of the most widespread forms of recreation. Official reasons can always be found to take a trip—perhaps to visit political constituencies or a new hydroelectric power plant or to confer with political activists. When traveling abroad one can be a delegate to sundry meetings and symposiums; when there is no objective reason, journeys are undertaken for "study and research."

Often the new class tries to disguise privileges by pretending to pay for them. In its 1965 state budget, the Republic of Serbia had foreseen expenditures of 137,629,130 dinars for clubs, villas, lounge cars, and similar privileges, but receipts of those items were estimated in the budget at 5,188,130 dinars.[24] In this manner many benefits seem superficially to be paid through legal channels. Although formal budgeting is ordered, there is a huge discrepancy between the price and the value of a privilege. In most instances, the price does not even begin to cover the actual value of the article or cost of the service.

Privileges are kept secret from the general populace and also from others in the new class. The fewer at table, the longer the feast. Discretion is also necessary because privileges are rarely definable in legal terms, and those who abuse them sometimes feel guilty; thus a new facet of moral decline in Yugoslav life has developed. In such an atmosphere of decay it is not surprising that corruption and crime abound in the general work force of clerks, attendants, secretaries, bodyguards, waiters, chauffeurs and directors, as well as in the new class. Participating as an accomplice to activities which are in a gray area of legality, if not actually hidden, one first finds his small, modest, and comfortable niche and eventually may be led to stealing or embezzlement.

For example, the conductor of a reserved sleeping car on an express from Belgrade to Pula (Brioni) knows that those aboard his car did not pay for a ticket because they legally have free travel privileges. He also knows that comrade minister, his wife, and his children are entitled to the privilege. But how should he deal with their maid, the minister's secretary, and a few in-laws? Sometimes when all compartments in that special car are empty, while there is not even standing room in the rest of the train, the conductor finds it difficult to understand why he should be held responsible for violating his official capacity in allowing other passengers in the special car, for a tip. Or, perhaps a waiter in a club is ordered by his chief to wrap a package of fine pastries or dried meats for a certain comrade to take home. Should the waiter's own family be denied the same privilege? Similarly, a state farm storekeeper is ordered to make up a package of Swiss cheese and butter for a visiting comrade. The storekeeper will see no harm later in preparing a similar package for his relatives. In a 1966 interview, the Mayor of Belgrade said, "Packages are still being wrapped sometimes. Only the techniques have been improved to make them so inconspicuous that the receiver himself believes that he has remained an honest Communist."[25] Thus privileges are a temptation to disregard the law. The capacity of moral differentiation is lost.

Property capital is no longer private in Yugoslavia. It is not state owned but "social"; in other words, it belongs to all. One might logically conclude that since everybody owns everything, each person can help himself. Garnering or, more accurately, stealing property from society is no longer considered a transgression, but a sign of cleverness. Kardelj complained that "for some Communists and Party committees it has become standard practice . . . that one acquires benefits on behalf of the social community. When common property is distributed according to political pressure, then, of course, everything is allowed and no one is responsible. It is even considered a mark of meritorious distinction when one succeeds in appropriating for himself more than his share."[26]

Thus the character of crime and corruption is different in the Yugoslavia of the new class than elsewhere, especially the West. Since all capital is automatically expropriated under the Yugoslav socialist system, there is no grab for big money or real estate. Criminal practices are oriented more towards consumption than production, more towards consumer goods and services than factors of production. It is therefore more attractive to use an automobile (with chauffeur, services, and gasoline included, if possible) than to own it. In general, money has utility if it is in foreign currency, but a somewhat restricted utility if in domestic dinars. For this reason present-day Yugoslavia can deservedly boast that its citizens are not involved in huge money scandals, yet there is great misuse of public (state and social) money, property, offices, and authority. Yugoslavs consequently tend to commit legal transgressions more in their capacity as officials than as private citizens. A functionary may often be imperturbable when offered a large financial bribe, but he may be very receptive to an insignificant gift or service.

The specific nature of Yugoslav crime can be misleading. Its most dangerous aspect is the fact that a submerged crime, the committing of a legal or moral violation, may well appear to be honest or, perhaps, even justified. In the dialectics of the new class, the crime surfaces, disguised as cleverness, efficiency, or deft performance of directives. To those who look closely, one new angle of the ethical confusion and distortion brought about by the Communist new class is uncovered.

3 *Mentality of the New Class*

INVERTED MORALITY

Between two world wars, many honest and idealistic people supported the Yugoslav Communist movement. Feeling that previous ideologies had failed to improve the living conditions of the peoples of the world, in disillusionment and despair they turned to communism, which promised them equality, self-respect, and quick results. They accepted Soviet primacy and Tito's leadership without questioning or understanding the implications of future developments. When Communist rule was established in Yugoslavia, the promise of a centralized dictatorship was the only one to come true of the numerous promises made by the revolutionaries. Although their ultimate expectations did not materialize, many old Communists, especially those who now constitute the new class, still believe that their ideology has not changed since revolutionary days and that they are honestly fulfilling their revolutionary vows. If to this conviction one adds the fact that Marxist evaluations and judgments are considered infallible, one can see reason for an attitude of expansive confidence and, above all, self-righteousness. These qualities are deeply ingrained in the mentality of the new class.

When the now dignified and privileged members of the elite ponder their achievements, they conclude that their present high status results not only from the accuracy of their beliefs but from their abilities, too. It is no small satisfaction to them to recall the difficult situations they were in, from which they somehow escaped. The entire sweep of the past twenty-five years marks a series of clever political maneuvers. Through every great historical upheaval (the revolutionary war and conflict with Stalin, the defection of Djilas, the Rankovic crisis) leadership of the Yugoslav Party avoided self-destruction and even gained advantages. The leaders boast, with some justification, that since the last war, Yugoslavia has made great technical advances, built modern highways, created new cities, and constructed factories and power stations. Asphalt has replaced mud, and high-frequency electrical lines have supplanted the village scare crows. Before the war a few hundred thousand semi-employed unskilled workers barely eked out a living; today about three and a half million workers are employed. The new class takes credit for all this.

The group firmly believes Lenin's dictum that there is no situation so difficult that a way out cannot be found, provided one knows what he wants. And the new class knows very well what it wants. From the Communist Party it has taken its ideology, from the state its authority, while during the war its members had created a comradely *esprit de corps*. Yet the new class still lacks an ethical doctrine to guide the moral integrity of its adherents. There is decided advantage in dividing its adversaries, but the dialectical paradox is that new-class unity itself is complete only when each man in it stands alone against the other members. The sinister mechanism for protecting Communist unity is the permanent, ubiquitous vigil of all over each. To maintain discipline the new class resolutely, unhesitatingly, and immediately rids itself of those whose loyalty wavers. Losses are great, but for the new class there is no price too high for retaining power. While it appears on the surface to be strong, monolithic, and telepathically conformist, it actually consists of a large number of lonely creatures who are frightened, fearful, and suspicious of everyone. Individuals in this group do not confide in their wives; they distrust their children, spy on their friends, and fear even themselves. One mistake and they are out. Neither cynicism, which generally accompanies success and pacifies the conscience, nor prosperity of the class as a whole can assuage the feeling of individual failure and frustration. The more successful they are as individuals, the more frequently they come into conflict with what remains of their integrity and past ideals. Let it suffice to consider the many receptions at which one almost always meets a comrade who, under the spell of liquor, becomes introspective and looks for someone to whom he can explain his "case."

Although there are other symptons of weakness, the entire group is basically obedient and disciplined. Obedience is inherent in the structure of power, and discipline serves a common goal. Under such circumstances one would hardly expect criticism to be as widespread as it actually is in Yugoslavia today, but, as a matter of fact, it is one of the most important means by which the present Yugoslav system is managed. There are many kinds of criticism, but that from one's superiors, not to be questioned, has become a form of governing in which simultaneous ordering and condemning, instructing and admonishing, exhorting and correcting are the major divisions. Criticism from above is applied so profusely that it creates the impression of unrestricted free speech in Yugoslavia. One finds, for instance, that Tito's political analyses are very often directives presented in the form of critiques. The same kind of criticism is also used by functionaries of the new class on behalf of the state and the Party.

But the new class is also shrewd enough to allow criticism among peers as a safety valve for dissatisfied people who are less inclined to rebel when given the opportunity to complain. Moreover, criticism makes it easier to discover weaknesses or rebellious intentions which should be promptly eliminated, and it also immediately indicates cadre weak points to which the new class is particularly sensitive. Even when a complaint is not justified, it serves as a useful reminder to everyone that investigations should be conducted.

With an almost artistic deftness the new class has removed itself from the spotlight of popular scrutiny and criticism and directed public attention to foreign political events or politically neutral national issues. The average person is deeply concerned with economic enterprises, schools, communal life, literature, and the like. Every day in Yugoslavia one hears about the poor quality of bread, the irritability of bus drivers, the tardiness of trains, the inefficiency of administrators, the overcrowded conditions of hospitals, and the unavailability of physicians. Because the brunt of criticism falls more on persons than on problems, those criticized are often victims of coincidence and rarely have the opportunity to clear themselves. Criticism itself is sufficient. In this way people can bicker with one another and forget the more substantial political issues which are not being resolved. For this reason the new class avoids becoming identified with its own system or accepting responsibility for its deficiencies. Such behavior differs greatly from the practice of the late forties, when Yugoslavia was still under the unsophisticated dictatorship of the Communist Party. At that time even the most insignificant backwoods official was representative of the full majesty of the Party and state. Woe to anyone who dared stand up to a plain village militiaman.

The mentality of the new class is such that it likes to criticize, but hates to be criticized. To extricate itself from suspicion or responsibility, the new class prefers its victims to be ordinary citizens, Party members, and even functionaries. Scapegoats are shrewdly chosen from real or potential adversaries. Sometimes the person sacrificed is unimportant, but the procedures of the witch hunt are often useful. When cases of "popular justice" are staged, national indignation is adroitly provoked, remotely controlled, and purposefully channeled. But the regime's cold and calculated political astuteness comes to the fore when, to protect, to punish, or simply to admonish itself, it throws a member from its own ranks into the arena of public wrath. Then hysteria sets in and falls upon an offender who often has no connection with the political issue; he is persecuted for a crime for which the new class did not dare charge him openly. This explains why newspapers are occasionally allowed to write about the transgressions of some high government or Party officials.

Sensitivity to criticism and a will to survive, even by sacrificing its own comrades, confirms the vitality of the new class. There is no place for a humane moral code in such a system of ethics; its sole desire is for power, for which no price is too high. The mentality of the new class is still evolving, but it leans to oppression rather than freedom, to deception rather than sincerity.

Behavioral Patterns

Since the new class is highly pragmatic, many incongruities characterize its behavior. One face is turned abroad, the other to the Yugoslav people; the former is presented to those beyond the direct control of the new class, but who should be influenced and used; the latter is for Yugoslavs who must be educated in mass dedication to the new leadership and its system. In both cases the Communist orientation of the new class is directed, as always, to preserving its hold on power.

When not in Yugoslavia, members of the new class strive to acquire personal prestige and shape their behavior accordingly. They assume the right to associate with the most important and influential people of other nations. The group likes the company of influential foreigners, even those disagreeing with various Yugoslav policies. Following an almost medieval code of chivalry (which, by the way, can always be changed), they try to foster feelings of professional solidarity among groups in authority in their home countries. For example, during the French struggle in Algeria, Yugoslavia incessantly accused France of the most heinous colonial oppression, sharply attacking France and its politics. All of France, including the French Communist Party, was open game. One day when *Politika,* the largest daily newspaper in Belgrade, published a cartoon of General de Gaulle with a somewhat oversized nose, very few noticed it. But Tito himself sharply intervened. How dare anyone ridicule the sovereign of a country! "What would Yugoslavia do if the French printed such a cartoon of me?" fumed Tito.[1] It was the feeling of professional solidarity of one sovereign for another which moved him.

The new class feels much the same and expects the reciprocity of all ruling classes regardless of their political view, skin color, religion, ideology, or philosophy, but with full regard for their attitude toward Yugoslav rulers. The Yugoslav elite is aware that solidarity of the international "elite" has great advantages. Solidarity, however, necessitates certain rules of behavior which Yugoslavs apply strictly. International rules of protocol and courtesy are also observed. If a representative of even the most unfriendly country (e.g., Communist China or Franco's Spain) happens to travel officially through Yugoslavia, he receives in full measure the deference due his position.

In addition to formal international etiquette such as flying flags, wearing dark or evening clothes, rolling out the red carpet, and saluting by cannon, the new class has established its own customs, one of which is the arresting of a number of people for "courtesy" reasons. When Nikita S. Khrushchev visited Belgrade in May, 1955, the secret police were uncomfortable because there were no prominent anti-Communists and reactionaries available to jail for the duration of Khrushchev's visit. So they arrested a number of citizens who had never participated in politics and were thus considered anti-Communist. After a week or so, the police explained in a comradely way that those arrested were not really guilty or even suspicious. They were arrested out of courtesy for the important Soviet guests. The new class expects reciprocal action from other countries. One French move was especially appreciated, when several Yugoslav emigrants in Paris were arrested and moved to the island of Corsica for the duration of President Tito's visit to Paris.

The group, conversely, is displeased when authorities in other countries do not show sufficient understanding of new-class protocol. During Tito's visit to Latin America in 1963, it was requested that "for security reasons" several Yugoslav political emigrants be temporarily arrested. The mayor of Belo Horizonte, the capital of a Brazilian state, refused the request, and Tito's route was consequently changed at the last moment. For similar reasons and the lack of "courteous accommodation," Tito's short and informal visit to the United States in 1963 was partly revised. The new class was not so naive that it could see only formalities in international politeness, but it was interested in gaining substantial political advantages.

Knowing that prestige outside Yugoslavia must be earned, its members adapt to the accepted norms of behavior in foreign countries in order to be respected and at ease socially. Often there is a psychological advantage in the fact that Yugoslav representatives seem a bit extravagant to non-Communist foreigners. Yugoslavs are openly, officially, and actively Communist, yet their manners are socially correct by Western standards of behavior. Those belonging to the new class have usually developed conservative artistic tastes which cause interest, often even admiration, when they move in Western society. For these reasons, Yugoslav diplomats and delegates are frequently invited to social gatherings in the Western world.

The regime is especially aware of the advantages in being a host rather than a guest. True, entertaining is more expensive, but everything is charged to the official account. The new class likes to entertain foreign guests lavishly, and it is rare indeed that a visitor leaves Yugoslavia unimpressed by the personal charm of his hosts or unappreciative of their hospitality. On every occasion, therefore, especially social gatherings, the new class presses its point of view. If its efforts are not completely successful, they at least soften unfriendly opinions.

Points of agreement are naturally emphasized when the Yugoslav regime turns to the East. With Russians, notwithstanding occasional rifts, the new class acts like an allied Communist government sharing the same heritage of Lenin and, though applying different methods, dedicated to the same goals. Above all, its policy is to delineate the Soviet Union as an older and stronger comrade and perhaps also as a protector. With East Germans the regime stresses Marxist unity; with Poles and Czechs there is basic suspicion of Germans, etc. Even with Chinese the new class points to common Partisan warfare experience. With all Communists it rallies as with socialist brothers, while in Asia or Africa propaganda is primarily anti-colonialist. When representatives of the new class are favorably received in Moscow, Washington, Rome, or New Delhi, its prestige inevitably rises in the world—and in Yugoslavia. That is the point at which prestige ceases to be social acceptance but becomes instead implicit approval and even justification for the existence of the new class and its rule.

Behavioral attitudes and practices of the elite group differ when directed toward the Yugoslav people. Since the fundamental issue is to sustain and further strengthen a position of dominance, two facets characterize this behavior: One is the intensification of the cult of personality which focuses on Tito, but also includes other leading personalities in lesser degrees, as well as the new class as a whole; the other facet is the increased formalization of behavior, including ceremonial activities.

During and after the war Tito was only the symbolic embodiment of the Communist Party, the armed forces, and the state, always a *primus inter pares*. In time, however, functions were transformed into the attributes of Tito's personality. The cult of personality has developed to huge proportions, with Tito in Yugoslavia being treated in much the same manner as Stalin was in the U.S.S.R.* The cult of personality eventually

* Speaking at the meeting of Croatia's Central Committee celebrating the 30th Anniversary of the Croatian Communist Party, Bakaric said, "Comrade Tito has

became a system of rules for group and individual behavior. Complete and minutely detailed palace etiquette was established and is strictly and pedantically observed. To break a rule is the equivalent of simultaneous violation of state laws and Party directives. Centering on Tito, the new code of behavior manifests itself in the increased elaborateness and number of official ceremonies. This makes the new class feel good and emphasizes the difference between ordinary men and the elite, between those who take part in a certain kind of ritual and those who are merely onlookers. The new class usually does not participate openly as a class in public ceremonies because to do so would remove its disguise. But a façade is always found to stress the greatness of the state, the Party, the nation, the government, history, and culture, behind which the members of the new class appear as officials and dignitaries.

One ceremony in which the new class does distinctly appear is the honoring of Tito on his birthday. Published statements emphasize his greatness and the importance of the occasion and those participating. On Tito's birthday, May 25, which is also celebrated as the National Day of Youth, there is a public display of the new class in its various costumes. On May 26, 1965, the official Yugoslav news agency *Tanyug* issued the following statement:

> Yesterday morning, on the premises of the Federal Executive Council, the President of the Republic, Joseph Broz Tito, received congratulations from his closest collaborators, then from representatives of parliaments, social-political organizations, the administration, and other institutions.
>
> First, the President received birthday wishes in his office from the members of the Executive Council of the Central Committee of the Union of Communists of Yugoslavia.
>
> A little later, in the salons of the Federal Executive Council, President Tito received congratulations from the functionaries of the Federal Parliament, chairmen of governments and parliaments of the Yugoslav Socialist Republics, and members of the Constitutional Court.
>
> Birthday congratulations were also submitted by the representatives of the Central Committee of the U.C.Y. of the Federal Committee of the Socialist Alliance of the Working People of Yugoslavia, of the Union of Youth, of the Conference for the Social Activity of Women, and the Union of Veterans of the Yugoslav Liberation War.

---

continued to be the creator and initiator at all crucial moments. In doing this he has earned the gratitude not only of our party, our people, and *the world workers' movement, but also of mankind.*" *Borba,* October 1, 1967. Our italics.

> The Federal Secretaries, their deputies, undersecretaries, assistant secretaries, then representatives of the Yugoslav armed forces, of the Yugoslav Economic Chamber, and of the Institute and High School for Political Science also joined with their best wishes.
>
> At the same time congratulations were submitted by the representatives of the Serbian Parliament and Constitutional Court, then by the judicial bodies of the Serbian Republic, secretaries, functionaries of the Republic's Economic Chamber, and social-political organizations of Serbia.
>
> On behalf of the City of Belgrade President Tito was congratulated by the functionaries of the City Council, and social-political bodies of Belgrade.

May Day, celebrated with vast splendor, is another occasion on which the new class can present itself to the people as the state, the Army, and the Party. One day before the parade about 800 to 1,000 invitations are delivered by special messengers to those to be admitted to the reviewing stands. The numbered invitations are printed in a luxurious paper-money design with the name written by hand in black Chinese ink. Invitations vary in color and design according to the stand for which they are valid. The stands are arranged by category and rank, proximity to Tito marking the degree of greatest importance. Well made, finely carpeted, and with comfortable chairs, the stands include a free buffet.

If the parade begins at 8:00 in the morning, all those invited must occupy their places by 7:30 A.M., when the gates close. At 7:57 Tito's motorcade arrives, surrounded by motorcycle guards in red and blue uniforms. At 8:00 Tito steps on the platform as cannons open fire in salute and all stand to attention. The national anthem is played. Twelve long silver trumpets adorned with silk streamers are blown next to announce the beginning of the parade. At that moment, the commanding general, on a white horse, rides close to the platform and, in a loud voice, asks Tito's permission to start the parade. An impressively disciplined military machine then moves into place with Prussian precision. Red flags and representative units lead off. The parade climaxes with a thundering of heavy Russian tanks rolling over the gently sloping avenue, while low-flying American-made jets roar overhead. This spectacle is observed by the many thousands distinguished and reliable enough to receive the passes, distributed through local Party units, allowing them to stand on the sidewalks where they had to have been, at the latest, by 6:30 in the morning.

The May Day parade impresses the people with its display of military might and massive popular attendance, in addition to the message that communism will triumph over all the world. On November 29, the Day of the Republic is celebrated in honor of the victory of communism in Yugoslavia. On this occasion Tito hosts a great reception, which in reality is a comradely gathering of those who directed the Communist victory and are now the wielders of power. The reception is a new-class affair with no outsiders. For the populace there are fireworks and cannon salvos. Other receptions, parades, celebrations, and ceremonies are held in which the new class discreetly participates while the ordinary people watch long lines of official limousines moving to the entrances of the White Palace or the Federal Executive Council Building.

The main behavioral trait of victorious Partisans was informality, but today the new class has become increasingly formal. After the war a dark suit was not official attire, nor was black recognized as the color of mourning. Partisans dressed according to their own whims as a matter of course, for most of them either had no knowledge of correct dress or considered such rules to be prejudices from the past. When comrades met, they were more interested in eating than in proper dress. The new society was forming, however, and there was need for social order. The standardized drab military uniforms also encouraged the change to vivid colors and decorations.

Russian customs in dressing and manners, however, were generally accepted by civilians after the war. Imitation of, a sense of responsibility to, and admiration for Soviet communism began with a certain reluctance because many Russian habits were considered *petit bourgeois* in Yugoslavia. The 1948 conflict with Stalin afforded a good opportunity to discard the Russian and find new models of conduct more applicable to Yugoslav circumstances and the needs of the new class, and shortly thereafter the elite more or less adopted the conventions of Western society.

The first official event at which the new rulers appeared publicly in formal evening clothes was a reception honoring Emperor Haile Selassie in the summer of 1954. During preparations for the visit of the ruler of Ethiopia there was no difficulty deciding the reception's guest list because the pinnacle of the new class had already been formed. It was far more difficult to decide how to dress. The vast majority of those invited did not have evening clothes and sincerely disliked them. The problem was finally solved in the Communist spirit: Opposition to evening clothes was defeated by making such dress obligatory. A "special temporary store" supplied all men invited with free, custom-tailored, formal evening clothes. The women fared even better because evening gowns, along with all accessories, were ordered directly from Paris. Rank determined whether the wife of a functionary got one or several complete outfits.

Haile Selassie did not realize that he was the first man in history to see the coming-out ball of the Yugoslav new class. There have been many receptions since then, and the new class has become so accustomed to formal evening wear that it now feels comfortable so dressed. The only change has been in abandoning formal clothes in favor of black tie; women follow the current dictates of Western fashion.

An interesting confrontation of opposing means to achieve the dictatorship of the proletariat occurred when Khrushchev visited Belgrade in 1955. Yugoslavs, still dizzy from their political victory over Stalin, appeared ostentatiously in semiformal dress while the Russians stubbornly wore ordinary dark suits. In the interim, however, Yugoslavs have soberly realized that the Russians are allies, and it was not wise to blatantly copy the style of the West. That is why, at present, black tie is recommended for receiving non-socialist visitors, but when Communist allies are entertained, or in Yugoslav domestic circles, only a dark suit is required. Otherwise, clothes do not differentiate rank and position in the new class, as everyone dresses alike. Difference in rank is shown mostly by the grouping together of inner circles.

It is difficult to learn all the conventions of new-class conduct because they are rarely clearly formulated and certainly never published. Complex rules vary for almost every occasion. On the other hand, conformity in Yugoslavia does not mean uniformity because of inequality in the power pattern of the new class. Thus there is a certain vagueness about behavior, and no one knows precisely what form of activity is prohibited, or under what conditions. Certain rules take shape, but they vary according to the situation and persons involved. One leitmotiv is evident. What at the very top is a sign of condescending magnanimity (such as criticizing socialism) may constitute a right for those below the top; for those further down, such behavior can be tolerated; for those even lower, it is prohibited; while for the bottom levels, it becomes a punishable transgression. Gradations of freedom in new-class conduct depend on the degree of authority possessed. Authority at higher levels has few limits or inhibitions, but lower-echelon authority becomes increasingly restricted in a network of regulations. Members of the elite must therefore learn rules and proceed with extraordinarily acute eyes and ears, but even then there is danger in misunderstanding the meaning of complex rules. It is permissible, for instance, for a person of high rank to enter a salon where Tito is present or to crack a joke about Yugoslav socialism. A person of lower rank who cracks such a joke makes a mistake which could ruin his standing in Yugoslav public life.

At official receptions, everyone knows where to go and what place to take. It is rarely necessary for protocol attachés to conduct a misinformed person from a salon reserved for a higher group, and for this reason Tito is seldom seen by the majority of those present at his receptions. He either greets the guests at the entrance and then leaves or, more frequently, arrives later, stops at the door while the national anthem is played, and then goes to the salon set aside for the highest group.

One of the rules of the political game is that each person must discover his own range of action. This is not easy because an even more important rule of conduct is that nothing may be said about the new class and its way of life—to an outsider or even within the group. Nevertheless, reliable sources of information can be found, frequently in an intimate friend or colleague, more often in subordinates. Important people have the careless habit of talking freely among themselves, taking no notice of chauffeurs or waiters who hear parts of conversations not directed to them. Chauffeurs and waiters are not security risks because almost all of them are agents of the secret police and, without exception, have been thoroughly checked and approved by corresponding police and Party organs. Chauffeurs relay the latest gossip, such as important personnel changes, often a month before official notification.[2] In the same way, a chauffeur tells his "boss" indirectly what should and should not be done, relating how so-and-so blundered or another acted wisely. There are other varied methods of obtaining information. A friend, with a well-timed signal or nod, will indicate what to do, while an ingenious secretary can provide all important information on what not to do.

Since the new class does not wish to publicly acknowledge its existence, its behavior is often contradictory. It would like to assume a public form, yet it is afraid to do so; it is torn between the logic of long-term strategy and the passion for immediate power. Low social origins encourage new-found opportunities for extravagance, but at the same time, caution and common sense remind the new class of discretion. That is why its social life is hidden as much as possible. It is easy for the new class to avoid publicity by holding its gatherings in private homes or in secluded places inaccesible to the general public. As a rule, those in the new class live together in selected suburbs or in separate buildings. Outsiders are removed quietly from such areas for reasons of security as well as privacy. Even special Communist Party cells and "dwelling units" are often established for families who live in separate houses or clusters of houses. In this way the group can maintain a segregated political life without mixing with other Party members in "ordinary" basic units.

Clubs provide the principal means of social contacts within the new class. They are usually nameless and not to be confused with such professional clubs as those for journalists or economists. Initially labeled "additions" to "special" supply stores, they were later justified because after the war the leaders did not have adequate entertainment facilities. When guests were invited to lunch or dinner, one's home was not (yet) suitable and public restaurants not recommended; the best solution was the organization of a club. Clubs are comfortable, even luxurious, and have three basic forms of recreation: a restaurant, a motion picture theater, and convenient equipment for billiards and cards. In addition, there are lawn tennis courts and Party guest houses where leaders stay when they come from other cities. The intent, at first, was to make it easier for Central Committee members and other leaders to have accommodations when traveling, but in practice this soon became free (or nominal-charge) lodging.

Club membership is an important sign of belonging to the new class. When even high functionaries are not members of a club, then they are merely tolerated socially and used professionally by the new class, not accepted into it. But in the clubs one can also find obscure persons without any function, achievement, or importance, who in some way succeeded in entering the new class and enjoying its privileges. Divisions of class otherwise hardly visible are clearly delineated in the clubs. Belgrade has a federal club; there are republican clubs in the centers of the republics, and so on. A "club of federal and republic representatives"[3] was even established in the Serbian provincial town of Vranye. Even though rooms, tables, and chairs are not reserved, there is no question where a certain person belongs. Intolerant of any deviation from the norm, the cream of the elite hardly mixes with lower-level members.

A club novice has a difficult time of it until he learns his exact place in the new surroundings. It is wise to accept the tutelage of a waiter (for a tip) because he is an informal and underground protocol expert acquainted with the latest changes—current promotions and demotions. It is good practice to observe which tables are served first and how long it takes, since the principle of "first come, first served" has no meaning there. Guests are received from related clubs, but the door is closed to outsiders. Avoidance of one's circle of associates can have more than superficial meaning for a club member, for does not absence from the club, a failure to associate with one's comrades, mean that one is drawing away? If so, then withdrawal means disagreement; disagreement is opposition; opposition is not tolerated. Absence from a club is the easiest way to detect a member's defection from the new class, or the beginning of it.

It would be a mistake to assume that clubs are purely recreational in nature, as there is always a great deal of conversation, especially while playing cards. Free conversation during the game is long, often interrupted and disjointed. In such informal circumstances the elite develops opinions, exchanges information, and becomes acquainted with the latest valid political evaluations, forming a common stand on issues, people, and courses of action. Not by telepathy, but by meeting and exchanging views almost daily, the new class acquires a far greater unity of thought and conduct than might be expected.

Clubs also instill a certain sense of belonging, an *esprit de corps*; thus, despite obvious inequalities of rank, a certain sense of fellowship and intimacy is found among people belonging to the same club, who have a common bond and gather together whenever they meet outside. If there are only a few, rank is ignored; if there are many, groups form as at the clubs.

Because silence is the rule in Yugoslavia, many things do not exist overtly. Clubs are never discussed. Vagueness surrounds talk of reserved beaches, summer resorts, hunting grounds, hotels, villas, and the like. Off the southwest coast of Istria in the Adriatic are the Brioni Islands, the President's official summer residence and retreat, where he spends a large part of the year. Although the public is informed in careful detail of who is officially received there by the President of the Republic, the Brioni Islands resort is covered with an absolute blanket of silence, the place where the cream of the new class gathers and lives several months of the year. It would be risky for anyone in Yugoslavia to recall that, before World War I, the Brioni Islands were the summer resort of the Austro-Hungarian Emperor.

Hotels there are apparently businesses like others in Yugoslavia, but access to them is obtained only by reservation which, in turn, can be made only after an invitation is sent by protocol. Those who have visited the Brioni Islands never talk about it, nor do they show any snapshots. Picture taking on Brioni—with any buildings in sight—is strictly prohibited. A novice guest who arranged a trip to the Brioni Islands for himself, after successfully passing through the security screening, and after arriving at a Brioni hotel, would be politely asked, "Why didn't you notify us of your coming? Comrades usually arrive by the morning express, and our cars are always at the station then. Comrades frequently come by special airplanes, and our cars are at the airport. We send cars, when needed, to Zagreb and Lyublyana."[4]

The attitude of the new class toward its privileges is wisely cautious because many were formerly workers or peasants who fully realize that prosperity and privilege provoke the hate and envy of the common people. There is no feeling of guilt on account of their privileged position, however, because they are unable and unwilling to comprehend that what they are doing is not right. Even more, each notes what others in the new class are doing. Availing one's self of privileges is not just a matter of comfort but also a permanent adaptation to a system of behavioral and "ethical" conformity; if a person in the new class did not use privileges, his self-indulgent colleagues would be embarrassed.

Yet, notwithstanding discretionary tactics, the new class enjoys public displays. Once in power, comrades tend to brag and enjoy appearing important in the eyes of the people. They are gratified when they see and hear themselves on television, radio, newsreels, and in the newspapers. Public exposure is justified as a means of building up a political and authoritarian image. But leaders also realize that public exposure is not a personal show, but a collective expression. Public appearances, by and large, depend on the position one occupies in the state or Party, and are controlled by protocol. But protocol regulations do not suffice to meet all the needs of the maturing new class, which is increasingly exposed to contradictory pressures. In this manner, a dualism is created which manifests itself in pedantic and detailed rules of state, Party, and social organizations, and at the same time in an informal paternalism within the new class.

The new class pragmatically resolved the apparent contradiction between formality and informality of behavior by keeping itself apart from other social groups. In one direction, however, the new class does not hesitate to push itself forward when it assumes the exclusive right to speak for the nation and, to a degree, for socialism, world peace, progress, and the underdeveloped countries. The ruling elite calls itself the "working people" when speaking in the name of the proletariat or "patriots" when acting on behalf of the nation. It is flexible in these instances.

The attitudes of the elite toward other social groups are varied. Its suspicions are strongest with regard to the peasants, who exemplify the material weakness of the economy and, by extension, of the new class. Furthermore, the peasants are stubborn; they persistently continue to oppose Communist authority; they also constitute a possible basis for an attempt to restore the past. One psychological reason for disliking the peasants is the fact that the very members of the new class, for the most part, left the villages only after World War II—just one generation ago. Comrades do not like to be reminded of their own past, and many feel embarrassed by their origins.

On the other hand, the new class has maintained a cordial attitude toward the growing mass of industrial workers, seeing in them its own strength. Just as the elite regards the Party as its political vehicle and the present system of government as the legal form of its authority, so it views itself as the proletariat in the social sense. Members of the group use the term "worker" on the many and varied questionnaires in answer to the description of occupation. Priority is given to the title "metal worker" because Tito was one as a boy. If one is not a "worker," there is usually an indication given of "proletarian-working origin"; "working peasant" is less desirable, but it may be improved by declaring that the family was "sympathetic toward Marxism." It is not good form to state one's occupation as "intellectual."

The industrial working class, therefore, represents the source from which the new class intends to replenish the Party and, eventually, itself. Despite a favorable climate for the proletariat, statistics indicate that the actual percentage of workers among Party members is low. After twenty years of priority for the working proletariat, members with "worker's" or "working peasant's" origin formed, at the end of 1964, only 43.9 per cent of the Party. This figure was in fact 3.7 per cent lower than in 1957. On the other hand, the percentage of "officials" as Party members is on the increase, despite all directives, and reached 38.4 per cent in 1964, compared with 32.3 per cent in 1957.[5] It remains a fact, though hidden from the public, that the majority of genuine workers are reserved towards the Party.

Among other social groups, remnants of the prewar traditional *bourgeoisie* are more a thing of the past in Yugoslavia than is generally believed. Economically destroyed, politically suppressed, socially humiliated, abandoned by the West, and forgotten by its own members in exile, the old *bourgeoisie* has almost ceased to exist. Unlike the new class, which denies its own existence, the old *bourgeoisie* is constantly discussed and attacked; yet it is almost nonexistent. Many who belonged to the prewar *bourgeoisie* try to infiltrate the new class, for instance, by marrying their daughters to new generals and ministers. A few of the old group alternate between jail and parole. While on parole they ostentatiously attend church, refuse to vote (if by some error of administration they were not disenfranchised), and stolidly maintain their integrity. In other instances, members of the prewar *bourgeoisie* endeavor to merge with intellectuals.

There is also a new *bourgeoisie* in Yugoslavia, consisting of private entrepreneurs (contractors, painters, tailors, butchers, mechanics, etc.) who make use of profitable loopholes in the socialist system. The new *bourgeoisie* is not allowed to accumulate large capital or to establish itself as an economic or social force. Although profits are sufficient to make its members affluent, individuals are too weak to imperil the new class, having neither the integrity of the intellectuals nor the traditions of the old *bourgeoisie*. Members of the new *bourgeoisie* are, nevertheless, despised by the new class as speculators and profiteers and used as the targets of faultfinding, censure, and tax burdening.

The attitude of the new class toward intellectuals is entirely different (see Chapter 10). From the point of view of the Party and the elite, intellectuals are adversaries in principle: Clever men always know more than is safe. The new class feels that the intellectuals can see it as a concealed parasite and are thereby capable of penetrating its moral shallowness. When dealing privately with intellectuals, comrades develop feelings of inferiority, but they cannot resist associating with them, doing favors for them, and trying to befriend them. By and large, intellectuals in Yugoslavia are accused of smuggling decadent and inimical ideas from the West and debasing and undermining Yugoslav socialism. Since it cannot destroy the intellectuals, knowing that a modern society cannot exist without them, the new class seeks to subdue and control them.

Disregarding the particular social group at issue, however, the essential point of strategy is intolerance of any political criticism of the regime. Anything even remotely resembling oppositional political activity is ruthlessly suppressed. For example, when Mihaylo Mihaylov, a former faculty member of the University of Zadar, indicated his intention to publish a non-Communist paper, he was sentenced to one year's imprisonment for "spreading false information." In addition he was harassed by "activists," or as he put it, "We are in a very difficult situation as far as obtaining food is concerned. As we leave the house, several persons follow us to the stores and tell the grocer not to sell us anything."[6] The Zadar Socialist Alliance chapter held a public meeting which resolved: "We ask those whose duty is to protect our citizens and the country to take all necessary steps to prevent his [Mihaylov's] activities, to punish him for everything that he has done, and to remove him from our midst in any way, for we shall no longer tolerate him here."[7]

As noted, the new class failed politically to assimilate other social groups which conform to its policies only because they are not strong enough to resist. In Yugoslavia, in other Communist countries as well, it is important for the regime to find adequate methods for dealing with both society and individuals. Through agitation and propaganda the new class tries to saturate society with its ideas and views. In this approach it is essential to understand that all the lines of communication which normally connect individuals in society are severed. In order to have a man at its exclusive disposal, the new class, using the Party channels, first cuts him off from his social group and then subjects him, lonely and isolated, to its influence. Skilfully, and with great psychological insight, it concentrates on systematically disrupting communications even within the family—conditioning parents to shy away from their children and children to weaken the authority of their parents, thus estranging the children from home and attempting to transfer their loyalties to political instructors both in and out of the schools. Along with this maneuver, the new class also seeks to weaken and eventually to eliminate religious activities.

This tactic succeeded beyond all expectations; disregard for parents turned into the negation of all authority, including the school, the Party, and the state. But the emancipation of youth struck the new class in its most sensitive spot, its children, who with increasing frequency turn against their fathers and their regime. It was not by mere chance that the son[8] of a very high official, who had been prominent in the new class for some time, publicly opposed communism and President Tito. Apparently, new-class parents have erred in neglecting their political vigilance, especially at home. In this case, the comrade father in question was sufficiently wise in Communist ways to be the first to condemn his son and then ask to be replaced in his upper-echelon job, partly as punishment and partly to devote himself to the re-education of his children. It is unnecessary to stress that he was pitied, but his resignation was accepted without hesitation. Since then he has lived in not uncomfortable obscurity, happy that heavier penalties were not inflicted.

The new class severs not only parental ties, but also the others by which a man normally lives. Husband and wife must bear their own burdens and disappointments, afraid to confide in each other. It is wise to keep friends at a distance and, in their presence, to measure carefully each word and intonation. In Yugoslavia there is a general tendency toward harmless topics; ordinary conversations are frequently only contests in praising what has to be praised or in denouncing those who have fallen. A man must behave consistently because different reports about him will eventually arrive at the same bureau, and they had better agree. Confiding in a physician or sometimes even confessing to a priest can be fatal for the one who fails to report to the person in charge. There are endless examples of broken relations with superiors, inferiors, relatives, peers, colleagues, mere acquaintances, co-workers, the old, and the young. Nevertheless, of all these severed communications, man's alienation from himself pains and erodes him the most.

Consistently conditioned to stifle his instinctive feelings of honesty, without trust in men and afraid of coming to love them, deprived of God, knowledge, and faith in ethical values, the individual is finally alone with a terrifying emptiness. There is no longer any honest confrontation with one's self because the criteria of conscience have been distorted or lost. After a frustrated quest to affirm himself as a person in his own right, the individual, soon bereft of hope, is left defenseless before the Communist system. Isolated, separated from his values, forced to be an extrovert, the individual must follow the only path left open—participation in the regime—which means submitting himself to the material and spiritual rule of the new class. People in Yugoslavia, therefore, do not make long-range plans but live from day to day, always bending with the wind. A man simply seeks and finds a kind of existential oblivion, glad that yesterday is over and forgetting about tomorrow, ceasing to be sincere with himself and trying somehow to justify his own identity to himself.

This is exactly what the new class wants; when the individual has been isolated, disarmed, and demoralized, it seizes him, occupies each moment of his time, and holds each particle of his feeling. Alienation is achieved by including the person in the "socialist way of life,"* which manifests itself principally in political gatherings (the Party, the Socialist Alliance, the Union, etc.). Meetings, however, have been held so frequently and have lasted so long that they have become boring; the new class realized this in time and introduced, in addition, other gatherings with more interesting topics but always with the same political substance. Their main purpose is to deprive everyone of the time or opportunity to think freely; in other words, no one can be alone with himself. Man must always—by the means, among others, of self-management—be activated, occupied, burdened, criticized, exhorted, and pressured until he is exhausted. But even when trying to relax, he is further harried by the radio, movies, and television. It is deemed particularly important to spend as much spare time as possible in the Socialist Alliance, clubs, youth centers, or farm cooperative lodges, labor union chapters, company recreational "Red Corners," or the sports stadium, but not at home.

These methods are applied not only to the people but even more to the new class itself, the victim of its own strategy. It moves in its own circle (of "collective leadership"); of course, some get tired and try, for instance, to spend a summer alone. Relaxation is sought in travel, especially abroad, because it is then possible to idealize the reality left behind and to enjoy a foreign reality instead. This point was highlighted by the spouse of a ranking official who, in a state of rare sincerity,

* For this reason, in the late fifties Kardelj prepared, but never realized, a detailed plan for the establishment of "dwelling communities," intended to encompass the entire life of individuals within collective units. A similar plan, with minor changes, was tried in Communist China under the name "commune."

exclaimed, "Everyone in Yugoslavia, from janitor to general, dreams only of going abroad!" Another new-class member, becoming weary of working, chose to be an ambassador in a remote capital, just to rest for a few years from comrades in Yugoslavia.

If this situation continues the new class will not benefit in the long run from disrupting the informal but essential lines of communication among men. Attempting by Communist methods to creep into the most intimate corner of each personality, the new class does not realize that it is creating a profound boredom which can be far more dangerous than political opposition. A single spark, under certain conditions, might suffice to detonate this boredom into a huge explosion.

Through the methods which it applies, as well as the goals which it is striving to achieve, the new class has formed a dual mentality. In order to double-cross the entire society, the new class double-thinks in its application of dialectical philosophy; it double-behaves as a class in a prospective classless society; it double-talks by its democratic vocabulary and undemocratic practice; and it double-deals by concentrating power in the trappings of liberalization. In this way the new class achieves within itself the same moral vacuum and debased ethics which it is forcing on the entire society of Yugoslavia.

4 The New Class and the Communist Party

CONFLICT

A class set apart from the nation and above the people and specific social groups, the ruling elite recently began to appeal to the people through self-management as a means of keeping the Party in check. The new class has simultaneously reorganized the Party, also through self-management, in order to rule the people more efficiently. As the top stratum of the Party, the new class fights the Party's subaltern branches right down to the bottom with every means at its disposal. It has been forced to do so because the Party apparatus has become an obstacle to the further development of the new class, that is, insuring its monopoly of power.

The genesis of the conflict between the new class and the Party was apparent during the last few years. The conflict itself, however, exploded into the open in 1966 and has profoundly encompassed all areas of Yugoslav life since 1967. This conflict jolted the public because it seemed almost absurd that the new class, led by President Tito, could turn against its own progenitor, the Communist Party. The 1966 ouster of Alexandar Rankovic,* the leading figure of the orthodox Party, was the turning point in the relationship of the new class and the Party and has confirmed the depth and gravity of the conflict. The Rankovic case also revealed that within the new class, beneath the surface of formal unity, there exist disagreements which are expressed in factional strife. The conflict is characterized by a power struggle, but it also implies differing viewpoints on fundamental ideological and political stands such as the role and character of the Party in society. This is why the clash

* Until July, 1966, Rankovic was the vice-president of Yugoslavia, one of the three secretaries of the Party, a member of its Central Committee and Executive Committee. He was in charge of the Party apparatus and of the secret police. He was also the heir apparent to Tito—the No. 2 man in Yugoslavia.

transcends the confines of the struggle for power in Yugoslavia and becomes an open question concerning the further development of communism in general.

While the new class as a whole does not wish to share its power with anyone, seeking rather to create an intensified monopoly for itself, at the same time it wants to widen and decentralize the responsibilities connected with the implementation of power. The classical Communist Party, which concentrated both power and responsibilities in itself in the form of a dictatorship, became simultaneously too broad and too narrow for the new class. It is too broad because new-class power reached a point where its administration required a more compact structure than that of the present Party. Besides, the Party had meanwhile grown excessively in numbers and officials. In 1940, the Party had around 12,000 members, of which about 9,000 were killed during the war and the first postwar years; it had 448,175 members in 1948. Large-scale purges ensued, though without extensive bloodshed, and while a substantial number of Party members were expelled, a large number of new, mostly young, men were enlisted. In 1964, the Party's more than one million members were organized in 35,240 units (cells).[1] In addition, the Socialist Alliance of the Working People of Yugoslavia forms a kind of antechamber to the Party. The Socialist Alliance presently has 8 million members (including Party members for whom membership in the Socialist Alliance is mandatory).[2] Still another appendage is the National Youth Organization, which by 1964 had about 1.7 million members. Yugoslavia has a total population today of about 20 million.[3]

The Party also became too narrow because the character of power changed, intensifying and tending to embrace the entire people and society more fully. Thus the new class realized that its rule through the Party mechanism and by old Party methods had become obsolete, inadequate, and even dangerous for itself. The era of revolutions in Yugoslavia had already passed long ago anyway, according to the new class. From its inception in the early fifties, the new class has busily reduced and adjusted the state bureaucracy; it continues, in the sixties, to dismantle the hierarchical structure of the Party apparatus[4] as well as to establish self-management, through which the system of rule will directly include and activate all social, political, and economic units. Self-management is actually a device by which responsibility is decentralized and shifted to all who participate in social processes. The top (the new class), of course, remains highly compact, following a model thoroughly analyzed and resolved by Lenin, who indicated precisely what should be centralized and what should be decentralized in a developing Communist system: "While *the greatest possible centralization* is necessary with regard to the ideological and practical *leadership* of the movement, *the greatest possible decentralization* is necessary with regard . . . to *responsibility* to the Party [read now the new class]."[5]

The two major factions in the new class, let us call them reform Tito's and orthodox Rankovic's, do not disagree much about the character of power; their primary concerns are whether the new class will hold the power monopoly through the Party, or independently of it, and the methods of exercising power. The decision of the new class to jettison the bulk of the Party apparatus was a long time coming. Under the disguise of monolithic unity, leadership was torn between opposing views which eventually became true factional strife and, in 1966, surfaced in a major political crisis. Kardelj, prominent in Tito's group, is against the old Party hierarchy and for a narrower concentration of power in the Party's top stratum, in the new class. Rankovic's group, on the other hand, prefers that power be held by the entire, strictly organized hierarchy of the Party, which is generally much broader than the new class, though narrower at the summit.

The difference between the two factions becomes more obvious when one examines the manner in which each would implement its rule. Kardelj's "anti-bureaucratic" group seeks to generalize and channel responsibility through the system of self-management springing from below from every unit and enterprise. Rankovic's conservative group relies primarily on a firm organization of power, centrally enforced by orders from above, requiring precisely defined responsibilities and obedience to directives or commands (*postanovka**). In other words, the character of power is identical for both factions: in the former, power is attained by conditioning individuals to cooperate and participate in social and political processes; in the latter, power is attained by coercion and minute supervision. But one should not naively assume that in either case there is any alternative to the Communist order.

Some analysts correctly regard the Rankovic faction as conservative because it seeks to preserve the old, tested, classical forms of a Communist dictatorship. It is highly incorrect, however, to think of the other group as liberal, because it in fact explores new roads and seeks more effective methods as well as strategic goals to implement the same undemocratic rule. Kardelj's readiness to accept new methods does not mean progress toward liberalism; it merely represents greater Communist flexibility regarding methods, organization, forms, and even ideology. Conservative Communists label anything that deviates from their understanding or interpretation of classical Marxism toward more

* *Postanovka* comes from the Russian word *postanovleniie,* denoting an obligatory general political directive.

flexibility as "revisionism." But, from the point of view of the mainstream of the new class, opponents whose rigidity retards or distorts Communist development are denounced as "dogmatists."

Tito settled the issue by firmly determining the course of the new class and explaining that there is no swerving either to the right, "bureaucratic" dogmatism, or to the left, "anarchist" liberalism. "The knell has sounded simultaneously to dogmatism and liberalism," he said. "There are no differences—one is as dangerous as the other."[6] In the light of this statement any illusions regarding the course of liberalism in Yugoslavia become groundless. Political concessions to anyone are not foreseen or allowed, but public opinion is assuaged by the promise of self-management and a "direct socialist democracy."[7]

It is of tactical interest, and generally characteristic, that the struggle of the new class against the Party is being waged in the name of the Party and from the position of the Party's political program. The logic behind such action is that the Party ought to be "saved" from its own apparatus and functionaries and be enabled to play, as President Tito said, ". . . the decisive role in the entirety of our social life, particularly in the development of self-management and the correct guiding of socialist development."[8] Because of this confusion, not only a foreign observer but also the average Yugoslav citizen, and even the Party member, is often perplexed.

The latest purge of the Party, and with it the inseparable police apparatus, was initiated in the summer of 1966 and represents a ruthless struggle, but one which is implemented with as little noise as possible. For instance, no arrests were reported at all, though it is certain that they have been made.[9] The efforts of Tito and the new class were aimed particularly at reshaping the Party's organization and personnel. The Yugoslav Party has passed through many purges, but the latest is perhaps the most intricate. In the first purge of 1937, when Stalin established him as the leader of the Yugoslav Party, Tito restaffed the entire Party personnel, removing all those he did not know or who were considered unreliable for any reason. In the rift with Stalin in 1948, Tito relentlessly weeded out all Stalinists, creating a new and larger but also weaker and diluted Party swollen with many young members. The new Party, however, was controlled by a broader hierarchy, as well as by a more compact commanding elite. The purge of 1966, intensified in 1967, was also intended to create a "new" Party even larger in number but deprived of direct power in its apparatus and conditioned to duly implement the authority of the new class. Stating that "class privileges are being eliminated,"[10] the new class—if not by explicitly confessing, then by inadvertently conceding—showed that at least one of the aspects of the struggle between the new class and the Party is the controversy over privileges.

Tito compared the purges of 1948 and 1967 and concluded that "What had happened in 1948 ought to be both the lesson and marker for the future." Reminding his audience that unreliable Stalinists had been excluded from the "ranks of the revolution in 1948," Tito emphasized the need to undertake a radical weeding out of all the " 'class enemies.' . . . This is proof that whenever internal difficulties in the Party appear, whenever there are disagreements, it is always necessary to undertake the most energetic measures. I believe that we today also have a situation in which the Party must energetically eliminate whatever hinders the building of socialism. . . . Without the purge from our ranks of those elements which do not belong to our Party . . . it cannot successfully lead our socialist development."[11]

This statement reveals a profound political crisis in which the ruling stratum undertakes far-reaching measures to liquidate the power of the Party and its ". . . privileged position linked with the statist structure."[12] The decisive year 1967 was spent in thorough Party and state reorganizations, which were clearly outlined in the *Borba* report, "Theses on the Further Development and Reorganization of the Party," published in April of that year. The document has become the cornerstone and main directive channeling the activities on reorganization.

Once the purge is completed as intended, the long political process of the shift of power—from the Party to the new class—will end. The three stages of dictatorship (the Party, Tito, and the new class) were consecutive in time, but they were also organically related to each other. The present Yugoslav situation demonstrates that the new class, by subordinating the Party, is about to form a new dialectical synthesis since the current phase of the metamorphosis of the dictatorship tends to resolve dialectically a series of mutual contradictions—of Tito, the new class, and the Party. Each unit gives and takes what is essential to the others. In other words the new class vitally needs an unquestionably compliant Party from which ideology, organization, and basic attitudes can be taken. Just as Tito uses the new class to create a solid social background for his dictatorship, so he gives himself to the new class as a symbol of its unity. Finally, the Party is supposed to submit faithfully to Tito and the new class, but if it did so, it would become again the cradle of exclusive power. Today Tito, the new class, and the Party are to be welded into one new whole, each unable to exist or survive without the other; thus the completion of these cycles will mark only the beginning of new contradictions.

It is impossible to rule a Communist country without the Party, regardless of the attempts of the new class to activate the people politically through the Socialist Alliance or various forms of self-management in the state, society, and economy. As a matter of course, whenever non-Communists are freed from coercion, they inevitably come into conflict with the Party's ideology and power—both of which are embodied in the new class—in their search for the promised and publicly proclaimed principles of self-management. These principles are officially described as ". . . becoming the basis of a developed system of a direct socialist democracy."[13] That is why the new class is bound unconditionally to be a sincere guardian of the Communist essence. While in definite need of the Party, the new class nevertheless denies it the authority which has already been condensed within its own group. The Party is not only an external shell but also an organism of individuals who, conditioned to view the world through a Marxist-Leninist prism, must execute the directives of the ruling stratum. The new class for its part is also personalized, and therefore its direction is determined by those who are the strongest at any given moment. In the summer of 1966, the crisis in the new class was manifested in the conflict of the two most prominent men: Tito, whose power is still growing, and Rankovic, who had ruled Yugoslavia in fact by a kind of invisible government.

Since power relations among individuals inside the new class are the determining factors, an analysis of socio-political relations and movements becomes meaningful only after the leading personalities have been included and evaluated. That is why the present conflict was so difficult to detect before it surfaced in the open clash of specific persons. Even then it was hard to realize what was happening because each, regardless of faction, used the same terminology and defended the same positions as the Party, the people, and socialism. In reality, however, they were attacking each other. Although the Central Committee plenary meeting of March, 1966, indicated that Rankovic placed himself on the side of the Party apparatus, no one could have guessed at that time that Tito's allusion to a need for a purge referred to Rankovic. Only later, in July, 1966, after Rankovic was ousted, could an analyst recognize not only who was on whose side, but also how those sides had been grouped.

Many earlier puzzles have now become clear because the conflict concerning the relationship of the elite and the Party appeared also in the form of a personal struggle within the new class between Rankovic and Kardelj—to succeed Tito. For quite some time Kardelj completely controlled the press, foreign policy, and the legislature; Rankovic firmly held the Party and the secret police, while both fought over the economy. Around 1956, a trend appeared indicating that Kardelj had prevailed over Rankovic in the control of the economy. From 1960, however, matters turned more in Rankovic's favor, though in a confused way. Often one of Rankovic's men would take over a very important position, but simultaneously Kardelj would succeed in pushing in as deputy one of his followers, who then completely isolated his boss, Rankovic's man. Also, when a Rankovic man was transferred from a higher position to a lower one, just when it seemed that he was degraded the lower position suddenly became more important.

The stalemate of Kardelj and Rankovic in the Foreign Office was also very interesting. Kardelj's word had always been crucial in the shaping of foreign policy; without him not a single foreign policy question could have been decided. However, the secret police, controlled by Rankovic through personnel switches, gradually infiltrated diplomatic functions in Belgrade as well as abroad, so that foreign policy was finally determined by Kardelj but implemented by Rankovic's men.

When the Constitution was changed in 1961–63, Rankovic established himself as the leading influence as Tito's deputy (vice-president of the Republic). It then appeared as if the competition had ended in Rankovic's favor because Tito turned to representing the state and traveling abroad. It was widely known that Tito personally favored Kardelj, but it seemed that he had decided in favor of Rankovic, who appeared more capable of the responsibility of leading the state. As Djilas observed when he and Kardelj encountered Molotov and Stalin in Moscow, Kardelj becomes easily flustered under pressure, and he cannot be depended upon to remain poised and cool-headed in difficult circumstances.[14] It is characteristic of Tito's behavior that he ostensibly favored Rankovic when actually he had serious doubts about him and was working against him. In fact, speaking at the plenary Central Committee meeting, July 1, 1966, on the occasion of Rankovic's removal, Tito confirmed that he had already had suspicions about him by 1962.[15] On the whole, the same pattern followed by Tito in the treatment of Djilas in 1954 was used with Rankovic. Just preceding the ouster of Djilas, Tito had allowed the publication of articles against the Party and the new class. When Djilas had played all his cards, the trap was sprung. Djilas was gradually pushed into isolation and then jailed twice in a solitary cell in Sremska Mitrovica prison. Eventually he was conditionally released. In the case of Rankovic, Tito allowed him to assume actual power in the Party and the secret police; just when it seemed that Rankovic was strongest, however, he was toppled. Rankovic was blamed for inciting factional cleavage in the Party and for plotting against the regime (he had planted microphones in Tito's home), but no legal action was taken against him or his collaborators (Svetislav Stefanovic and Voykan Lukic). The whole matter was suddenly and shrewdly played down to pacify domestic Party circles and foreign Communist parties.

Tito's behavioral pattern in the treatment of his adversaries is glorified in Yugoslavia as the archetype of an ingenious strategy known as the "Battle on the Neretva River, 1943." Even Yugoslav children read in their primers how Tito had ordered the retreat of the overwhelmed Partisans to the east bank of the river, while taking along about 4,000 wounded. After the passage, he ordered the bridge blown up and all heavy weapons which could not be moved across the river destroyed. As soon as this was done, Tito commanded a general crossing back to the west bank. The Germans and Italians, convinced that the Partisan forces were east of the river, launched their decisive offensive attack into empty space while the Partisans were recovering undisturbed.

Through Djilas, Tito disposed of the liberal democratic elements in 1954; he rid himself of orthodox Party elements through Rankovic in 1966. This does not mean that Tito found an ideal solution to his problems but that he eliminated immediate obstacles to the further development of the new class. The new class tried to take full advantage of the dissatisfaction of the people, accumulated during the last twenty years, in directing it against both Rankovic and the bureaucratic methods of police rule that have plagued Yugoslavia. Yet Tito's popularity was never at such low ebb as it is now. Surrounded by second- and third-rate new-class leaders at his public appearances, Tito seems to be increasingly deserted by both his top aides and the people; it is probable that he will seek strange and unexpected allies in the future.

Although everyone knew that methods of police rule had been implemented for the benefit of the regime in general and of Tito and the new class in particular—with full knowledge and even enthusiastic approval—the responsibility for such changes was thrown fully upon Rankovic. The formal pretext for closing in on Rankovic and the police was their widespread practice of checking on everyone, regardless of position or function. The microphones which had been secretly planted in Tito's residence were viewed by him and the new class as an insult and a sacrilege. Although the police had behaved in accordance with new-class directives, the elite wanted an excuse to liberate itself as a group from police surveillance, to set itself beyond general security precautions. So the police were blamed for their methods and activities. Since 1966 the new class has remodeled the entire security system of Yugoslavia, creating a body that will protect rather than control it. But with its turnabout concerning the police, the new class harmed itself and added to the demoralization and disorientation of those very security organs which must serve and protect it; members of those security organs still cannot understand why they are considered guilty of that which they performed as conscientiously as possible and for which they had previously been hailed and decorated. The new class even went so far as to sharply criticize the security personnel and stated that prior to 1967 the dictatorship of the proletariat in Yugoslavia was not Marxist but a "police dictatorship."[16]

There was no doubt that Rankovic had succeeded in infiltrating all areas of Yugoslav life with his men, and he even held some sectors, such as the Party apparatus and the secret police, as a monopoly. Though strange, the monopoly of the secret police was not as pervasive as might have been expected. For instance, the police apparatus in Slovenia, though shaped and controlled by Rankovic, had remained loyal to Kardelj, its national Slovene leader. A roughly analogous situation also existed in Croatia, where the police were loyal to Rankovic but clashed sharply with the federal and Serbian police apparatuses. Serious conflicts were recorded in business operations, especially foreign trade, which were penetrated by the secret police. Under the protection of law and the inviolability of the police, large-scale smuggling (both national and international) was carried on, for example, in cigarettes, bringing enormous foreign exchange profits which gave the secret police a copious income independent of the budget and hidden from everyone.

Thus the purge of Rankovic's followers was an immediate consequence of his ouster. Yugoslav purges are not as bloody as some purges once were in other Communist countries, but they are efficient, quick, and ruthless. After all, this is best known to Rankovic's men who, as police personnel, had conducted so many purges in their day. For that reason they are trying to retreat into limbo to weather the present political storm. The number of security personnel foreseen for dismissal in Slovenia in 1966 was "50 per cent of them at once."[17] It was reported that 24 per cent had already been fired in Croatia;[18] the target was set for 64 per cent in Macedonia[19] and "more than 50 per cent"[20] in Serbia.

Under Communist conditions, personnel changes become deciding factors but also illuminate the weak points of the regime since cadres are only fallible mortals. Personalization of authority causes unexpected developments, since much activity depends on human unpredictability in general and on those persons holding position of high authority at any given moment in particular. In countries where power is embodied in a single dictator such as Stalin, Mao, or Tito, the personality of a single man becomes paramount. All things being hypothetically equal, any two such regimes differ simply because one of them is headed by Stalin, for example, and another by Tito. Dictators created by a Communist environment influence that environment in turn and inevitably create a personality cult. The cult of self is only one among many of the means of strengthening the dictator's personal authority. Yet the advantage of such a situation is that the dictator overshadows all factions, presenting and simultaneously enforcing a platform on which the unity of the movement, regime, Party, or in this case the new class in Yugoslavia is maintained.

Under such conditions the importance of those under Tito is not eclipsed but, on the contrary, approaches proportionally the dictator's authority. The personality factor amplifies and reproduces itself, moving from the dictator downwards. This is why the supreme leader surrounds himself with men whom *he* trusts or whom *he* personally favors, and the process is imitated by leaders under him. Each tries primarily to strengthen and better entrench his own authority, but the entourage is usually dependable only while the leader's power is growing. When the leader begins to fall, the entire pyramid of his authority usually starts to crumble like a tower of cards.

The advantage for members of the new class is that they can place their supporters in more important positions while removing their real or suspected opponents from those functions. In this way the purge technique favors the new class because the enthusiasm of the promoted personnel outweighs the desperate discontent of those who have lost. While the former are zealous and therefore useful to the regime, the latter are passive, often terrified, and thus less dangerous. The distribution of available posts and the sharing of new benefits or spoils are also important incentives for the turncoats, who are always in a hurry to assert their new loyalties.

The system of the political purge nourishes new regroupings which, if carried to the extreme, would produce anarchy in the present Yugoslav crisis. But Tito gathers his quarreling brood under the wing of the tested Marxist concept of "collective leadership." Just such a leadership, and not an heir atop a pyramid, is what Tito considers the best solution for himself, for the new class, and for Yugoslavia. A kind of national *vrkhushka* (a word of Russian root denoting the controlling group at the top) would correspond to the aspirations of the new class; they could divide supreme authority among themselves. It is probable that in this way a mutual, though temporary and unstable, balance among the stronger men in the ruling stratum could be established. Then, after a period, the more representative positions could be filled by weaker comrades—with the subtle intention of easily pushing them upward now and out later. In such a case Kardelj's chances of becoming president are fairly good since he is not the kind of man to be a national leader. Those functions which are filled today by Tito could be distributed conveniently among several individuals: one would become the president of the republic; another the chairman of the Communist Party (or, as earlier, the secretary-general); the third commander in chief of the armed forces; while other important positions such as prime minister, the speaker of the parliament, chief of the security apparatus, etc., would be alloted to other members of the ruling elite. Such a solution, however, could not be permanent because instead of consolidating the new class in the form of "collective leadership," a new process of condensation of power would have to begin. That process will manifest itself in factional maneuvers until one of the leaders finally does not succeed as the new dictator. The tragic fate of the new class is that it is constantly and persistently struggling to become a monopolistic ruling caste. But the more it achieves this end, the more it will have to subject itself to the unlimited power of its own dictator. Unable to free itself from the process of ever condensing power, the new class repeats the cycle of moving from collective leadership to personal dictatorship just as it fights the Party, always to emerge from it again.

In this endless struggle the new class meets many objective obstacles —in addition to the chronic economic crisis—the most complex of which is the problem of nationalities. The question of nationalities became acute within the new class itself, though it professes to be Yugoslav and international, since the group consists of individuals who belong to particular Yugoslav nationalities. Individuals in the new class often become the symbols of nationalist tendencies, either consciously as fighters or spontaneously as a result of circumstances. Tito, however, as the leader of the new class, admonishes its members that they are primarily, and above all, Communists.[21]

Never solved or, better said, well-camouflaged by the federalistic form of the state, the nationalities issue surfaced in the recent political power struggle and also found expression in the economic unevenness among the more- and less-developed Yugoslav republics. The nationalities question today does not only mean the extent to which one feels himself a Serb, a Croat, or a Slovene, but also the amount of per capita income in one or another republic,* as well as how many adherents of which nationality occupy the more centrally important positions.

* The economic reform of 1965, discussed later, accentuated the economic aspects of national relationships. In the 1960's the average annual per capita income for all of Yugoslavia was about $605. At the same time the average for Slovenia was $935, for Croatia $725, while in Serbia it was $480, in Bosnia and Hercegovina $348, Macedonia $339, and Montenegro $330. See Rudolf Bichanic, "Economics of Socialism in a Developed Country," *Foreign Affairs,* XXXXIV, No. 4 (July, 1966), 645.

Just as the economic reform has become a hotbed of political conflicts, so the problems of nationalities—minorities, languages of Cyrillic or Latin characters, history, cultures, and even religious affiliations—have become the fiery bases for another type of conflict. Thus, for instance, Rankovic, whether he wanted it or not, appeared as the leading representative of the Serbs; Kardelj, in like manner, became the head of the Slovenes; Vladimir Bakaric of the Croats; Krste Crvenkovski of the Macedonians, etc. Nationalistic pressures in the new class and Party are becoming so strong that the framework for proletarian internationalism and Communist solidarity is cracking under them.

Multiple contradictions in Yugoslavia's political, social, and economic life have pushed to the fore the nationalities issue in a demand to recognize the separateness of the Croatian language, which by now is officially considered a component of so-called Serbo-Croatian or Croato-Serbian. Rarely has an event inflamed public opinion to the extent of the Croatian "Declaration about the Title and Status of the Croatian Language," of March 17, 1967, and the corresponding Serbian "Proposal for Reflection," of April 2, 1967.[22]

Both acts of "chauvinism" surprised the ruling elite, which interpreted them as hostile political actions. Confirming this interpretation, President Tito sharply stated, "We could not have imagined that some people would dare to do such a thing. . . . They have been working secretly preparing the Declaration, and they have kicked us in the back. . . . Such things shall never happen here again."[23]

In a violent and massive political campaign, the Party was condemned for lacking political alertness, for weakness, for "mutual amnesties," etc. These deficiencies have been declared the main cause of political deviations by which nationalism has become one of the forms in which "the ideological and political alliance of the remnants of reactionary forces"[24] is established. The leader of the Croatian new class, Vladimir Bakaric, has even gone so far as to state that "foreign countries . . . and various foreign services are involved in this matter as in the case of Djilas and Mihaylov."[25] Blaming the Party for dogmatic and bureaucratic-centralistic deformations, the new class has in fact been attacking Rankovic without even daring to mention his name, always referring impersonally to the "the decision of the Fourth Plenary Meeting of the Central Committee" at which he was ousted.

Yet, the price is too great which the new class must pay for maneuvers to subdue the Party, blaming it for the activation of the nationalities problem. While the settling of national relations through federal state organization brought about Communist rule in 1945, the resurrected nationalities question threatened both the new class and the unity of

Yugoslavia in 1967. "How much it cost to put this country together, and how little it would take to wreck it."[26]

Although this and similar evaluations about internal disunity were sharply criticized and officially interpreted as wishful thinking on the part of the enemies of the regime in Yugoslavia, it is impossible to deny the depth of the present national crisis. The new class has even been forced to reconsider the character of class power in Yugoslavia. Blaming the Party for stripping power from the "working class," the new class states that the working class is "endangered by the isolation of the managerial stratum which performs the functions of power and by the bureaucratization of its own political vanguard [the Party] which is beginning to merge with the state apparatus."[27] In fact, the new class has become entangled in its own dragnet by attacking the Party in the very name of the same Party under which it is disguised. Speaking of itself, the new class concludes that ". . . it is the historical merit of the Communist Party of Yugoslavia to have uncovered the essence of these tendencies, to have forged the strength to consciously oppose them."[28] "To have forged the strength . . ." is seen by the new class as self-management, by which the new class simultaneously implements, justifies, and hides its own exploitative character. The way in which the new class will rule by the "direct democracy" of the working class without the Party apparatus and how the Party will respond to increased subordination for Communists, whom Tito calls "the soldiers of the revolution,"[29] remains to be seen.

SUBORDINATION

Once formed as the Party's principal stratum, the new class did not dissociate but merely differentiated itself from the Party. In fact, the entire structure was divided into the commanding group, the new class, and the subaltern (apparatus and members), similar to the split personality of every Communist—a dictator when facing downward and a slave when looking up. Such a development within the Party, however, required the purging, reorganization, and reeducation of the new Party from its former role of ruler to the role of executor of policies.

Formerly, particularly under the conditions of the Party dictatorship, an ordinary Party member represented authority; now, however, even the officials have been deprived of authority. Of all the former prerogatives there remains the obligation to be dutiful and the right to elevate one's self ideologically in order to function as a "leading ideo-political force."[30] It is constantly drummed into the consciousness of Party members that they are the best citizens of all, a condition which they must keep proving through activities described as vitally important to the building of socialism in a new Yugoslavia. But the middle and lower officials in the Party are not enthusiastic about such a change because they realize that their functions command less power and fewer material advantages. The privileges which previously were also shared by Party officials are being transferred into the exclusive circle of the affluent new elite, which is also relieving the Party apparatus of administrative and managerial responsibilities in assigning them to self-management. The unrewarding and even dangerous aspect of political responsibility, however, will still remain with the Communists.

The pressure of the new elite on limitations of Party authority is not a recent phenomenon; it has been, rather, a lengthy process which accompanied the development of the new class from its very inception. Pressure has resulted mainly in the dismantling of the "old" and the building up of a "new" Party, by which the new class assumed the role of caretaker, trustee, representative, and protector of the Party. But as the new class succeeds in condensing the power at the top of the Party and state, it fights to prevent the emergence of strong men at the bottom level of Party cells. That is why the principle of personnel rotation (see later), a most effective antidote to the entrenchment of Party bureaucracy, was increasingly applied in the period preceding the reorganization of the Party.* Thus, for instance, every year since 1964, at least one-fourth of the cell's secretariat and one-third of the municipal Party committees have been replaced.[31]

The organizational changes of breaking down the Party hierarchy and separating it from the state were accompanied by the introduction of new methods of work. The aim was to incapacitate the Party so that it could not act by itself or in its own name, but only on behalf of socialism, i.e. the new class. Furthermore, the new methods encompass a fuller integration of the Party with social processes—no longer as an external force above society, but by infiltrating into all organisms by the osmosis of ideas and arguments.[32] Were it not so tragic, it would be amusing that the new class charges the Party to guide correctly, or rather to persuade convincingly, the self-management organs to make ". . . the decisions at which they have arrived in a sovereign manner . . . to be correct."[33] While complimenting the Yugoslav system and the Party for being "socialist, humanitarian, and democratic," Kardelj stated clearly that the

* The composition of members of county Party committees changed in Serbia by only 17 per cent in 1959 and 19 per cent in 1961, but in 1963 it rose to 32 per cent and in 1964 to 53 per cent. In 1959, 37 per cent of the Serbian municipal committees were changed, 30 per cent in 1961, 33 per cent in 1963, and 57 per cent by 1964. *Politika,* May 5, 1965.

essential goal of the Party is "decision-enforcing," meaning the policies of the new class, in addition to seeing that the "decision-making" of self-management is correctly attuned to the above policies.[34]

Instead of issuing clear orders, the Party must stir the very soul of the people and insure that each citizen, according to his own knowledge and ability, makes his own decisions, provided of course that such decisions follow the current political evaluation of the new class. Compulsory directives, orders, prohibitions, and restrictions are conveniently shifted from the Party to the bureaus of self-management, where competent professional decisions are made, and later appear as state laws, business rules, financial obligations, health quarantines, traffic rules, etc. In this manner the Party is relieved of authority and the new class freed from responsibilities.

While stripping the Party's authority, the regime is also anxious to transform Party members by developing a different image of Communists. Devoted and unconditionally reliable, Party members are led to believe that they possess exceptional ideological qualities and that they must work faithfully in public affairs. They are expected to discover and sincerely confess their weaknesses and doubts to the entire Party unit and to practice self-improvement by ever more intensive and dedicated activities. Party members accept this course reluctantly because they have no alternatives and are unable to protest. Complying, but with a growing resentment, Communists remain increasingly unrewarded for their political activities, often even punished for what was formerly considered an exceptionally conscientious fulfillment of duties as shown, for instance, by the 1966 purge of the secret police. Moreover, Party members constantly risk making a political mistake, offending someone, or getting involved in the whirlpool of intra-Party intrigues.

Also included in the Party purge are old members who "have been corrupted by power,"[35] which is indeed true. At the same time many new persons are being admitted to improve the balance of membership composition. The system of purges not only removes political waste but also shapes new loyalties; yet, this slow and lengthy process seems to be becoming more complex with the passage of time. The individual Communist's acceptance of a more operative and less administrative Party is the main objective of the present so-called Party life which seeks to enable members to act, but not to rule. In consequence, Party life has been split into two dimensions: the internal part directs the molding of the Communist personality—its reason, feeling, and action—into appropriate ideological-political modes; the second dimension follows with the establishment of Communist group behavior in which individuals turn outward to integrate themselves into all areas of society. This is an extremely arduous task to implement, and the new class is as vague in describing the procedure of accomplishing it as it is precise in critically examining the chronic crisis of the "old" Party in both its content and method of work.

In the period immediately preceding the Party's reorganization, the new class had brought about its impotence after depriving it of authority. From the organizational point of view, this meant that the basic cells of the Party had stagnated in boring meetings which almost exclusively discussed trivialities such as the orderly payment of membership fees, unexcused absences from meetings, or questions of discipline, "instead of directing their political activities into the self-management units of society."[36] There was nothing in the dull meetings to attract those frustrated members who avoided them; meetings were of such poor quality that they frequently turned into a caricature.[37] Secretly, the clock was checked to see if enough time had passed to adjourn reasonably. The only distractions occurred when one member criticized another who, as a rule, was not present, and for that reason there were no inhibitions about discussing him. Criticism included bizarre personal characteristics of the individual and even denunciations.

The new elite and their families did not see any need to be bothered by attending cell meetings regularly. In 1964, therefore, the Party congress amended the bylaws to allow "certain" members to be excused indefinitely from regular attendance. Previously, nonattendance for three consecutive months meant mandatory termination of Party membership. Older members often skipped meetings and then brought legitimate excuses. Such behavior finally became an absurd form of permanent nonattendance, or "Party retirement," in which those of the age of sixty years or more would be automatically excused from cell meetings. Although already enacted in one Montenegrin organization—in the spirit of promulgating self-management in the Party—the decision had been quickly withdrawn since it challenged the notion that Communists are to be active until death.[38]

The decreasing interest level of the cell meetings, discussed exhaustively in the Yugoslav press from the early 1960's, was an interlude in a deliberate policy to transform the "obsolete" Party. Once the "old" Party had been compromised, the drive for its renovation and rebirth in 1967 started more easily. The new-class attack on the inefficient "old" Party was continued as "deprofessionalization"* of the Party personnel ap-

* Hardly mentioned at the March 1966 Plenary Meeting of the Central Committee, deprofessionalization became a ripe political issue by July, 1966. In the edition of June 2, 1966, *Komunist,* the official Party organ, discussed it under the headline, "Deprofessionalization [of the Party personnel] Does Not Hinder Political Activities."

paratus to rid it of politically strong Party men. Deprofessionalization consisted of the replacement by amateurs of earlier full-time professional Party officials, particularly of municipal committee secretaries. When it is kept in mind that "amateur secretaries" fulfill their Party duties in addition to their regular employment, that their time is limited, and that they are, finally, given little or no remuneration, it becomes clear that neither are they able nor do they wish to affirm themselves as functionaries of power in their own right.

With regard to the formal organization of the "new" Party, the approach of the new class was highly flexible. It insisted on a few essentials: democratic centralism would insure both the involvement and subservience of the Party; basic "home units," where members could be accepted and registered and pay their fees, would provide a place to attend to other membership technicalities. Other intra-Party activities and communications, especially between lower and higher units, would be conducted by "delegates." This new device is of remarkable interest, because the delegate system may develop into an informal Party hierarchy as well as the form in which the existing hierarchy might submerge itself. It is much more probable that the delegate system is intended to allow the new class to staff intra-Party communication lines with its own men.

In addition to defaming, deprofessionalizing, and reorganizing the Party, the new class separated it from the state security with which it was formerly closely intertwined. Prior to the purge of 1966, policemen gave their primary loyalties to the Party. Security organs were above all political factors. In separating the Party from the police, the new class deprived the Party of its main hold on power, leaving it, weakened and helpless, at the mercy of the ruling stratum. Furthermore, the Yugoslav police force has been substantially reduced in number, and its functionaries are increasingly professionals.

By taking power away from the Party but making its organs responsible for social and political developments, the new class wants to establish, within the Party and throughout the country, an order through which it can direct all activities of Yugoslav life. The new class seeks to control the whole society firmly, if not through a single center, then by a single system of ideas. Under the conditions of self-management, it is possible to enforce this intention if all activities which function autonomously remain in harmony with the directives of the leadership. For that reason the new class no longer needed and was actually hindered by Party organs as direct wielders of power and enforcers of professional authority.

Consequently, in the same way that self-management came to be a part of the state and national economy, the new class introduced a form of self-management into the Party organization. The Party was reorganized into units with increased autonomy. Such units are invited and actually conditioned to initiate and further develop an intensive and pervasive political life. This means that Party units, and even members, may be quite on their own if they maintain a clear orientation and line formulated in "programatic documents and by political development,"[39] "orientation" being the new class as it is, and "line" being what the new class says. The new pattern is reminiscent of an army in which all units march separately but fight together. The dialectical resolution between the thesis of the self-managed nonconformity of Party units and the antithesis of their synchronized conformity of political function is achieved in the synthesis of Party unity. That unity is not of democratic nature, ". . . not a mere consequence of all existing trends in a still heterogeneous society"; it is, rather, an imposed master plan consisting of a clear and definite political platform.[40] The essential point in this attractive "democratic" self-management model is the sharp restriction that if there is any ". . . disagreement with the basic concepts of the Party program and bylaws, disciplinary measures are to be undertaken."[41]

In actual life, however, relations are much more complex. Social life is replete with contradictions and conflicts. Theoreticians of self-management, among whom Kardelj is prominent, concede that the state must exist. If the state exists, it must then be fully controlled. Control was formerly held by the Party and its apparatus, but now it is the responsibility of the new class and its self-management master plan in which the Party, as an instrument of the new class, has the focal position. In either case, "As the state exists, there is to be the dictatorship of the proletariat," which means further that it is "necessary to maintain permanent direct influence on all levers of power, insuring that authority will be utilized in harmony with the fixed socio-political system."[42]

In stating that internal social contradictions exist in a socialist society, Kardelj shattered the illusion of those who believed that "socialism is a state without conflicts, and the building of socialism is a planting of flowers."[43] Kardelj warned that difficult problems are ahead, and that it is therefore necessary to find adequate weapons to overcome "new situations," "new resistances," and even "new fronts."[44] To deal with the situation, given the circumstances and a common political platform, the new class needed a practical instrument to insure Party unity. For this purpose it increasingly utilizes the well-tested organizational principle of democratic centralism. Since that principle had been the backbone of the "old" Party, the new class denounced its former usage but simultaneously extolled its future possibilities. Thus we are informed that democratic centralism had been, in practice, outright "bureaucratic centralism." After more than twenty years of praising the method of democratic centralism for managing the Party "from the bottom upwards," one was told in 1967 that this kind of centralism had never been democratic.

"The discussions began only when political decisions were made," as stated at the Belgrade seminar on topical problems of the reorganization and development of the Party, June 5–8, 1967.[45] Although the former Party was characterized as a "fetish of false unity,"[46] the new class still conceded that the use of democratic centralism was justified in the past because it acquired different meanings in different periods and under different conditions of the Communist movement. Anyway, the point today is that in the Party and its activities, it is "possible to apply this principle [democratic centralism] in an ever more consistent manner, because communications between 'higher' and 'lower' leadership bodies by the introduction of self-management have been freed from narrowness."[47] The Party's secretary-general, Todorovic, added his explanation in a report to the Seventh Plenary Meeting of the Central Committee: "Democratic centralism is the fundamental principle for the Party's efficient activity under the new conditions."[48] Bakaric put it clearly, relying on Tito's words as the highest proof: "Why does comrade Tito ask for democratic centralism? Not because of some abstract principles . . . but to stop certain discussions . . . and to achieve unity . . . within the Party."[49] As the reorganization of the Party progressed during 1967, the image of democratic centralism improved even further. Crvenkovski stressed that it would be *"absurd* to liquidate or abandon democratic centralism because *without central decision-making a modern society cannot exist."*[50]

Generally speaking, the Communist Party as a given organization and under existing conditions has lost utility for the new class. In Marxist terminology, ". . . the societal productive forces have outgrown the given system," the Yugoslav Communist Party, that is. Bakaric stated, in *Politika,* November 5, 1967, "It was quite evident . . . if the old organizational pattern had remained as before—that the Party would have to hang in the air." Thus an extensive reorganization—it might also be called a new technique of subordination—was begun by introducing self-management to the Party. To avoid misunderstanding, self-management was described as continued rule by the Central Committee rather than actual autonomous behavior by the Party itself. Clarifying the official position, Bakaric, in the same article, said, "Does [self-management] mean that . . . the Central Committee must do what is decided by basic Party organizations? . . . This thesis, of course, we could not accept because the Party must lead the working class in its historic assignment, must represent its consciousness." Elaborating further on the implications of a self-managed Party, Bakaric said that the Party can be subordinated to no self-management but to that "which is in agreement with the historical role of the working class," which is simply the realization of communism.

Party organs, thus, are indispensable to the new class as instruments for control over all social activities. As the new class views it, the Party ought to be transformed into some sort of operational nervous system that would properly start, as well as energize, the semi-automatic mechanism of self-management to implement directives. Or, as the chief new-class leader in Croatia said, "It is the main duty of the Party to see that self-management operates without great frictions and develops normally."[51]

The present chairman of the Federal National Assembly, Milentiye Popovic, emphasized that it is "not sufficient" for the Party "only to agitate and explain certain measures," but that it must also fight to persuade the elected bodies to adopt freely what is expected of them, that is, "progressive decisions," or the policies of the new class. He therefore considered that the Party, in order to lead the society to communism, ought to be "organized in such a manner that it could work in every circle and at every level," even without a formal command.[52]

The problem in the struggle between the new class and the Party is that the new class does not allow the Party to issue orders. Neither does the elite want to issue any orders itself, preferring them to be anticipated, almost intuitively grasped, guessed, and proposed from the lower levels of political administration where the people are processed by self-management. From experience, the new class knows that when the Party issues orders it becomes a power by itself and develops into an independent bureacracy. The new class is determined not to allow this to happen again. It intends to mold the Party into a body that does not rule yet is responsible as a kind of simultaneous advisor, seducer, teacher, preacher, hypnotizer, fascinator, schemer, tipster, publicity agent, guiding star, conscience, and psychologist—but never a ruler. The paramount objective is to condition Yugoslavs to think, feel, live, behave, and work as the new class thinks they should. The role of the new class is, by means of the Party, to let self-management know of the decisions it should make, achieving in this way a direct socialist "democracy." The Party's new role, in which it has been relieved of authority and has had to integrate itself into the society, again by means of self-management, insures that the long and persistent struggle will continue in the future. The new class realistically faces the conflicts which, though diagnosed in advance, have already appeared here and there, and "are becoming severe and dramatic."[53] In a deep crisis even social self-management, as conceded in *Borba,* is not as it should be, and the Party itself, which ought to direct developments, frequently violates the principles of self-management.

In fact, in the entire process, which represents a profound transformation in subordinating the Party to the new class, the regime hides behind the majority decisions determined by democratic centralism in the Party and self-management. Finally, or rather initially, after all this talk about self-management and democratic processes of the people and the Party, it was Tito himself who clearly said, as the Yugoslav press headlined on the front page, "the reorganization of the Party must be executed from the top down."[54] To avoid any misunderstanding of what this means, Todorovic told the Seventh Plenum of the Central Committee, "We shall discuss and *we must* adopt the proposed decisions on the change of the manner and form of organizing Communists."[55] And the Central Committee unanimously approved the theses for the reorganization that same day, July 2, 1967.

There is the other side of the coin, however, when the Party, by self-management, and even in its own name, counterattacks the new class, as seen in the discussion in the next chapter.

Resistance

The pressure of the new class to limit and eventually to eliminate the Party's authority elicited the Party's resistance in many forms. The ordinary Party members, the lower and middle officials, cannot avoid accepting the challenge of the new class. But it is only with profound reluctance that the Party apparatus rises against the new class which acts on behalf of sacrosanct Communist unity, hierarchy, and ideals. Violation of Party discipline, moreover, is absolutely incompatible with Party spirit.

Because of their conflict with the new class, Party officials look back with longing to the days when their jobs were secure and well paid, but they also realize that it would be counterrevolutionary to oppose the new class overtly. Fully understanding that present circumstances represent a struggle for survival, they also realize that their every move is open to political risks; they are exposed to thorough supervision from above and to the alert scrutiny of self-management personnel from below.

Party functionaries thinking of guerrilla tactics do not have the ambition to become martyrs under present conditions. Basically opportunists, they carefully weigh their chances of success in order to side with whatever faction they think is going to win. While the new class requires subordination and responsibility from them, the majority would prefer to lie low and wait to join the victory procession. Many prefer to keep their mouths shut, but the new class sees through their subterfuge and challenges them to speak their minds openly. To counter passive attitudes the new class has established a policy of "political responsibility for silence when the words of a Communist ought to be heard."[56] Squeezed by the new class, Party officials are also caught in accelerated political developments and crises in which they are tested to prove their political alignments.[57] In the meantime, time is running short, and, especially since 1967, the Party functionaries have been losing their hold on power.

Party apparatus men consider demotion unjust, recollecting how faithfully they had sacrificed themselves by collaborating with Party leadership (the present new class) during the war and the seizure of power in 1940–45. They also remember how they toiled when the Communist state and society was being organized from 1945 to 1950. They are convinced that it was mainly a result of their support from 1950 to 1960 that the rank and file of the Party were made into errand boys while the Party leadership was being transformed into the new class. Party officials, however, must now pay the bill and lose their power under the same logic which earlier permitted them to outmaneuver the rank and file of the Party. In sum, there are indications that the Party apparatus is becoming so embittered at losing face that it is ripe for resistance against the new class.

In resisting, the Party apparatus finds itself in a strategically unfavorable position—lacking organizational unity, the apparatus appears as dispersed individuals or, at best, as local groups. The regime, however, occupies the commanding positions and has material means at its disposal, as well as a monopolistic grip on Party ideology. The Party apparatus, on the other hand, has a tactical advantage in the field, where it constitutes, controls, and implements authority. It holds the communications media, performing as an isolator as well as a connector between the new class and the people. Men of the Party apparatus, through self-management, address the people in the name of the new class and speak to the new class on behalf of the people. Furthermore, as local authorities, they have the advantage of utilizing the inertia and distrust of the people and the Party rank and file who are fed up with ceaseless changes and reforms.

In the spring of 1967, Party resistance appeared as taking advantage of the newly introduced quasi-democratic procedures by which citizens could nominate several candidates for the posts of representatives and communal delegates. By this innovation the new class intended to gain publicity for democratic "free elections," while it reasoned that nothing could be lost since elections are fully controlled anyway. But the apparatus of the Party endangered the entire scheme by nominating its own men or groups in many locations. Although such "independent" candidates were Communists, some with prominent war records, they were publicly censured since they were not selected or approved by the new class. Condemning such cases as "underground agitation," "unallowable methods of campaigning," etc., the new class sharply repressed such practices, blamed local Party officials, and undertook the measures necessary—notwithstanding "free elections"—to nominate and elect proper candidates.[58]

Under such circumstances Communist opposition is moving gradually from apparent subjection to passive resistance, to hidden sabotage, and eventually to more open deviations, distortions, and open disagreements which can become the prelude to the rebellion. In reaction to internal political unsteadiness, Tito appears to be tempted to repeat his strategic (Neretva) pattern of doing the opposite of the obvious. This would mean an attempt to move nearer to the Communist bloc and to establish better relations with the Russians in order to be able to use them against his own Communists. In the meantime, sporadic and localized Party opposition turns to a widespread and increasingly common stand against the new class. Simultaneously, these resistances are taking organizational shapes, among which the most typical is the *vrkhushka.*

The *vrkhushkas* ("topniks") are an informal group of local leaders and officials who command varying degrees of authority and influence. Local leaders can be found in administrative units of counties, cities, and villages, in offices, institutions, and economic enterprises, depending on local conditions and personal relationships. All are Communists with an occasional non-Party expert in their midst. Usually the local *vrkhushkas* consist of the secretary of the corresponding Party unit, mainly a kind of group leader, and representatives of the local administration—police, court, union, business workers' council, and bank. When the local leaders achieve a balance of authority and divide it among themselves, the *vrkhushka* then wedges itself in, severing connections between the general populace (peasants, citizens, workers) and the new class. *Vrkhushkas* insulate the new class not only from the people but also from authority; instead of the new class enforcing authority on behalf of the people, the *vrkhushkas* enforce it on behalf of the new class.

The struggle between the new class and the *vrkhushkas* can be seen in various forms. One characteristic of the local leaders is conformism in words but opportunism in actions. They reconsider directives from the top in light of their own interests, and they execute them to serve their own convenience. As a rule, lip service is paid to the directives, which are duly accepted and rarely criticized openly; most often, though, the directives are poorly obeyed, frequently ignored, and filed away in archives. Sometimes directives are intentionally carried out so excessively and literally that their execution only harms the regime; it sometimes happens that their content is even perverted and changed. In short, what *vrkhushkas* decide is actually done. Whenever the new class, in the form of high Party leadership, criticizes such actions, the *vrkhushka* readily and humbly bows and loudly joins in the criticism. Since the culprits must be found, the *vrkhushka* takes matters into its own hands, determines its adversaries, and sticks on them the label of guilt.

For several years now a fierce campaign has been waged in the Yugoslav press against those Party members who distort the decisions of the leaders, but the press did not dare record or directly name organized resistance until the ouster of Rankovic in 1966. In the meantime, the *vrkhushkas* succeeded in setting up their ambushes somewhere at the middle and lower levels, and are now fighting against the aggressive new class while still maintaining their own power. The cleverness of the *vrkhushkas* is in establishing their own authority by skilful maneuvering in imitation of the new class.

Party apparatus resistance to the new class assumed specific shapes after self-management was intensively implemented and Rankovic was ousted. The new class, as noted before, established self-management for direct collaboration with the people with the intention of freeing itself from the Party apparatus; the people, on the other hand, saw in self-management an opportunity to gain more freedom from both the new class and the Party apparatus. The Party apparatus also accepted self-management, realizing that in association with people, those elected to the bureaus of self-management, that is, it could bring them over to the Party line. Through self-management, finally, the *vrkhushkas* are cementing themselves into positions of strong local authority and immunizing themselves to pressures from above.

The role of the *vrkhushka* in the struggle of the Party against the new class is better seen when one remembers that the mechanism of self-management moves generally in two opposite directions. The more subtle movement comes from above and consists of the application of the policy guidelines of the new class; the other movement, from below, is found in self-management's responsibility to act in accordance with the new class. Under these circumstances, the emphasis of self-management is placed on decisions reached in the field—in enterprises and local units. The new class does not like to interfere; it allows the organs of self-management to establish their own rules and mechanisms, which usually can produce better results (e.g., higher labor productivity or lower costs of production). This also means that, though the new class does not relinquish its authority, it does grant authorization for action. Only when decisions in the field do not suit the new class does interference come from above.

The new class, therefore, does not hesitate, indeed it prefers, to utilize self-management as a convenient channel to purge those Communists who do not pass the test of faithfully accepting the subordination of the Party. Appealing to Communists to ". . . elevate themselves above the low horizons of their momentary partial interests and professional status . . . and work against the strivings for preserving the monopoly of ownership and petty-ownership egoisms," the new class interferes by expelling undesirables from the Party. The new class rids itself of "those members who are exponents of the bureaucratic usurpation of power of turning self-management into a mere façade."[59]

Since matters are not developing as they should, a fact confirmed by the deepening chronic crisis in several areas of Yugoslav life, the new class is compelled to undertake more or less systematic measures in different forms, one being the Party reorganization, another the "economic reform" of 1965. Although such measures proclaim the principle of self-managed autonomy, they in fact consist of exceptions and limitations which fundamentally negate the very principles introduced. For example, the economic reform established the free market as a principle but simultaneously put almost all prices under much stricter control. This was explained, of course, as an interim measure, but thus far it is still in practice. So complicated a conglomeration of contradictions exposes the Party apparatus and the *vrkhushka* to great difficulties, but it also gives them important opportunities. *Vrkhushkas* are always on the spot because they are organs of the new class whether the new class likes it or not.

The new-class regime publicly conceded that "frequently they [basic Communist units] are more closely linked with the enterprise's administrative apparatus and with the factory and communal committees of the Party than with the direct producers; . . . they are interwoven with the administrative apparatus."[60] Furthermore, Party units were criticized for either closing themselves off from the organs of self-management or "manifesting a tendency toward taking over operative affairs and direct responsibility from the self-management organs and socio-political organizations."[61]

It is an advantage for the *vrkhushkas* that the new class must interfere in the implementation of state policies. By this interference, though hidden under the form of guidance, the elite causes discontent among the people, by the increase of unemployment or fall in real wages, for instance, and provokes resistance in the self-management organs responsible for all failures and difficulties—such as the fact that extra workers in factories must be fired by the organs of self-management, i.e., the workers' councils.

Since *vrkhushkas* are in constant contact with the people, they feel undercurrents immediately with well-developed political perception; they even anticipate, join, and take over political leadership to exploit the mood of the people promptly. Thus a widespread practice of compromise appears between the local Party apparatus and the self-management organs (directors, union leaders, top men in the workers' councils, etc.). This compromise actually represents the essence of self-management in Yugoslavia in the form of local autonomy at present. From compromise comes an inversion in the attitude of the citizens, workers, and peasants, who, though disliking the local Party organs which are constantly on their backs, still find a community of interests with them. When various local, parochial, nationalistic, regional, and other similar considerations are added, it becomes understandable why the local *vrkhushkas,* assuming that they represent a form of local compromise, appear as spearheads of different opportunistic movements. Through compromise, the Party apparatus seeks to retain control, and the people seek to resist pressures from above; both give rise to political ferment.

Thus shaped, *vrkhushkas* are already a material and political danger to the new class. In fighting to retain authority, *vrkhushkas* do not allow the new class to implement its policy. In delegating responsibility for difficulties which constantly appear in the society and economy, the new class could no longer single out erring individuals or incompetent organs of self-management; criticism consequently fell increasingly on the state, the system, and, logically, the regime itself. Explanations, directives, warnings, and commissions for investigations are in vain. All is lost in the labyrinth of flexible defences of the lower Party apparatus which is protected by the methods of self-management, doubletalk, and double think.

The alert eye of the new class noticed this development in the field, but it was Tito who first struck out against the *vrkhushkas,* calling them by this name. Only since 1964 has the new class directed its main effort against the *vrkhushkas,* the local officials whose power seems the strongest and most incongruous. Throwing itself vigorously into the fray, the new class seemingly failed to realize that it thus exposed not only its own existence and tactics, but also the conflict between the top and bottom of the Party. The fight against the local officials caused an internal division of the Party, enhancing the polarization of resistance of the lower Party leadership and rank and file, on the one hand, and the pressure of the higher leadership, on the other. The new class has also gone overboard in applying one set of rules to itself and another to subordinates. It has even neglected the fact that whatever is represented by a *vrkhushka* for the local level is represented for the whole of Yugoslavia by the new class.

Having lost sight of the variables of a potentially dangerous political situation, the new class revealed its blindness and negligence in a newspaper publicity campaign against the *vrkhushkas.* Typical of the campaign is an irregular ode written by a young Yugoslav, Vlado Bulatovic (Vib), printed under the heading "A Note With A Message," and entitled "The *Vrkhushka* Exposed."[62] Bulatovic's satire was so sharp, and his exposé of local Communist rule so complete, that in the long run blame falls on both the new class and communism:

> There is a nice way to change a working unit into a miserable mess.
>
> As soon as five leaders become glued together, a new body is created: the *vrkhushka.*
>
> At this point those remaining in the working unit had better sprout wings and fly away.
>
> The working unit is divided into "topniks" and "sheepniks."
>
> How does the *vrkhushka* function?
>
> The *vrkhushka* arranges, disarranges, mixes, and gossips in a hushed tone.
>
> In working units voices are then muted, and all know that whispers mean trouble.
>
> To repeat: the director and his president one, president two, secretary of this, and secretary of that take each other's hands and make a circle.
>
> That is why a *vrkhushka* can also be called a merry-go-round.
>
> They hold hands and whirl right through regulations, rule books, bylaws, and statutes.
>
> The others silently look upon this. After all, if not part of the circle, a comrade rates low.
>
> The *vrkhushka* is a wind-*ushka* that whisks the people away.

> The *vrkhushka* is an ominous bird of prey that crows, and with each raucous sound someone is retired, or fired.
>
> The *vrkhushka* is a dragon. It swallows a man and excretes a reptile.
>
> For the *vrkhushka* self-management means self-service, and the so-called workers' council is but a disposable paper napkin.

That members of the new class do not yet feel involved with the *vrkhushkas* and that they continue to draw distinctions between that group and themselves, the *vrkhushka* being blamed for all problems, is evident in the fact that Bulatovic, on January 1, 1966, was awarded the *Yugoslav Distinguished Order of Work with the Golden Wreath* by Tito.[63]

The power struggle continually motivates the Party to set itself against the new class. The clash loses the character of internal disagreement, therefore, and gains the quality of a political battle between two mutually inimical groups. In a situation like this it is not difficult for Communists to recognize the exploitative character of the new class and to compare it with other exploiting classes in history. It would be only one step further to accept the orthodox Communist prescription that a hostile class ought to be annihilated. The *bourgeoisie* of Yugoslavia was annihilated by expropriating its capital; the new class can be eradicated only by expropriating its authority.

At the present stage of the struggle, the Party apparatus is in a better tactical position than the new class because it is able to camouflage its appetite for power and to present itself to the people as a fighter for upright social ideals. Although slogans such as "classless society," "equality," "freedom," and "prosperity" have been thoroughly discredited in the development of postwar Yugoslavia, they have been taken out of mothballs by the Party apparatus, and are again being mobilized —but this time against the new class. In trying to acquire popular trust, Communists in the field pose as the protectors of the interests and freedom of the people. From their position of authority at the head of the people, the *vrkhushkas* declare that here workers ought not to be fired, that there labor conditions must be improved, and that everywhere wages are too low and prices too high. The new class, however, though firmly holding control of the state and power, lacks a bit of convincing sincerity when the President from Brioni or other members leaving their ministerial villas in luxurious limousines deliver their weekly exhortations to the "working people."

Yet, the bare truth remains that the *vrkhushkas* themselves are only a small new class adapted to a local framework. In the beginning the *vrkhushkas* wanted to be a part of the new class only to be able to behave locally as the new class did in Belgrade or on the Brioni Islands—to maneuver, to manipulate, and in general to play the exciting, profitable, and dangerous game of authority over men and materials. Permeated by opportunism, the *vrkhushkas* would like most to achieve a compromise with the new class to retain their local power. But the new class refuses the limited interests of Communists in the field since its own further development requires a change in the present structure and content of the Party.

But, as in similar situations of conflicting tensions, the more the new class pressures Party members, the more they resist, not only locally (the *vrkhushkas*) but also individually. They do not organize themselves in formal units, but they do align themselves with current issues and political conditions. Communist resistance is spreading, and the issue was well characterized in the plenary meeting of the Serbian Central Committee when it was stated that ". . . a bond among those who have the same ideological views is often made spontaneously. To a great extent it comes about when people find each other on the same wavelength, and, playing it by ear, they carry out a common action without any organized preparations. This is a typical method of operation for opposition ideological forces."[64] While there is no uniformity in the methods or motives of resistance, there is a tendency to create an ideological community, and though incapable of forming a new progressive movement, Communists are returning to Leninist concepts of the Party.

The initial opportunist discrepancy concerning the sharing of power between the new class and the Party apparatus turned into a conflict over personal monopolization of power. The struggle remains unclear because both sides are hiding their real motives while trying to appropriate the same Marxist-Leninist ideological platform. The new class claims that it is developing Marxism creatively under modern and changing conditions. "Marxist thought," as stated at a recent plenary meeting, "is Marx, Engels, and Lenin, the October Revolution and *our revolution, and all contemporary developments,*"[65] referring of course, to the policy of the new class. On the other hand, the Party apparatus prefers the safe ground of the classical Party dictatorship that flourishes in the Soviet Union and also existed in Yugoslavia until the early 1950's.

Substantial ideological support for those Yugoslav Communists who oppose the new class comes, unsolicited, from the Soviet Union. Present developments indicate that the Soviets are moving in the direction of strengthening the type of Party dictatorship which is now counterposed to the dictatorship of the new class in Yugoslavia. This, of course, does not exclude the possibility that, at some later stage and perhaps in a peculiar form, a Communist new class would be created in the Soviet Union—but of course it would be different, as the Soviet type of communism is different.

The new class and the Party are basically of the same quality though they represent different stages of Communist development. Their family disagreement about how Yugoslavia should be ruled or, rather, how the power should be shared has moved far beyond its initial causes and goals. It has now become not only an internal struggle but also an issue of international communism.

5 Foreign Relations

POLICY

Had international political conditions been different in 1945, it could have been very difficult to establish a Communist regime in Yugoslavia.* Despite the Great Britain–Soviet Union secret agreement of 1943, in which the two powers pledged that their respective interests in Yugoslavia would be a stalemate, the Yugoslav Communist Party, with substantial Soviet support, took over the government of Yugoslavia, and the Western Allies promptly recognized the new regime. Otherwise, deprived of outside help, the regime hardly would have been able to entrench itself. With these lessons constantly in mind, Tito's regime has been acutely aware of the importance of foreign relations, and endeavors always to take advantage of international political developments.

The government weighs foreign issues primarily according to their relevance to its internal political stability. In so doing, the Yugoslav new class is gradually shaping a rounded system of international relations consistent with its own interests. Foreign policy, however, was exposed to the strong pressures of the economic reform in 1965 and the new-class rout of the Party hierarchy in 1966. The former apparently developed self-management and attempted to apply it in the foreign service, while the latter reduced bureaucratic influences. In 1967, the Yugoslav State Secretary for Foreign Affairs, condemning the earlier Party monopoly in "foreign service operations," indicated that "far-reaching changes also encompass the administration, of which the foreign service is one part. Within the over-all reorganization, the foreign service too must be adjusted . . . to consider *the framework of its activities and its responsibilities in a new light.*"[1]

* In May, 1944, when German forces attacked Drvar, Bosnia, the headquarters of Tito, and a near collapse took place, Tito escaped in an airplane to Bari, in southern Italy, an area already liberated by Allied forces. Tito later returned to Yugoslavia, but this time to the island of Vis, deep in the zone of Allied protection, and led the Partisan movement from there. Very much like Lenin, who traveled through Germany en route to Russia in a sealed train in 1917, Tito returned to Yugoslavia on a British destroyer, H.M.S. *Blackmoor,* on June 7, 1944. *Borba,* July 23, 1964.

While the economic reform (see Chapter 9) tries to assert elements of business profitability, the practice of self-management formally shifts initiative and responsibility for foreign policy from the government to the entire society, involving national assemblies, enterprises, institutes, scientists, writers, sportsmen, etc., even to the private citizen who happens to be traveling abroad, or who by chance meets a foreign tourist in Yugoslavia. All are transformed into instruments of the ruling-class interests in the international field. In this way members of the diplomatic service have now supposedly become professional experts and advisors, the Party being the ever-present and ever-active spiritual and political coach, and the self-managed enterprises and associations offering, by means of declarations, resolutions, and other official forms, this support or that condemnation of foreign political events—according to the instructions they receive. At the same time, the new class is elevated to the position of incontestable leadership.

Criticizing simplifications and dogmatic clichés otherwise characteristic of Communist diplomacy, the new class insists that its foreign political views, usually described as "our policies of international cooperation," be applied consistently in a world of complicated relationships, situations, and forces. Members of the elite, though accepting the fact that international relations and movements represent an objective agglomeration, still strive to influence international politics and exploit them to their own advantage as far as possible. Although its operations are flexible, the new class firmly believes that its vital interests lie with the "socialist" countries or, freely described, the "democratic . . . independent . . . progressive" ones,[2] in a "broad confrontation with the forces of reaction,"[3] with "conservative, aggressive pressures," or, simply, with "opposed interests."[4] These "forces of reaction," which include particularly the Western democracies, should be fought, weakened, isolated, discredited, taunted, misled, used, and abused; thus a world revolution eventually will be achieved. In this framework, "imperialists" are accused of "trying to arrest the further offensive of progressive forces, to regain the old, and possibly to acquire new positions."[5] Consequently, the new class is interested in various revolutionary or "progressive," peace-loving movements, wars of national liberation, nationalistic ferment, anti-colonial uprisings, and the economic progress of underdeveloped countries—even when economic development is successful it causes sudden social changes which are apt to lead to political unrest.

New-class attitudes on world issues are contained in a series of postulates that determine Yugoslav foreign policy. The postulates are manipulated with varying intensity according to specific needs and occasions. One of the most important of them is the unconditional refusal to allow any interference from abroad in Yugoslavia's internal affairs, yet the new class maintains the right and obligation to be actively concerned, even to the point of meddling, with the internal issues of other countries. In addition, the new class sees Yugoslavia as justified in requesting the support from abroad needed for its economic development, in fact, for its stability.

Appealing to traditions of liberation, democratic inclinations, national pride, and the unity of the people, the regime deliberately presents its foreign policies as being so significant that the Yugoslav people ought to forget their potential disagreement with it, if for no other reason than the "progressive" quality of its foreign policy.* In this fashion the new class dually assures itself that foreign countries should support Yugoslavia because it is a sovereign and independent country and that, domestically, Yugoslavs should support their government because of its positive foreign policies. The new class not only devotes an excessive amount of careful attention to achieve this end, but it also indoctrinates the populace in foreign affairs. Important newspaper coverage is given to developments abroad and commentaries on foreign affairs; stressing foreign issues is in fact one among the many ways in which the elite seeks to de-politicize and de-emphasize internal problems. In sum, foreign policy is an important and potentially decisive factor in preserving the authority of the new class. Power being the ultimate goal, the new class pragmatically and flexibly, but always persistently, implements a type of "realistic foreign policy" in which the main principle is that there are no principles beyond its own interests.

The most prominent positive feature of Yugoslavia's foreign policy is its apparent insistence on the preservation of peace in the world and the effort to avoid war. War is considered the most serious threat that can come to the regime from the outside world, not only a war aimed directly at Yugoslavia, but any war—especially a world war that would without doubt disturb the existing national and international balance. The new class knows that a war would be too great a risk for its existence, regardless of the involvement or the outcome. If Yugoslavia were on the losing side, its present regime—if not the Communist order then surely the rule of Tito—would automatically fall. Even a successful war would very likely cause a shift of forces in the victorious group involving significant, perhaps decisive, changes in the composition of the regime. This explains the regime's stand against war, particularly one in Europe.

* Speaking at Gospic, October 3, 1967, Tito said, "Yugoslavia's prestige has grown enormously. The words of Yugoslav representatives at the United Nations and elsewhere are listened to by the whole world. In every corner of the globe one knows about Yugoslavia and her people." *Borba,* October 4, 1967.

The need for maintaining international peace, however, is replete with contradictions for the new class, as well as for other Communist regimes. In addition to being dedicated to its national, internal dictatorship, a Communist regime is also dedicated to world revolution. Under present international conditions, the maintenance of world peace is equal to the maintenance of an over-all *status quo*. The latter, it is true, is a guarantee to national Communist regimes against foreign aggression or intervention, but it is also an obstacle to the Communist drive to achieve world-wide influence; yet this dilemma faced by Communist countries in safeguarding their dictatorships, is surpassed by a deep conviction that they are always threatened by the existence of democracies anywhere in the world. The present emphasis on spreading communism under the conditions of peaceful coexistence, therefore, is shifting from territorial expansion to a more subtle weakening of democratic countries, a task which underlies the very foundation of Yugoslavia's foreign policies. Tito defined it in his statement on the 50th Anniversary of the Bolshevik Revolution, "[Our] international policy is based on the implementation of peaceful coexistence, *which is not a status quo, but which presumes an active struggle against* imperialism and colonialism for the establishment of equal . . . relations between all peoples."[6] This actually means a change in the *status quo* in the direction of fulfilling Yugoslav political aims.

Tito understood well the contradiction of peace in the world as a safeguard for his dictatorship and the necessity to change the *status quo* in favor of a "world revolution." Under such conditions the new class approached the issue of war pragmatically rather than theoretically denying that war is a necessary method for the spreading of communism—except, of course, if there is no other alternative. The new class justified its own position and supported the cause of world communism in asserting Lenin's concept of world-wide national revolutions as the method by which communism ought to be extended.

Foreign revolutions are particularly convenient since there is no need to involve Yugoslavia in an overt or formal violation of its alleged neutrality. By giving aid in various forms and differing degrees, the new class can participate in foreign revolutions. No international complications arose when Yugoslavia supplied the Greek partisans with arms in 1946–49 or when it gave similar aid to anti-French rebels in Algeria or to the former pro-Communist Lumumba government in the Congo. But revolutions may differ in character, and they can cut both ways. The new class therefore categorizes revolutions as either progressive or reactionary, mainly on the basis of the enemy against which they are directed and of implied Yugoslav interests. In other words, because it is in power, the new class considers revolutions to be forever finished in Yugoslavia.

Thus the new class accepts revolutions in principle, provided that they are not in Yugoslavia and that they are "progressive" in character, in other words, not directed against a Communist regime. Conversely, determination of counterrevolutionary activities is made in accordance with the criteria of the new class and activities once labeled as counterrevolutionary are considered a violation not only of national but even more of international order. Other developments leading in this or that way toward socialism are called "national political processes," which ought to be recognized as the sovereign right of each nation and, consequently, protected from inimical foreign interference but not deprived of foreign support.

"National political processes" may appear as the formation of a socialist government through parliamentary majority in a country, such as a *coup d'etat* producing a regime which leans more to the left than its predecessor, rebellions, or various anti-colonial activities, national liberation movements, revolutions, and so on. Kardelj stated, "In some countries peoples will settle this question [of socialism] through open conflicts, as in our country; in other countries it will be solved through peaceful methods, even through the traditional institutions of their political systems. In some countries it will be solved by the working class led by the Communist Party; in other countries the question will be resolved through broad coalitions and all-people's movements."[7]

Combining a respect for the national independence of other socialist countries with a condemnation of counterrevolutionary activities, the new class arrived at the "ratchet" principle, a mechanism of international conduct and law which would prevent the loss of a socialist position once it had been won, thus allowing the world to develop in only one direction—toward communism.

It is from these vantage points that the Yugoslav government identifies itself with peace; it automatically places within the group of "warmongers" not so much those who in fact threaten world peace but those who in any way endanger or oppose the Yugoslav regime, directly or indirectly. For these reasons the new class opposes Western democracies and endeavors to impress the Yugoslav public that democracies deliberately obstruct social progress and are unable to prevent economic and political crises. In presenting the governments of democratic countries as reactionary and blundering, the new class implies that Western democracies are stagnating and, as a rule, destined to decay.

The new class frequently and publicly addresses the people of the West as "peaceful and freedom-loving," "progressive," and "democratic." Actually, the people of the West are seen by the new class as potential political opposition to its regime, and as systems which ought to be transformed into revolutionary forces leading to social unrest, revolution, and communism. Mindful of this kind of Communist reasoning, it is easy to understand another dimension of the statement of the Yugoslav political theorist, Veljko Vlakhovic. In the Middle East crisis of 1967, Vlakhovic, in accordance with Marxism-Leninism, saw a confrontation of the aggressive pressures of "imperialists" directed against "the progressive forces of the world." Vlakhovic utilized classical Marxist jargon in this sense, calling the United States of America the "gendarme of capitalism . . . which preserves the remnants of colonialism and creates a jumping board for neo-colonialism."[8]

Profoundly opposed to the ideology of the West, Yugoslavia also refuses to join the Eastern bloc formally, having learned by experience that that strong and firm group would deprive it of independent authority in both foreign and domestic affairs. It is not difficult, therefore, to understand Yugoslavia's foreign policy of nonalignment, especially in view of its acceptance of an international balance as a necessary condition for internal political stability. Aside from a strong dislike of war, there remains the fact of unavoidable international conflicts. In addition, the climate of the cold war allows international contradictions to be both sustained and further developed in the form of mutually counterpoised blocs or regional groupings of countries. Under such conditions, a country like Yugoslavia could be involved in and escalated into a war against its will or intention, but while sincerely paying its respects to the ideals of world communism, the new class values nothing so much as its own interests and security. One attribute of its peace efforts, therefore, is the attempt to remove Yugoslavia from blocs, shunning the Warsaw Pact and condemning NATO and similar alliances. Such new-class attitudes are often, but not very correctly, described as the "politics of neutralism."

Yugoslav policies of coexistence and neutralism have often been deliberately befogged by certain words to create the illusion of true neutrality or coexistence and of genuine peace. Another delusion is that the policy of nonintervention in the affairs of other countries is in fact respected. These matters are sometimes discussed openly in Yugoslavia. *Borba,* on October 4, 1964, published an article with the strikingly self-explanatory title of "Alignment, the Secret of the Nonaligned." That this title was not an accidental slip and that Yugoslavia is really aligned was confirmed by Tito, who later said, "We can be neither unengaged nor nonaligned."[9] Of the many interpretations advanced, Kardelj's was the clearest, and it expressed well the motives, aims, and methods of the

Yugoslav understanding of nonalignment: "Of course, our views on the policies of coexistence, and with that the politics of nonalignment in blocs, are not only the most adequate statement of democratic ideas about international relations, but are at the same time a part of our socialist ideas about the roads to socialism. [That policy,] however, does not mean that we are avoiding responsibility in the great struggle of contemporary humanity to find a progressive way out of the social contradictions that today divide the world. *Least of all does it mean that we are neutral*."[10] He later said that the "essence of peaceful coexistence and [the policy of] so-called nonalignment is not only that . . . it is *not neutral* toward the present progressive socialist, democratic, and peaceful forces but, *on the contrary, represents an inseparable part of that struggle*."[11]

With its qualities of initiative and leadership, Yugoslavia was able to take a prominent position among the nonaligned countries of the "third bloc." Yugoslavia capped its role as leader by initiating and hosting the Belgrade Conference of Neutrals in 1961. The Conference of Neutrals was arranged mainly to draw together those countries not wishing to belong to either major bloc; actually, it accused and condemned the leading countries of the Western bloc. The very idea of organizing the loose and varied multitude of nonaligned countries, however, proved a failure. The Conference also showed unmistakably that Yugoslavia was neither as neutral nor as nonaligned as was claimed.

Yugoslavia's policy of nonalignment operates in the diplomatic field from the heights of broad ideological and theoretical formulations down to the most minute and practical of details, a range which emphasizes the great value Yugoslav diplomacy places on international declarations made at various conferences of neutrals—at Bandoeng in 1955, Belgrade in 1961, Cairo in 1964, New Delhi in 1966, and so on. One objective of Yugoslav foreign policy at those conferences was to get as many countries as possible to agree to generalized formulations convenient to Yugoslavia such as peace, coexistence, the prevention of aggression, economic development, and neo-colonialism. Once formulations are hammered out and the declarations published, Yugoslav foreign policy then leans on them heavily to define, justify, and implement Yugoslavia's own demands in bilateral and multilateral diplomatic activities. When a situation goes against Yugoslav foreign interests, resolutions formulated in Bandoeng, Belgrade, Cairo, or Geneva are quoted, and the Yugoslav interests in the issue under consideration are presented as international interests, ethics, and law. Practiced diplomacy maneuvers the other party into a situation advantageous to the Yugoslav regime. There are many cases which illustrate the success of "neutralist" policies: promoting revolutions with arms received from democratic countries; building socialism with capitalist wheat and credits (which Tito understood, and Khrushchev did not*); saving Communist economies with Western trade and economic aid; and inducing Western countries to finance the development of anti-Western programs.

The foreign policy of Yugoslavia, usually described both at home and abroad as nonaligned or "actively neutral" (which means at least pretending to be neutral), did not pass the test in its relations with Israel. Anti-Semitism was almost unknown to Yugoslavs before World War II; common suffering during the war forged a deep Yugoslav respect and friendship for the young Jewish state. Nevertheless, since the middle of the 1950's the course of the new class gradually and thoroughly swerved to side with the Arab countries. The Arab nations, especially Egypt, were evaluated politically as hotbeds of revolution and potential contributors to the weakening of Western democracies. On the other hand, Israel has leaned toward the democracy of the West, and was automatically categorized by the new class as a member of the "forces of reaction."[12]

Instead of approaching both Israel and the Arab states in an effort to seek peaceful solutions in friendship, the Yugoslav government went overboard in violently supporting Nasser and those currents in Arab countries which wanted to settle problems by force. Immediately after the outbreak of war in June of 1967, Tito spoke officially on behalf of the Yugoslav government, without even consulting it, and expressed "full support to the UAR and the other Arab countries, [promising] to do all [we] can to help their just struggle."[13] Undoubtedly such resolute condemnation of Israel and abandonment of the position of neutrality came about from Tito's personal attachment to Nasser, but it was also a result of the intention of the new class to utilize the unrest to provoke and accelerate a broad revolutionary ferment in the Middle East and Africa. The policy of the new class against Israel, according to the *New York Times,* has caused "misgivings even among some members of his [Tito's] government."[14] These vacillations within the government itself certainly represented only a fraction of the discontent of the Yugoslav people with the foreign policy of the new class.

It would be erroneous, however, to conclude that foreign political interests were the only factors which led the new class to interfere in the Middle East conflict. The new class actually made a great effort to

* Khrushchev's criticism that "socialism cannot be built on American wheat" was refuted by Tito in his Labin speech of June 15, 1958: "Those who know how can do it, while those who do not know how will not even be able to build socialism with their own wheat." See Hoffman and Neal, *Yugoslavia and the New Communism,* p. 450.

amplify the scope and depth of the Israeli-Arab confrontation in order to divert Yugoslavs' attention from their own domestic situation. That Yugoslavia is in a profound crisis is indicated both by the political ferment of the Party reorganization and by the bogging down of the economic reform, so the new class selected or welcomed the Arab issue without hesitation because it offered tactical advantages. First, the new class stated that the Arab states had been exposed to the attack of "international imperialism [Israel] that has passed to an offensive on a broad front,"[15] with the implication that it would be only a matter of time until Yugoslav national sovereignty and independence would also be endangered. Second, since the common Yugoslav is far removed from the Middle East, political propaganda against Israel could be intermingled with anti-Semitism which, though rare in Yugoslavia, can be easily administered as a disease of the mind.

Yugoslav foreign policy, however, stubbornly pretends to "keep out of blocs," seeking advantage in the United Nations, counting especially on the vast number of new countries. This is the reason that Yugoslavia endeavors to cooperate constructively in the activities of the United Nations. Better than many other countries, Yugoslavia grasped the fact that the United Nations can give much while asking little. Eventually, the United Nations and its numerous activities and agencies offer a convenient forum in which a policy of active nonalignment may achieve great results in establishing international recognition, publicity, and respect for the present Yugoslav regime.

Well aware that Yugoslavia is a small country in international affairs, Tito did not select the path followed by large countries in world politics. He did not try to take Stalin's place in the international Communist movement, nor did he try to imitate his methods, knowing that Yugoslavia could not match the achievements and strength of the huge Soviet Union.

Although Yugoslavia was not able to gain importance by virtue of strength, area, or population, it could still be influential. Prestige does not depend on size alone but on astute leadership, flexibility, persistence, the ability to select the right issues at the right time, the capacity to weigh properly the force of various movements, and a brazen disregard for others. If these points are mastered, then even a small country can develop a stature which far transcends its material resources. Tito said, "We have our worries . . . but we must actively participate in international relations. . . . Our country plays a role today as if it had a population of 100 million, not 20."[16]

There is no doubting that, by the policy of nonalignment, Yugoslavia has succeeded in establishing itself as an important international force among the newly created and liberated countries as well as among countries confronted with the problems of economic development. Yugoslavia's influence was determined in considerable measure by its demands in the field of international relations for precisely those economic solutions which are attractive to regimes in the new countries. Yugoslavia requests generous financial and material aid but simultaneously insists that there be no interference from abroad, not even in the form of observing how the foreign aid is used. Yugoslavia attracts new countries because it, too, is relatively small and therefore not dangerous, nor can it become a competitor—and least of all a colonial conqueror. New countries in Asia, Latin America, and Africa visualize Yugoslavia as a teacher, but they do not realize that the aim of its foreign policy is to achieve the function of leadership. Yugoslavia also attracts new countries because of its record of dynamic development and full employment which accompanied its strong economic expansion. Yugoslavia claims that it has an efficient system of economic planning which seems to be transplantable without Yugoslav political forms and which, requiring less effort and resources, promises to achieve more in a shorter time than other plans. Furthermore, Yugoslavia claims to have created a national type of socialism, a type desired by new countries that have grown weary of centuries of European capitalism and yet do not like the prospect of being adopted into Russian or Chinese socialism.

Yugoslavia also showed political acumen in being at once defended by its allies and supported by its adversaries, and this ability to find itself several sources of support is of great interest to newly established states. Finally, the Yugoslav regime can now boast of more than twenty years of unbroken political stability, an important asset in a time of frequent *coups d'etat,* particularly in the younger countries. The formula of enduring authority is attractive to many beginners in the art of government, and it is a necessary tool in learning how to consolidate one's own rule. Thus many new countries view Yugoslavia as a kindred spirit. Most of them can find certain pertinent experience there and, possibly, viable advice for their most pressing and complicated problems. Yugoslavia gladly provides counsel and, in addition, begins with extending economic aid to other countries, even though it is a poor nation itself and suffers inflation. Primarily in order to establish prestige in the world, "especially with the newly liberated countries," though itself receiving substantial foreign aid during the last fifteen years, Yugoslavia has granted $650 million in credit.[17] That is the price being paid by and the manner in which Yugoslavia creates its international image, which, in the final analysis, is only another means of insuring the international prestige of the new class.

Yet, notwithstanding all these efforts and the lavish granting of credit, Yugoslavia's foreign policy began to stagnate sometime in 1961, after the Belgrade Conference of Neutrals, and economic relations even began to "shrink alarmingly."[18] The Yugoslav Secretary for Foreign Affairs, in May of 1967, stated: "During the past few years our activity, though somewhat less spectacular, has become considerably more intricate."[19] It is of course difficult to concede or diagnose the real reasons for such developments, but the new class had to find appropriate explanations and excuses.

As a matter of fact, it was with disappointment, almost indignation, that the new class found its numerous international activities increasingly frustrated. Although failures are conveniently blamed on the pressure of "reactionary forces," Yugoslavs are beginning to realize that many of the advertised policies of "international cooperation" are wrong, costly, and troublesome. Sukarno, Nasser, Ben Bella, Lumumba, Nkrumah, and similar men are markers along the road of unsuccessful Yugoslav foreign involvements. Because of such failures the new class introduced self-management into its mechanisms of foreign policy in order to make everyone responsible on a broad front. The economic reform emphasized the profits of business, while self-management, i.e., the Party and the social reform, obligated all concerned to actively "engage more directly in the establishment of the country's foreign policy interest. . . . This guarantees that Yugoslav foreign policy will support and defend the increasingly intricate over-all interests of our society."[20] The entire matter becomes crystal clear when one keeps in mind that "our society" means primarily the regime of the new class.

The Communist World

Tito became well known because of his military successes and his assumption of authority after World War II. He became famous, however, only after his conflict with Stalin in 1948, because he organized and led Yugoslavia in a struggle against all other Communist parties. That was the first big rupture in modern world communism, and there were many Western experts who, according to their hopes or fears, asserted that the Yugoslav schism, the first crack in its monolithic structure, forecast its coming disintegration.

Since 1948, a great deal has been written about that conflict and the problems of unity within and between Communist parties. But it now seems that many predictions did not come true; communism as a world movement is stronger and more widespread than twenty years ago, notwithstanding its internal difficulties. When events, relations, and conflicts in the international Communist movement are analyzed, it is apparent that they simultaneously represent the ferment of growth and a crisis in the whole system. This can be observed in the development of Yugoslav communism and especially in the appearance of the new class. While the conflict with Stalin initially represented a crisis within communism, subsequent developments, as well as the efforts of the new class, suggest the creation of certain new guidelines, such as polycentrism, to elevate the entire world Communist movement to a higher and more rational phase as a substitute for the obsolete patterns of Stalinistic satellitism.

The problem of unity in communism did not appear while Communist rule existed in only one country, as was the case in the Soviet Union from the Revolution of 1917 to the end of World War II. Other parties not in power, and precisely because they were without power, were not considered "sufficiently equal" by the Soviet Communist Party. At that time world Communist unity was formally expressed in the Third Communist International, the Comintern, which was fully absorbed by the Soviet Party. Also at that time, any action or statement against communism was automatically considered to be directed against the Soviet Union, and, similarly, anything hostile to the Soviet Union was regarded as anti-Communist. The spreading of Soviet authority was tantamount to the spreading of communism, and Stalin stated at one point that world revolution advanced on the bayonets of the Red Army.

The end of World War II revealed a completely different situation of Communist unity, since Communist regimes arose in several countries of Central and Eastern Europe, among them Yugoslavia. The problem became even more complicated because the Red Army was located not only in defeated countries but also in allied ones while, at the same time, Communist ideology persistently advocated the principle of national independence and sovereignty. However, the existence of national Communist states did not pose an obstacle to the broadening of Soviet authority. "Democratic" and "people's" republics merely underlined the difference in quality, and therefore in rank and priority, which set the socialist Soviet Union above other Communist countries and the Soviet Party above other parties, especially, paradoxically, above those in authority in their own countries.

Under these circumstances the Stalinist interstate relationship known as satellitism was formed among Communist countries in Central and Eastern Europe. Superficially, national differences remained, but a complete homogenizing of authority occurred in fact and was embodied in the leadership and domination of the Soviet Union, which came increasingly to represent international communism. The totalitarian power which ruled the Soviet Union was broadened and applied to other Communist countries. Although Communist parties remained national in form, even maintaining different names—such as the "Worker's Party" or "United Socialist Party"—from which it could not always be seen that they were Communist, the point remains that a Central and Eastern European Communist group, including Yugoslavia, was subordinated to the Soviet Union. The satellite system became the Soviet form of conquest and expansion. Consequently, the spread of communism had sooner or later to encounter the same problems faced by every other conqueror in history.

The introduction of communism in Yugoslavia represented the application, development, and strengthening of the same principles and rules that were valid in the Soviet Union, but Yugoslav Communists did not imitate Russian Communists. The Yugoslav Party, led by Tito, sincerely tried to implant Soviet achievements and prototypes in Yugoslavia, taking the best of the Soviet Union; for example, the same type of Party, state, and organization and the same type of dictator at the top evolved fairly rapidly in Yugoslavia. Thus, inevitably, identical points of view made the Yugoslav Communists resist the domination of the Soviet Union. Acknowledging that the Soviet Union under Stalin represented the highest authority, to be obeyed and respected, Yugoslavs also felt that they knew what was in the best interests of communism in their own country. Assuming that in Yugoslavia they legitimately represented both world and Soviet communism, they became more self-confident. Thus, on the one hand, Yugoslav Communist power was strengthened gradually in proportion to the growth of Soviet strength and influence in Yugoslavia during and immediately after World War II; yet paradoxically, on the other hand, as their power grew, Yugoslavs turned against Stalin's satellitism. On this point Yugoslavia differed from the other Eastern European Communist countries which were more fully subordinated to the Soviet Union because their parties had been weaker.

The conflict between Stalin and Tito in 1948 was a crisis of Communist relations within the satellite system. With increasing heat, the conflict—the facts of which were not brought out fully by either side—focused on the issue of how to arrange relations among Communist countries and parties. It became more and more obvious that the satellite system could not serve as a basis or framework of unity among Communist countries. The Yugoslav new class, just beginning to walk, attacked satellitism as a form of Soviet, Stalinist conquest just as it attacked colonialism as a form of capitalist expansion. Stalin never condescended to acknowledge the depth of the crisis in intra-Communist relations, which, however, was eventually understood by his successors. Rebellions in East Germany (1953) and in Poland and Hungary (1956) and the looming problem of China in the Far East confirmed the crisis in world communism. Thus far the Soviet Union has failed to offer a workable formula for the unity of the world Communist movement, perhaps because of an unwillingness to abandon its commanding position. What the Soviet Union had tried was a lukewarm and unsuccessful revival of Comecon (the Council for Mutual Economic Assistance), in which the Soviet Union would again dominate. Actually, the Soviet Union did not at all intend to change the substance of the satellite system but, rather, to find more convenient forms of it behind a new façade. The less successful were these maneuvers, the more the Soviet Union was willing, or forced, to give in.

While Tito and the new class were keeping a tight hold on power within Yugoslavia, they had to wait for—and possibly encourage—the maturing of the de-Stalinization process in other countries, primarily in the Soviet Union. The new class eventually considered it opportune to activate, cautiously, the issue of intra-Communist relations. The issue is still wide open. The Yugoslav regime, nevertheless, is vitally interested in developing an international Communist system in which it intends to find its ultimate national and international security. Obstructions to the new class in Yugoslavia and to the Communist system internationally could then be condemned as counterrevolutionary, and dealt with successfully.

Deliberations about a new type of relations among Communist countries were directed primarily at those points of satellitism causing the most friction. Foremost among these was Stalin's concept of monocentrism, the total power of a single national center established within an international Communist framework. Monocentrism was considered inadequate by the leaders of the new class because it made them dependent on an outside power. Monocentrism is also difficult to implement and dangerous, since inefficiency at the center poses a serious threat to the vitality of the entire movement. The new class deemed it inadmissible to rule the world from one center. Instead of weakening the international Communist system by extending the power of a single center directed by a Stalin, the new class believed that power could be more effectively expanded if adapted to specific national and local circumstances. In practice, this adaptability, even with today's systems of mass communication, could be better realized in a national framework. The new class therefore rejected the principle of a monocentric, exotic center in the Kremlin or, even worse, Peking; it requested instead the supremacy of national Communist power in each country—in Yugoslavia, of course, of itself. On the other hand, the new class considered a coordinated international system of national Communist regimes necessary in order to establish and develop the dictatorship of the proletariat as a national category, while simultaneously developing proletarian internationalism as a world-wide system of cooperation among Communist regimes and parties.

Actually, it is clear today that the Stalinist system of satellitism has failed and that it is gradually being replaced with a new structure whose basic postulates are apparent, but not yet fully operative. According to data available at present, relations are being developed toward a polycentrism of several, even numerous, parallel centers within the world Communist movement.*

The new class does not view international Communist unity as a formal entity but as a network of informal ties of relations, attitudes, and behavior. Having developed through practical experience itself, and being pragmatic, the new class wants no formal forum, body, charter, agreement, federation, state, commonwealth, or confederation; it does want a supplementary force to preserve its regime as well as all other Communist regimes. International unity would consist, for example, of direct aid against internal counterrevolutions (as in Hungary in 1956), help against "outside" pressures (as in Vietnam), a common effort to aid the Arab countries against Israel (1967), or efficient "political processes" anywhere which would tend to extend assistance to communism.

The basic approach is obviously not geared primarily to an international framework of unity but rather to one that is national. Or, more simply, emphasis falls not on a formal new international Communist organization as such but on the strengthening of each national Communist regime and party—and consequently of the new class in Yugoslavia. The new class views collaboration with nations and parties as specific according to the need for help and the ability to provide it. In other words, all Communist countries and parties belong to the world movement commensurate with the degree of their participation, and they participate according to their potential resources and capabilities. In this way actions undertaken by and within the international Communist movement are indeed individual, but they are becoming more coordinated.

* Although the term *polycentrism* is associated today mainly with the late Italian Communist leader, Palmiro Togliatti, the basic principles undoubtedly were first postulated in Yugoslavia. Yugoslav attitudes and behavior are also the closest to a practical application of polycentrism.

The goal is to create a common stance which will be felt throughout the world as an effective protector of national Communist regimes and also as a catalyst for "political processes" in various nations for a "world socialist," i.e., Communist, system. The unity of Communist parties, by a dialectical interpretation, is therefore equated with "the diversity of our political positions, conforming to the situation and degrees of development in each country," Togliatti's well-known death-bed memorandum, in which he also stated that "Any proposal to create again a centralized international organization" should be rejected.[21]

The new class favors a type of unity which is not rigid because centralization would minimize, even paralyze, its ability to adapt to complicated and always changing world-wide revolutionary movements and requirements. No computer can calculate in advance when, where, and in what form events will occur. Similarly, no one can formulate a plan or plans for each and every situation. That is why the new class prefers to place emphasis more on common objectives than on methods. In this way a competent Communist agency can always be found to provide the necessary initiative and to take over the guidance of political movements. It would then be possible to consider promptly and effectively each case of support of a Communist country, to enter into more diverse activities such as anti-colonialism or the development of underdeveloped countries or giving help to national liberation movements. Leading the involvement would be the country, person, or agency most qualified to deal with each particular situation, and the country, person, or agency most qualified is precisely the one most concerned with the action.

The new class does not conceive of one world-wide Communist organization whose rules stipulate, for instance, that headquarters be located in a certain city, that meetings be held in rotation in every one of the capitals of the member countries, or that the host always presides—as is written in the statutes of Comecon. In the Yugoslav concept of polycentrism, a community of interests, according to which all the remaining questions can be arranged, is essential. Because of the necessity of cooperation, the future of the world Communist community acquires new dimensions when compared with earlier Stalinist ideas. The community should always be *ad hoc* but not chaotic, always current but never tied to an a priori set of rules or rigid forms. This was cleverly formulated by Togliatti when he said, "One needs to be on one's guard against forced exterior uniformity, and one must consider that the unity one ought to establish and maintain lies in the diversity and full autonomy of the individual countries."[22]

The above quotations illustrate that the concepts of the new class, once created in Yugoslavia and repeated by one Yugoslav Communist to another, became widely recognized by other Communist parties. For the new class such recognition was a great international victory, climaxed when the Communist Party of the Soviet Union eventually joined the polycentrists. The Yugoslav press gave wide publicity (in July of 1966) to the new Soviet view that "life showed again that the time had passed for guidance over the Communist movement from one center." It was also emphasized that the development of communism had become so complicated that "no organization would be able to guide the movement from one center without, at the same time, exposing the movement to the enormous danger of a steady decline or, rather, of insufficient consideration of the specific concrete conditions of its struggle."[23]

It is difficult to conclude whether or not Belgrade believes the new Soviet views on polycentrism to be sincere, but it is certain that the new class is wary of Soviet domination in the world Communist movement. For these reasons Yugoslavia's Party also decided not to attend the international Communist meetings at Karlovy Vary, Czechoslovakia, in April of 1967, nor the Budapest meeting in 1968. The points argued by the Yugoslav press indicated that not even an international meeting was seen as sufficiently capable of appreciating the diverse conditions and experiences of individual Communist movements and countries. By their refusal to participate at the meetings, Yugoslavs actively resisted the establishment of a general policy which might again be resurrected and which would be obligatory for all Communist parties.

That the Soviet Union is indeed trying to achieve or strengthen its domination of the world Communist movement was confirmed by *Pravda*'s explanation and interpretation of Communist unity: "The main ways to strengthen unity are common activities, coordination of foreign policy, mutual assistance and aid, constant improvement of political unity, and cooperation on the principles of Marxism-Leninism and proletarian internationalism *on the basis of documents which were commonly approved by the brotherly parties in 1957 and 1960*."[24] Having in mind exactly these documents which had formulated the common line for national parties, the new class avoided the meetings since it would only add new authority to the same obligatory line.

A characteristic of new-class philosophy is that the emphasis in achieving international Communist unity is placed on the freedom of action of each country, that is to say of each Communist Party. Yet this cannot be interpreted outside the context of communism and consequently does not mean that every Party can do as it wishes without limitations. That would not be communism at all, and certainly not international communism. "But this does not mean, of course, that they [the Communist parties] should follow the dictum, 'each for himself.' An attempt to interpret the independence of parties as an evasion of a solution of common international tasks, as a sort of 'neutrality' in the solution of common affairs, can in no way be regarded as either a sign of independence or a sign of maturity."[25] The focal point is that every Party is sovereign within its own national framework to make its own decisions and to conduct its internal (national) affairs. As formulated by the Italian Communist newspaper, *Unita*: "[Communist] unity ought to be complex and must, first of all, guarantee respect for the autonomy of each Communist Party."[26] This would mean sanctioning the most important practice of every national Communist regime, for once attained, authority is recognized as supreme and final.

The objective of the new class is how to place all the Stalins, Titos, and Maos past, present, and future, next to each other so that everyone can be perfect and impeccable in his Communist qualities, even though each follows various ways and uses different procedures. Then unity really will be unity and not a uniformity under which only one rules.

For the intended world Communist political community, it is best not to adopt a name used before. Thus the word *consociation** is used here as an unburdened term which will not lead to confusion, nor will it camouflage intent. Regardless of the term, there is no doubt that in international Communist relations a new quality is being sought and possibly created; it naturally tends to be expressed in new forms. According to the thinking of the Yugoslav new class, consociation will shift the emphasis from organization to action and from rules to common attitudes and a common behavior. Consociation will very likely have many façades, varied and elastic programs, numerous titles and names, but always the same objectives—the development of a world Communist system granting support to national Communist regimes and parties whenever, wherever, and in whatever form necessary.

The participants, it is perhaps too much to say members, in such a consociation are to be joined in a common defensive league, even without any formal written agreement or charter. Mutual aid is to be obligatory for all, always and everywhere, with any means necessary, and at the disposal of an individual adhering country. Each participant is to cooperate according to its skill, capacity, position, and, finally, its maturity to understand and accept responsibility in the common struggle for survival. In North Vietnam, for example, the Soviet Union supplied arms and experts; Bulgaria and Czechoslovakia delivered machines and

* Webster's Third International Dictionary defines *consociation* as an ecological community with a single dominant.

consumer goods; East Germany and Hungary gave mechanical tools; Poland used its ships; Yugoslavia sent medical supplies and initiated actions for peace on North Vietnamese terms; Rumania endeavored to mediate between the Soviet Union and Red China, while Western Communist Parties organized anti-American protests. As in this manner, each participant would no longer be defending just another Communist country but the world system of communism, including his own regime. Consociation would thus represent, according to the new class, a completely safe system of mutual and automatically renewed guarantees. Each regime would be able to manage its own problems, and in solving them it would contribute to international unity. This does not mean that international obligations would be ignored or nullified; on the contrary, it means that they are increased and intensified. "Each move of any Communist Party, especially of the one which is in power, has its own broad international implications."[27]

The reorganization of the Yugoslav Communist Party in 1967, therefore, was deemed by the new class to be a task which, among others, helps fulfill the Yugoslav Communists' "international obligations."[28] Tito has elaborated this view, which is not shared by several other Communist parties: "Our success in the realization of the social and economic reform will mean much for our country, but it also will represent a contribution to the affirmation of socialism as the world social system."[29]

The views of the new class on Communist cooperation and development through a specific international form, in this case consociation, provide a formula for tackling international issues. Further growth of communism would be possible; the crises of the satellite system would be corrected or eliminated; and above all, Communist regimes would be stabilized. The establishment of a consociation in which the world Communist movement could exist and function would be an enormous advantage for Tito and the new class. They would be unassailably secure in their foreign policy and strategy. When the regime could be guaranteed that no external force would overthrow it, the new class could occupy itself exclusively with internal stability, and each national Communist regime would be a kind of trustee to maintain power for international communism. And even if matters did not go as they should nationally, allied support would be automatically guaranteed, in this case by international Communist intervention.

The desire for these results motivated the new class, under Tito's leadership, to engage actively in the building of a polycentric consociation of the world Communist system. Meanwhile, the need for such action became urgent because intra-Communist conflicts intensified in the mid-1960's, particularly between the two strongest Communist empires, the Soviet Union and Red China. Accepting the hard fact of mutual differences such as territorial claims, national interests, and economic unevenness, but simultaneously seeking over-all political stability and security, the new class sees a consociation as one means by which Communist governments and parties could smooth out their differences with fewer difficulties and emerge strengthened, both as national regimes of dictatorships of the proletariat, and as representatives of a Communist international movement.

6 Administrative Structure

Pseudo-democratic Forms

Another characteristic of the new class is its contradictory attitude regarding laws. On the one hand the new class wants all laws to be respected since in the area of public administration it was confronted with the important issue of legalizing and perpetuating itself, while at the same time insuring that all possibilities through which it could be replaced were outside the law. The issue may appear formalistic, however, because the new class already holds authority firmly, so that it does not seem practical to suppose that anybody could easily dislodge the regime. On the other hand the new class is permeated with a profound disrespect for the law which evolved partly from orthodox Communist opposition to the bourgeois state in general and partly from the desire to eradicate any imposed limitations on its quest for power. Once power had been seized, and as the regime strengthened itself, legality became relative to new-class authority in its dependence on new-class interests. Although present laws in Yugoslavia seek to establish and enforce a comprehensive "socialist" legal system, the new elite considers itself above the law. Failing to understand its responsibilities to the people and the restrictions imposed by the very laws which it created for its own protection and convenience, the new class sees that the higher the rank held by an individual, the less subject is he to the law.

Power has also been subjectivized in the Communist regime. This means that the entire legal system is no longer a framework in which the rulers must function; it is, rather, an instrument utilized by them. The legal system has thus been deprived of its objective character in being transformed into a set of political or administrative tools for the ruling class. Laws became politics just as new-class interests have been proclaimed as national interests and as economic rationality was subjected to "social-economic planning."

The new class wants to preserve a relative validity in the legal system for its own benefit, but the new socialist legal system must at the same time be presented as objective justice to the general public. Within this paradox the new class endeavors to establish lofty legal principles which are treated in practice, when needed, like scraps of old paper. But consolidation of authority in the executive branch does not allow freedom or license to Yugoslav officials in the administrative apparatus. On the contrary, they are part of a strict system in which they must carry out each directive meticulously, even to the extent of ignoring and transgressing the law. Each official is concerned primarily with fulfilling his administrative responsibilities, but he also understands that emphasis is on his actions, not on the law. Use of legal principles depends on current political appraisal, interpretation, timing, circumstance, and last, but most important, on the persons or groups who actually manipulate the laws. Not dogmatic, the new class is proud of its ability to apply, enforce, adjust, or ignore any law or legal provision as it sees fit.

Every official is the trustee of a certain amount of power, but, of course, all officials are not equal. Earlier, when the new class was merged with high bureaucracy, the higher one's position, the greater one's power and the lower the restrictive value of the law. At present, however, the regime wants to subject and bind its administrative apparatus by state regulations which are in fact those of the new class. While each man must execute the instructions of his superior, he is also the superior of someone else. For this reason a Communist official has difficulty envisioning the obedience due the law as an objective validity. He knows only that orders which come from his superiors are law for him, and he wants his commands to be law for those under him. Thus officials tend to respect orders unconditionally, but to ignore laws. The Mayor of Belgrade defined this phenomenon in an interview: "Of course we have always been doing everything according to the laws and regulations. However, since I had to interpret the rules, it sometimes appeared that the laws were created just to be handy for me when I needed them and not made to be applied for themselves."[1]

Consequently, one feature of Yugoslavia today is a profound inversion of the notion of legality; namely, conduct depends more on actual circumstances and needs than on the impartial validity of laws, ethics, or morals. The ruling strata, therefore, can never violate laws because current practices are constantly being legalized and justified—with the result that law ceases to be a set of objective rules but becomes instead a set of generalized current policies. Immediate needs become absolute and permanent principles. In this light it is easy to see why Communist regimes are always torn by an unusual contradiction; while they are aware that they must be pragmatically flexible and capable of dealing with each new situation, it is difficult for them to change or modify current policies in practice. Each alteration in the political situation first causes a crisis then a change of laws and numerous regulations. Since Communist power is also personalized, shifts in policies are as a rule connected with substantial changes in personnel; thus, a time of policy change is also a time of general change characterized by vulnerability and weakness.

The tendency to overrate current policies is augmented by the fact that, even in times of peace, a Communist regime is a form of civil war. Djilas called it a "latent civil war between the government and the people."[2] During the Communist revolutions and wars, battles were fought with guns. Now the battle is to "build socialism," for which purpose both laws and justice are utilized as important additional weapons. In consequence, justice in Yugoslavia cannot be impartial but must be subordinated to current political needs. Tito outlined the function of judiciary mechanisms and the responsibilities of Communist lawyers in his address to the Yugoslav public prosecutors: "Not only do our comrades in public prosecution await the opinion of political organs, but they often wait a very long time. However, you should make your decicions without waiting for evaluations by political organs. If sometimes you are unsure of yourselves, then ask them."[3]

It was clear that previous judiciary practice had been to wait for directives from Party organs and that judiciary organs had been mainly passive instruments which applied the law in the political struggle as they were directed. In his address Tito did not change the principle that a law must have different meaning depending upon the political expediency of a situation; on the contrary, he confirmed this principle and even strengthened it by shifting direct political responsibility to judiciary personnel for the proper political interpretation and application of the law. This move was part of a greater maneuver by which the new class, as shown in Chapter 4, seeks to reduce its dependence on the Communist Party.

Yugoslavia, like other Communist countries that espoused the methods of a proletarian dictatorship, nevertheless practiced democratic procedures and forms, frequently with an almost religious pedantry. There are parliaments in Yugoslavia, and elections are held regularly, even though the parliaments are obliged to build socialism and the elections are not entirely free. One who reads the Yugoslav newspapers, however, will note an unusual richness in descriptions of the freedom of the people. As a matter of fact, the new class is neither against freedom nor against the people, provided that each is properly defined. In new-class terminology, "freedom" is considered to be participation in the building and strengthening of socialism—no longer a right, it is now an obligation. Since the new class sees itself as the representative of socialism in Yugoslavia, there are no restrictions on the freedom of the people to collaborate with or support the new class. Consequently, the new class views "the people" as those who are actively on the side of its regime. This definition was confirmed in a conversation between the American writer Louis Adamic and Kardelj almost twenty years ago, when Adamic asked Kardelj, "Who are the people?" Kardelj was precise in his answer, "All those are the people who in any way, with physical labor or mental effort, make a positive contribution to the totality of the constructive process in the state."[4]

Since 1946 Yugoslavia has experienced several fundamental reorganizations: Three brand-new constitutions were enacted (in 1946, 1953, and 1963, the latter amended in 1967); the national economy was centralized and then decentralized; economic enterprises have been deprived of all and then allowed some autonomy; self-management was introduced into the entire society; and even the Party has been thoroughly transformed. Nevertheless, Kardelj's definition of the people did not change in substance. New socio-political forms have merely been substituted for old ones. As the people were evaluated previously according to their positive contribution to the state, they are measured now by their degree of active participation in the "self-managing socialist society," as Kardelj stated in his updated definition of the people.[5]

It is not coincidental that the concepts of 1952 and 1967 have a common denominator concerning the treatment of the people, since each reorganization, though often giving the impression of confusion and even chaos, has followed a consistent line in elaborating the socio-political system of Yugoslavia. To overcome the difficulties of reorganizations, the new class is willing to compromise, but it never abandons the resolute ideal of building up its own system according to its needs. Again citing Kardelj, "[It] is vital . . . that we never lose sight of the basic directions . . . of our political system, . . . that in this path compromises will be necessary, that stand-stills and difficulties will occur . . . but we must be consistent in our efforts of constructing the political system and adapting entire social and political instruments . . . gradually, but more and more widely, to the affirmation of self-management relations and their integration into a single social entity."[6]

Following the view of the new class, the methods of self-management ought to permeate the entire society deeply so as to establish a definite social and political substance which would consistently embrace the society from top to bottom as the power monopoly of the new class. In maintaining such control, the practices of self-management would have to move upward from the smallest commune and local enterprise to the summits of legislative, judicial, and executive authorities. Under these circumstances, a new social pattern is being constructed in which the individual is increasingly ignored as a citizen endowed with the unalienable rights of man. The individual, rather, is emphasized as an ingredient of the self-managed organism whose functioning ought to represent the life of the society.

The logical consequence of such a development is a change in classical parliamentary forms. Instead of an elected *representative,* one meets a *delegate* elected or rather appointed through self-managed organs to which the people belong. On the other side, national assemblies (parliaments) are becoming more subject to the process of "integrating them with the system of self-management and direct democracy."[7] It is highly characteristic that "direct democracy" is being emphasized in the midst of a transition to indirect elections by way of delegates. Also, just when the Party is being dislodged from its powerful commanding position it is expected to encompass the political consciousness of the people. Ceasing to effect a transmission of political power, the Party progressively becomes a transmission of political influence, ideally uniting all individuals in their respective self-managed organisms, and then merging all such organisms into a well-directed socialist society.

To grasp the real meaning of the self-managed society, from the local level up to the national assemblies, one must remember that in Yugoslavia each unit is free, i.e., obliged, to make its own decisions, provided *"that it should be clear to everybody that our socialist community will not allow us to deviate from the path of socialism, socialist self-management and direct democracy, and the social role of the Communist Party."*[8] In implementing the role of leadership, the Party is charged with the responsibility of guiding the society and the self-managed organs correctly and preventing any deviations or distortions. Those who could conclude that self-management means more democratization are deluding themselves since the Party "continues to remain the most important revolutionary catalyzer." Or, rather, "independent . . . responsibility of the assembly and the deputies does not contradict the leading role of the Party . . . which . . . is one of the conditions for the *deputy's really being qualified* to adopt an attitude and *make conscious decisions."*[9]

Aware that life is full of "contradictions" which tend to endanger its power monopoly, the new class is mapping the social and political patterns of a society very reminiscent of, and even related to, the ideas of the so-called corporate state. Insofar as the new class succeeds in realizing a system of self-management, it will demonstrate its great triumph by establishing a mechanism of social equilibrium. This equilibrium will not result from the elimination of social classes and other causes of class conflicts, as Marx thought possible by the elimination of private property and the creation of a classless society. Instead, the new class recognized the de facto existence of classes and other contradictions and has developed the all-embracing social mechanism of self-management through which it seeks to channel and contain contradictions in such a way as to make their resolution possible only on that political platform which it allows, and which it terms the "building of socialism." Different kinds of corporate states or societies have existed before in history as ideas or concrete experiments, and for each of them the main purpose was to freeze social conflicts in favor of the interests of the ruling class. But, differing from other corporate social systems, self-management in Yugoslavia does not seek an equilibrium between mutually counterpoised social groups, interests, and classes (e.g., workers, industrialists, peasants, etc.), but wants instead an equilibrium between opposed interests within each of the self-managed units. Thus self-management emerges as the tool to stabilize the new class politically and socially.

Since the units of self-management permeate Yugoslavia's entire social structure, the new class tries to solve its problems by atomizing and localizing the conflicts. In other words, problems should be dealt with where they arise. When problems surpass the local facilities for handling them and spill over to higher and broader levels, then they should be settled by the corresponding assemblies of cities and republics and the federation in order that solutions may evolve in keeping with the essential interests of the new class—building socialism, defending national independence, developing the national economy, and stabilizing political structures. By shifting the problems and conflicts to a local frame of reference, the new class wants to devalue them and let the self-managed units stew in their own sauce. On the other hand, the new class is being identified with the building of socialism, and its status is made inviolable. In this way the regime secures political stability for a time through a self-managed society. But in the long run the new class will be unable to avoid asserting its conservative and reactionary character as the ruling and exploiting class within or outside the self-managed society, a fact that will lead it necessarily to its historical and politicial defeat. In other words, the apparent settlement of the new class within its self-managed society signifies the beginning of a new cycle of the class struggle.

Although the people are seen as those who go along with the new class, the dominant theme of the present elective system in Yugoslavia indicates that there exists a profound distrust of even those people who are being processed by the Party and organized in self-management units. The new class does not want to recognize a principle which would permit free elections, nor does it desire to allow the people to choose their representatives directly; instead, nominations are tightly controlled, and delegates are substituted for representatives. In administering the state, the regime can now afford to manipulate the people deprived of sovereignty and to use the Party deprived of authority. A system of "direct democracy" with indirect elections and delegates has been established. In the present elective system the ordinary citizens elect "communal delegates" to the municipal councils, and only these delegates have the right to elect representatives to federal and republican national assemblies. National assemblies, in turn, are dependent for their decisions on two centrally positioned minority houses, which will be explained shortly. Also above the elective and parliamentary systems there is the practice of rotation which sweeps the political scene at regular intervals.

When the delegate system and the practice of indirect elections were introduced in 1963, it seemed that the relatively small number of delegates could be more easily manipulated to insure the election of the desired parliamentary representatives. Yet, changes in 1967 indicated that the new class is intent on reducing the importance of the parliamentary representatives in general in order to weaken the entire concept of the classical parliamentary system—again because it does not want to recognize any inherent rights of the elected representatives or, consequently, the citizens. As emphasis shifts from the citizens to the self-managed organisms in which they are employed, so too does importance shift from the person of the representative to the letter of the instructions he receives. The guiding principle of the representative system is that once elected, a representative has the right to make his decisions within the limits of his own competence in the bodies (parliaments) to which he is elected; a delegate, however, is elected less for his decision making rights than for his ability to follow instructions. The essential characteristic of a delegate is that he is bound by specific instructions received from various levels—from the self-managed units on the bottom to the highest national assemblies near the top. In this broad range of the Yugoslav socio-political structure the leading and directing function of the Party must be exerted as an instrument of the new class. With this in mind, Kardelj's meaning is clear in his statement that "The question arises whether the time has come to more speedily eliminate formal political representation in the so-called socio-political communities . . . and to adopt the delegate system more consistently. . . . The representative system hampers, to a certain extent even distorts, the proper sense of elections in a self-managed socialist society. . . . It appears that a delegate system, if carried out more consistently, would introduce more flexibility into all these relations."[10]

Technically speaking, another advantage of the delegate system for the new class is that delegates are easily rotated. In addition, for all practical purposes the elite can informally monopolize higher-level delegates for its own ranks. The important point remains that in the system of representatives it is necessary to retain the procedure-ridden, time-consuming, and politically odious device of recalling a representative if he does not behave properly, always with the risk of creating a political martyr. In the delegate system, however, no one can be recalled because a delegate cannot transcend his instructions. In other words, instead of controlling those persons who are elected, it is more expedient to control their instructions. Suffice it to note that instructions can be either in agreement or not in agreement with the policies of the new class. If not in agreement, then they are politically unpermissible and automatically voided. By means of the delegate system and an obligatory political line, the new class may have set a precedent in a kind of political automation.

The limitation of voter freedom begins with inconspicuously set requirements which have to be met by the prospective delegates in order to satisfy the new class. A candidate's personal qualities should be commensurate with the function that he performs. Kardelj pointed out that "the deputy who wants to take part properly in the work of the assembly must be able to lean on all . . . means for the solving of contradictory social interest."[11] Kardelj was evidently unable to realize that representatives should represent the people, not the government. Consequently, a representative's qualities should be such that he is capable of working for the new class in the national assembly, which means that he ought to be able to stand firmly against "partiality" of his constituents and to uphold "socialist practices."[12]

When indirect elections were established, Yugoslav propaganda attempted to convince the people that the new election system was both democratic and socialistic. In fact, the new class proclaimed that who elects whom is not important; the important fact is that elections do take place. That is why the Yugoslav press stated that: "Elections in the main have shown . . . that indirect elections do not in the least interfere with the direct participation of the voters. That which is seemingly lost because the voter does not vote directly for a representative

. . . is more than compensated for by the fact that voters can directly propose candidates . . . and confirm their lists. And that is essentially more important than the formal act of voting itself."[13]

In the above and similar statements, Yugoslavs were able to confirm what they had already known well; namely, according to each of the preceding constitutions (1946 and 1953), which in their day were hailed as outstanding achievements of democracy, elections were not democratic at all, since the voting was merely "a formal act," and since somebody else (the Party) had nominated the only available candidate. Yugoslavs were also informed that they had been given the opportunity to "propose the candidates directly." However, "it only appears that the voters exert a main role; yet elections are in most cases just casting the votes," as explained by Professor M. Zvonarevic at the Zagreb symposium on the election system.[14]

The manner of nominating and the introduction of a number of candidates, in addition to indirect elections, are the main innovations in the Yugoslav election techniques introduced in 1963. Emphasis was shifted from the "momentary formal act of voting" to the preelection political campaign, i.e., to the process of nominations, in which the dependence of the citizens on the new class is expressed. This was neatly explained in *Borba*:

> The substance of our voting rights . . . transcends the substance of voting rights in classical [bourgeois] parliamentary election systems, which basically consisted of the simple political act of voting for a candidate of a definite party. . . . The process of nominating a candidate consists of a prolonged prenominating phase in the political life of citizens, which affords the possibility of examining thoroughly the characteristics and the quality of numerous possible candidates before making a nomination choice.[15]

The choice of "numerous possible candidates" is, in fact, restricted to persons eligible for nomination. The eligibility of potential nominees is ascertained by an undisclosed and secret political procedure, which takes place somewhere within the political apparatus of the Party and the Socialist Alliance prior to nomination because, as Kardelj conceded "If the nominations were implemented spontaneously and freely, . . . various antisocialist and destructive influences would be asserted."[16] This procedure verifies and proves beyond doubt that the nominees are acceptable to the regime. Persons exhaustively reviewed are finally allocated a place in the appropriate and confidential card file of eligible candidates. Also, the card files apparently must be approved by higher political bodies. Eventually, when all procedures are concluded, a file of approved candidates is established—a reservoir from which nominees can be *freely* selected. The Yugoslav press praised the Republic of Slovenia's Socialist Alliance for being the first to organize, in February, 1965, a card file of eligible candidates. The Slovenian files at that time included "9,539 people who have already proved themselves capable of strengthening socialist relations."[17]

The essence of Yugoslav nominations is the manner in which the new class has broadened the democratic "rights" of Yugoslav voters. Instead of being given one candidate for each electoral seat, as previously, the voters can now participate in nominating more candidates, with the condition, of course, that each nominee be included in the approved card file. Yugoslavs are thus free to select and obliged to vote for one of several candidates since each has been tested previously for subservience to the regime.

While elections in democratic countries are occasions which ideally manifest the equal rights of citizens to vote and be elected, in Yugoslavia, in contrast, the entire election system points to the existence of an intricate stratification of citizens, each weighed for his political importance, usefulness, and reliability. On the lower level are the ordinary voters who, as a rule, belong to the Socialist Alliance; above them are those who are also plain voters but belong to the Party. Further up are numerous citizens who are eligible candidates, and who are alloted places in the card files of the election commissions.

Eligible candidates are generally graded in three levels of importance: a lower echelon of candidates for municipal (local) councils, a middle level of those standing for republic assemblies, and a higher stratum for federal functionaries. Within each of these divisions eligible candidates are further differentiated according to the body to which they might be elected. Finally, within each card file is another selection of preferred candidates. In a word, there are first- and second-class eligible candidates. *Borba* has reported that, "On the basis of this documentation of the card file and the leadership of the Socialist Alliance, the election commissions will suggest a more restricted group of 5,000 people."[18]

Once eligible candidates are screened, it is necessary to select the final mix of those who fit the desired order, all of which has little connection with the voters. The planning activities of the election commissions often go so far as to determine in advance the exact composition of the bodies to be elected in terms of profession, age, sex, ethnic background, social origin, war record, etc. "It will take little imagination to picture the election commission (or some other political body) in the role of a tailor who designs parliamentary houses, according to measure and order, to the exact centimeter."[19] In order to give the impression that the people really had selected the candidates, the new class encourages the nomination of a larger number of candidates than potential elective seats—a method indeed changed from the former practice of nominating a single candidate for each seat.*

The most important part in the entire nominating process is played by the election commissions, which are not provided for by the Constitution, being, rather, private institutions of the Socialist Alliance. The activities of the election commissions, however, are widely discussed in the national press; they exert full control over the election processes, and they not only determine the lists of eligible candidates but also instruct political organizations and other organs as to what to focus their attention on. When necessary, the commissions also take appropriate measures to have specific people elected or even defeated:[20] "It is not enough to have files of eligible candidates. It is necessary to invent a series of new forms of how to nominate candidates . . . I [Kardelj] must say that our 'election commissions' are still undeveloped, and we must move toward more differentiated mechanisms of election commissions which could broaden their operations in the formation of sections, groups, etc."[21]

If one inquires why the Socialist Alliance holds such broad authority in election procedures, the answer can again be found in this statement by Kardelj: "The role of the Socialist Alliance can be realized only under the condition that the Party, through the methods and forms of its work, becomes, to an ever greater extent, the internal moving force of the Socialist Alliance."[22]

In order to insure that elected functionaries perform satisfactorily, but that they do not stabilize themselves in power insofar as they do not belong to the new class, an elaborate system of personnel rotation was devised in Yugoslavia.[23] Rotation applies to all elective functions in the state apparatus (federal, republic, local), including all economic, social, and political organizations, particularly the Party. In practice, rotation means the systematic turnover of all personnel in such way as to strengthen the elite's hold on power. The practice of rotation in Yugo-

* The ratios of nominated candidates to elective seats in the 1967 election were the following: for the Federal Council, 81:60; for the republic councils, 425:325. By republics the ratios for the Federal Council were: Serbia, 42:25; Croatia, 16:13; Bosnia and Hercegovina, 11:10; Slovenia, 87:60; Macedonia, 53:50; Montenegro, 44:35. Data from "Elections of Delegates and Representatives," *Politika,* April 23, 1967. For the Belgrade communal councils there were 803 candidates for 430 seats; for the city council the ratio was 533 to 212, according to *Politika,* April 22, 1967.

slavia illustrates the skill of the new class in using a device, by its very nature the opposite of permanency, as an instrument for maintaining its own permanent power.

Since rotation requires the uncontested political stability of the regime as a precondition, there was no mention of it in Yugoslavia between 1945 and 1950, when the Communists were struggling for survival. Some time later, during his dictatorship in the 1950's, Tito did not need rotation because it would have been an obstacle to the creation of the new class. Once firmly in the saddle, however, the new class introduced rotation as a means of weakening and eliminating real or potential rivals.

The practice of rotation found particularly successful opportunities for growth under the conditions of self-management, creating "an ever stronger linking of the [national] assemblies with the systems of self-management as a whole."[24] According to the present Constitution, rotation limits the duration of elective functions, as well as some appointive positions, to terms from a minimum of one year in the workers' councils of factories to a maximum of four years at the federal level. There are, however, many provisions in the Constitution and other laws which make exceptions to the rule. As a matter of fact, exceptions at the lowest level of functions, as in the case of the workers' councils and managing boards of economic organizations, are limited strictly to consecutive reelections of up to two years.[25] Somewhat less strict are the rules for higher functionaries, who are limited to four additional years;[26] while at the very top the exception has been made for Tito to rule permanently: "The President of the Republic shall be elected for a term of four years, and may be reelected for one further consecutive term. *No limitation of tenure of office of the President of the Republic shall apply to Joseph Broz Tito.*"[27]

In the matter of rotation the new class succeeded in striking a spawning bureaucracy by depriving it of permanency—and especially of the right to office. Besides, since the new class can occupy the top levels of administration in the state, Party, Army, national economy, etc., it is the highest authority and undertakes appropriate measures to behead the middle and lower bureaucratic strata, weakening them and making them incapable of any organized opposition. On the other hand, rotation was complemented, particularly at the lower levels, by the intensive infusion of new and young personnel because it is easier to manage young people who have had less experience in resisting the new class. Moreover, it is advantageous for the new class to become involved, as soon as possible, with the younger generation, "charging them with their share of responsibility."[28] For instance, in federal and republic national assemblies, at the beginning of 1965, more than 25 per cent of the representatives were under thirty years of age. In 1967, one-third of all voters were younger than twenty-eight years.[29]

The aim of the personnel turnover is to create insecurity among those serving the new class and to force them to compete among themselves in service and usefulness. In addition, as time passes, those who by rotation have become involved in collaborating with the new class increase in number and percentage. The ingenuity of the system lies in the fact that it established a dialectical unity of rotation, applying it simultaneously in two opposing directions. On the lower, much broader level of those who serve as instruments of power, the new class rotates functionaries vertically by changing various people quickly and systematically in the same function. On the upper level of the new class, functions are rotated horizontally from one member to another. Thus the key positions remain in the hands of the same group, as "It is important that about 12 per cent of the functions remain immobile within the same group, notwithstanding rotation. This is a low percentage, but when we look closely at the function in question, then it is evident that in them is concentrated an enormous political power."[30] When, because of rotation, those in the new class remain temporarily without function, then, according to the law of April 8, 1967, they receive the privilege of the same income as before. (See above p. 33)

One may conclude that rotation, nevertheless, actually cuts both ways and that the new class was forced against its will to regulate its own privileges by enacting the new laws. It is also evident that rotation was necessary as a precious tool of the new class to break down the Rankovic faction or, in other words, "to achieve what was expected of it: a more rapid change of cadre."[31] Rankovic's ouster intensified the conflict between Tito and the Party, and rotation was a convenient and legal form to aid in the general purge of the Yugoslav Communist Party.

Events in Yugoslavia since 1966 have shown that rotation and purges are identical in substance though different in form. While a purge appears, usually in time of crisis, as a kind of emergency measure, personnel rotation is in fact a systematically organized and routinely performed chronic purge. Thus Yugoslavia, consistently Communist, has a built-in crisis—the purge—which is one of the essential fixtures of the entire administrative and political system. At present, the large-scale purge seems to be over; that is, the Party faction has been more or less defeated. But the new class, through its spokesman Kardelj, proclaimed that a "partial deprofessionalization of certain functions and offices in the representative and political executive organs,"[32] i.e., of the state and the Party, had been introduced. Yet it is now necessary to adjust the practices of rotation to the new needs of the new class, and therefore the negative consequences of the "rigid application [of rotation] which sometimes has had ill effects"[33] are now being considered. More political flexibility is called for, and the new class intends to achieve it by the delegate system. As Kardelj said, "It appears that a delegate system, if carried out more consistently, would introduce more flexibility into all these relations."[34]

By means of delegates, who are supplied with specific instructions, who meet *ad hoc* according to the issues and items on the agenda, and who are always adapted to the current situation, the new class makes rotation more permanent and also more consistent with its aims. The dialectical consideration is that a more flexible administration does not herald the weakening of the rotation system, but, on the contrary, it shows the definite integration of rotation into the Yugoslav socialist system.

But many complicating factors must be kept in mind. At the very outset of the Rankovic crisis in 1966, international-level implications were evident.[35] Also, when rotation was definitely established in Yugoslavia, it was abolished in the Soviet Union. "The compulsory turnover in leadership," said Leonid Brezhnev at the 23rd Congress of the Communist Party of the Soviet Union, "results in the loss of 'good experienced Party workers.' "[36] In both Yugoslavia and the Soviet Union rotation was introduced to arrest bureaucratic forces; in Yugoslavia rotation has to maintain the power monopoly of the new class, while in the Soviet Union it was intended to strengthen the Soviet Party as a whole. In 1961 Nikita Khrushchev hoped to establish a competitive system favoring the most capable members of the Party—by rotation. At that time rotation in the Soviet Union contributed to the intensification of the struggle for power within the Party and in the already vigorous bureaucracies in the state administration, the Army, and the economy. Khrushchev, however, underestimated the power of the Soviet bureaucracies, which, though rivals, were sufficiently strong to cause his overthrow and to abolish rotation itself by 1966.

Since the Yugoslav new class, by rotation, isolated the middle- and lower-level functionaries of the Party from power, it is not inconceivable that some day such functionaries might turn to the Soviet Union for consolation, inspiration, and even support. From the attitude and practices of the Soviet Union, the Yugoslav "good Party workers" can draw political and ideological conclusions which could lead them to resist the power monopoly of the new class and to rebel on behalf of the Party.

The Yugoslav state system does not maintain democratic concepts of legality. Its structure, for instance, does not provide for a division of authority into legislative, executive, and judiciary branches. Instead, while deftly manipulating democratic terminology, the Yugoslav Constitution lumps all three branches together in one undiluted unit of power.

Operations of the executive branch are not balanced according to a democratic structure of government but are justified by corresponding legislative and judiciary activities. For this reason, a plethora of laws and regulations is easily and frequently enacted, changed, cancelled, corrected, or amended, even with retroactive validity if necessary. In the Yugoslav Constitution the principle of non-retroactivity is quoted only to be denied in confusing legal terminology: "No regulation or other general act shall have retroactive force. Only by the law in question may provision be made that certain of that law's provisions and the regulations passed in accordance with such provisions shall have retroactive force" (Article 154). Thus by the deed for which one became a hero yesterday, he may legally be today's criminal. The executive branch sees the government (the Federal Executive Council) as an organ of the federal national assembly, responsible to it as an operative unit and bound by its policy decisions.[37] Similar control regulates the judiciary system; judges and public prosecutors are appointed and removed at will by the national assembly.[38]

As a result of its efforts to control the state and society, the new class has exposed Yugoslavia to endless administrative and other reforms and reorganizations. Each reform is pervaded by the leitmotiv of the stabilization of the elite, requiring permanent and dynamic regroupings of administrative mechanisms and personnel, implemented in various forms. According to the new class, the entire "political-organizational skeleton of the political system . . . detaches itself from the traditional ruts of bourgeois parliamentarianism."[39] The parliamentary political representative election system, it is stated, is still partially mixed in the present Yugoslav system, and "unprincipled political cliques" could thus be encouraged to appeal to the people from anti-Communist positions. Apprehensive that in the bourgeois-democratic type of election system one enters into "a political struggle for power," the new class, in its reorganizations, began to drift away from the general Communist pattern of pseudo-democratic forms and procedures. Abandoning the democratic cloak in which the dictatorship of the proletariat has been clad and hidden, the new class, hypocritically, in opposition to the bourgeois system, wants its own "direct socialist democracy."[40] What is behind this attractive terminology, "direct democracy," was shown in the above explanation of the delegate system in which the political value of a citizen is measured not in an absolute sense but empirically, according to the degree of his active integration "in the concrete social and work-relationship" of self-management. Thus, in order to avoid the process by which, according to Kardelj, "a poorly informed citizen certainly becomes an unskilled voter,"[41] the new class de-emphasizes the concept of parliamentary democracy which implies the sovereignty of the people. As a matter of fact, the new class needs pliable national assemblies, an efficient state administration, a docile self-managed society, and a reliable Party by which it can rule but on which it will not depend. In other words, the new class wants its authority to exist independent of the people, state, economy, and even the Party. By openly giving primacy to its own political system, the new class demonstrates that the need has passed for pretending that the people possess ultimate authority. For this reason the new class asserts that nobody, under any circumstances, dares to challenge the authority of its political system. In teaching the people about "democracy," the new class does not allow them to believe that they, the people, could change the government or the regime by elections. The regime of the new class must be clearly and unmistakably inviolable.

In the present Constitution the new class staked out its claim on Yugoslavia in trying to make any "democratic uprising" impossible—not only by the people but even by the Party. This explains the complicated maze of seven legislative bodies, constitutional courts, rotation, recall, etc. Similarly, and even more effectively, the elite has blocked any unfavorable election returns, referendum, or truly democratic reaction of the voters by means of delegates, election commissions, and candidate card files. The new class went even further in legally protecting itself from overthrow from abroad; it denounced as unconstitutional, illegal, and criminal any surrender or capitulation of the present regime: "No one shall have the right to sign or acknowledge capitulation or the occupation of the country on behalf of the Socialist Federal Republic of Yugoslavia. Such an action is unconstitutional and shall be punished by law. High treason is a crime against the people and shall be punished as a grave criminal offense."[42] Thus the new class sincerely, though perhaps naively, forbade the replacement of its regime by internal revolt, parliamentary methods, counterrevolution, or conquest from outside.

The Constitution of 1963 gave form to a new type of political and administrative system of Yugoslavia, one which is presented as the highest achievement of socialist democratization. "The Yugoslav socialist system, disregrading all insufficiencies in its theory and practice, represents, nevertheless, the most progressive existing model of social organization."[43] Comparing the 1962 draft of the Yugoslav Constitution with the constitutions of Western democracies, Kardelj stated, in reference to the latter, "The system is maintained and safeguarded while governments and parties in authority change."[44] The system in Yugoslavia at that time was undergoing fundamental changes. It is clear that Kardelj considered the substantial advantage of Yugoslavia's pattern to be the fact that the system could be changed easily, whereas the regime could not.

On the other side, as an essential difference from other Communist constitutions which automatically grant power to the Communist Party, the Yugoslav Constitution of 1963 preserved authority for that group, the new class, which was already in control. In this way the elite proved brilliantly that it was fully aware of the internal rearrangements taking place within the Yugoslav Communist Party by which power moves upward to the top Party stratum, resulting in an increased transformation of the Party apparatus and the rank and file into the instruments of the new class.

Control over the national assemblies is outwardly manifested in a tangled pattern of parliamentary chambers. This arrangement insures that no law or measure can be passed against the will of the new class. The Federal National Assembly consists of six different chambers with a total of 670 members; there is also a seventh chamber with vaguely formulated functions. The legislative functions of the Federal National Assembly are performed by four chambers, one each of which is responsible for administrative, economic, educational, and social and health sectors. There are 120 members in each of the four chambers, but members may function as legislators only in conjunction with the fifth and sixth chambers, the Federal Council and the Council of Nationalities, which were established as a single body with 190 members in 1963. The Constitution was changed, however, and the original chamber was split in 1967. The Federal Council and the Council of Nationalities may act separately or in common meeting, but they must always be in mutual agreement. Each has the right to pass judgment on matters relating to foreign policy, state security, and national defense; they also can make personnel appointments which are reserved for the Federal National Assembly, e.g., members of the federal government ("the Federal Executive Council"[45]).

The seventh chamber, the Council of the Federation with just over one hundred members, was established by the Constitution to represent the apex of the power strata. There are indications that it can become the real seat of supreme authority as a sort of top council with a function in the Federal National Assembly parallel to that of the new Presidium in the Party. Between the Council of the Federation and the Party Presidium,* of course, no conflict evolves because almost all members of the Presidium are also included in the Council of the Federation. The Council of the Federation convenes with Tito as chairman, and its members "can be authorized to act on behalf of the President of the Republic as well as the Federal Executive Council [the federal government] within Yugoslavia and abroad."[46]

Representatives for all chambers except the Council of the Federation and the Council of Nationalities are elected indirectly by communal municipal delegates.[47] Members are elected to the Council of Nationalities by the parliaments of the republics; each republic—Serbia, Croatia, Slovenia, Bosnia and Hercegovina, Macedonia, and Montenegro—elects ten members, while the autonomous provinces of Serbia (Voyvodina and Kosmet) elect five members each, making a total of seventy members. Members of the Council of the Federation are elected by a particularly distinguished procedure: the President of the Republic, Tito, nominates the candidates who are subsequently elected and confirmed by all six chambers in a common session.[48]

In addition to full procedural control of parliamentary functions, the new class established a constitutional court that can nullify laws found unconstitutional; it has the right, moreover, to interpret the laws authoritatively. Both the nullification and the interpretation of the law enables the new class to change positive law by controlling judges—who belong to the new class.

Finally, there is the right of recall by which the ruling elite can control an individual parliamentary representative by having him impeached at any time during his term. Since a simple majority vote of delegates (members of municipal councils) in each constituency is sufficient for recall,[49] it is not too difficult for the new class to initiate and execute recall whenever such action suits its purposes.

Concentration of Power

Convenient adaptation of the parliamentary mechanism, efficient application of rotation, and directed elections, in addition to the subordination of the Party, made the maturing of the power monopoly of the new class possible. Consequently, and almost simultaneously, processes were

* It is interesting that the government decided to put the offices of the Council of the Federation in the very same building in which the offices of the Party's Presidium and Central Committee are housed, on Marx-Engels Square in Belgrade. *Borba,* May 27, 1967.

being carried out which led to a greater power concentration on local levels.

Due attention of the new-class regime is directed naturally toward the administrative-political division of the country because authority is exercised, directly or indirectly, through that channel. Even though Yugoslavia has retained the federal form of state organization, the local authorities have been changing their patterns constantly. Immediately after the takeover in 1945, local administrative units (counties and communities) were very numerous but small in terms of population and area. Such units contained many functionaries who had been in connection with their respective superior levels by departments such as the police, the general administration, the Party, and educational and health services. Nevertheless, as the regime settled down and as power became concentrated within the Party, the number of power holders on the local level decreased while the degree of their authority increased. Fewer but more powerful functionaries controlled territorial units larger in area and population.

Simultaneously, different departments were slowly consolidated at the local level into corresponding "people's committees," which had been shaped as groups of local (community or county) department chiefs. A smaller number of more important chiefs, such as officials in the police and finance, soon formed a narrower "executive people's committee" as the top power group of the local authority. But from the beginning all efforts had been directed to subject each people's committee to the stringent control and "guidance" of the corresponding Party committee and its secretary. Since the Party committee could not control all members or departments of the people's committee, a tendency developed to authorize the Party secretary to act on behalf of the whole Party committee. On the other hand, the people's committee could be more easily managed through its key representatives who constituted the "executive committee of the people's committee."*

The political role of Party superiors grew in importance as local department chiefs in the people's committees and the executive people's committees were increasingly manned by appropriate professional experts. Under these conditions, the executive people's committee became a kind of obstacle actually tending to support less and limit more the

* To understand the machinery of this system of the new class, it is necessary to explain the role of committees under Communist conditions: In the revolutionary days of 1941–45, committees allowed the activities of the Party to be presented as democratic, simultaneously mobilizing the masses and attracting more co-workers. Committees were also convenient for the application of democratic centralism. The form of the committees was advantageous also because it established one person as a false front while another really ruled.

ability of the Party to act behind the scenes. About 1960, therefore, local executive people's committees were accused by the Party bureaucracy of having too much power.[50] As a result they were replaced by boards, each of which included several related departments of local government. Thus the role of the political coordinator was enhanced—at the time it became that of a "full-time professional administrator,"[51] usually in the person of the chairman of the people's committee. But the master stroke of the new class was in splitting the functions of secretary and chairman, and allowing the chairman of the people's committee to become more important than the respective Party committee secretary. In most cases secretaries were elected initially as chairmen, a change in title rather than authority. In this manner, when these two functions were split in two different persons, the way was paved to make the chairman, who had become the political superior, independent of the Party apparatus; also initiated the process by which the new class began to divorce itself from the Party apparatus. In this context the chairman of the people's committee not only became stronger in relation to the Party, but was also able to merge with the local organs of self-management. Actually, the new class began to use the mechanisms of decentralization and self-management as devices to strengthen central control, on the one hand, and to make the controlling functionaries independent of the Party apparatus, on the other.

A careful study of the functioning of self-management, particularly in the examples of local governments, confirms that the new class, in addition to transferring all responsibility to the self-managing units, utilizes such units as a medium through which it influences all levels of authority. While the power of local government appears to lie in the people's committees, councils, and boards, political functionaries are actually in charge. By and large, the focus of real local power, formerly always a Party secretary, became the chairman of a people's committee. This man stands on the very edge of the new class; to those who look upward he seems a part of the new class; when viewed from the top, however, he is but little more than an instrument.

While the concentration of power consisted in strengthening the new class, it was reflected outwardly in territorial changes of the units of local government. It is interesting to follow the constant decrease in the number of counties and communities and the parallel growth in size, as shown in Table 1.[52]

Ever since 1965 the elimination of counties has continued; by 1966 they existed only in Serbia and Croatia.[53] The drastic reduction in the number of counties and communities is well illustrated by figures which

TABLE 1
CHANGES IN YUGOSLAV COUNTIES AND COMMUNITIES

Year	Counties		Communities	
	Number	Average Population	Number	Average Population
Kingdom of Yugoslavia				
1921	370	32,468	6,575	1,827
1939	378	41,540	3,831	4,100
Communist Yugoslavia				
1947	—	—	7,951	1,960
1948	426	37,080	8,063	1,984
1952	—	—	4,076	4,120
1953	351	48,180	4,139	4,110
1955	107	164,000	1,479	11,850
1958	—	—	1,135	15,800
1960	—	—	809	23,000
1961	75	250,000	774	24,420
1965 (April)	24	812,000	543	36,500
1966	—	—	516	38,700

relate to the Socialist Republic of Serbia after 1954, as shown in Table 2.[54]

TABLE 2
COUNTIES AND COMMUNITIES IN SERBIA

	1954	1955	1957	1960	1963	1965
Number of counties	126	42	37	27	14	9
Number of communities	2,550	737	501	250	217	below 190

As the state power in Yugoslavia became more stabilized, it was shaped into bigger territorial units with increased populations or, in other words, more power in fewer hands. It is reasonable to expect that the county as a formal unit will be eliminated in Yugoslavia. On August 28, 1967, *Politika* reported that counties had already been eliminated in Serbia in March, 1967. Republic and autonomous provinces will be strengthened, but the growth of communities, in size and population, will be accelerated. The recorded changes in the form, size, and number of local governments, which resulted from the concentration of power and its elevation to the upper levels, also illustrates the history and the development of the new class.

While local governments underwent the relatively uncomplicated process of the concentration of power, manifested outwardly in the growth of local administrative units and inwardly in the transfer of responsibilities to local self-management units, the concentration of power on the federal level has been of a much more involved nature. By the mere fact that the new class was identical with federal authority, the processes of the condensation of power were more decisive and at the same time more subtle. To shape adequately the actual power relations, the elite employed the federal form of state organization, profusely embellishing it with democratic and socialist features, introducing, in addition, an apparent decentralization to camouflage its power structure.

Since those who occupied the highest levels of the state and the Party were members of the new class, it was natural that their mutual hierarchical lines overlapped. The new class, first of all, retained key positions in the structures of the state and society by controlling the government and other related departments of the federal authority (judicial system, legislature, labor unions, the Army, etc.). The new class took charge primarily of the Party leadership, especially the Central Committee in which important state and other decisions were made and implemented by respective organizational units such as the courts and the national assemblies. In practice, however, the Central Committee became too large and clumsy, and decision making was appropriated by the Politburo, officially known as the Executive Committee of the Central Committee. A supreme body, the Politburo consisted of fourteen persons, each of whom was put in charge of a particular area of the society, the state, or the Party. Membership in the Central Committee grew from 135 to 155 (in 1964), ironically but definitely reducing it to a body for unanimous approval. At the same time the number of members in the Politburo increased from 14 to 19, making it much stronger and more important than previously. But the entire Politburo, in turn, had been controlled by an inner, narrower body, its secretariat, which initially had five members. It was a characteristic action of the new class that the secretariat was reduced in number to four (the member dropped in 1964 was Svetozar Vukmanovic, the leader of Yugoslav Labor Unions) at the very moment when membership in both the Central Committee and the Politburo was increased.

Yet, the hierarchical ladder of the new class did not stop at the secretariat, since its members were never truly equal. They were ranged in two groups because Tito and Rankovic were much more important than Kardelj and Vlakhovic. Though there was never any doubt that Tito was the first in command, however, he could not tolerate anyone near to him as second in command, as confirmed in July, 1966, by the ouster of

Rankovic. Tito's views in this case, were not entirely a result of personal vanity (Rankovic's microphone in Tito's home); he was also acting as the leader of the new class. The logic supporting hierarchical alignment in the development of the new class had been maintained, possibly by inertia, perhaps under pressure from the bureaucracy of the Party apparatus, but certainly without any opposition from the new class. The result of hierarchical development—many of the elite did not appear to be fully aware of it—threatened to destroy the new class itself. Tito realized in time, however, that a strict concentration of power at the top levels (which must, of necessity, be narrow) would eventually transform the new class into either a Party or a state bureaucracy.

The point was the crux of the Tito-Rankovic, i.e., new class–Party, collision course. In this conflict on the basic issue of supreme authority, Tito transcended the interests of his own one-man dictatorship to protect and promote the combined interests of himself and the dictatorship of the new class. He consistently attacked the principle of the hierarchy, exempting himself at the summit, of course, and finally succeeded, in 1966, in dissembling the upper echelon of the Party. It was a windfall advantage that, by ousting Rankovic as his second in command, Tito also achieved a further elevation of his already supreme position while at the same time forcing the new class to return to the old form of almost collective leadership.

It was a kind of rebirth for the new class when, in October of 1966, a new reorganization of the Party structure resulted in sweeping changes. The highest Party body, the four-man Secretariat of the Executive Committee of the Party's Central Committee, was abolished—thus eliminating second-, third-, and fourth-place positions. Then the Executive Committee itself became an exclusively operative mechanism of eleven younger functionaries led by a secretary, thus liquidating too the roles of men from fifth to nineteenth place below Tito. The new Executive Committee is charged with the responsibility of promptly executing the policy decisions of the newly formed Party Presidium.

The Presidium, Tito's creation, has become the supreme policy-making body and the consolidation of state and Party authority. It stands in lieu of the former Party Secretariat and the Executive Committee. Simultaneously, the Central Committee underwent further dilution when it was partitioned to function in five commissions and directed to incorporate nonmembers to participate actively in its work. While the hierarchy of the Party was weakened, the new class itself was strengthened.

By establishing the Presidium with himself as chairman (the function also includes the title of chairman of the Party), Tito arrested the growth of the aggressive tendency of top-level Party members to accrue power, a tendency naturally leading to a Party dictatorship which, hierarchically ordered, would promptly and almost automatically deliver a new dictator right after Tito's demise or removal. Tito, therefore, did not hesitate in the least to express his apprehensions clearly in stating, "I felt that with this type of organization we could prevent the creation of the personality cult, because as it [the Presidium] is so broad as a forum . . . with its 35 members, it should be a little more difficult for an individual to stand out much, since there are so many people in it."[55]

The new Presidium represents a cross section of the top of the new class, manifesting its united, all-Yugoslav character by including representatives of the Yugoslav republics and even the national Hungarian and Albanian minorities. Fairly well balanced, the Presidium is composed of the most renowned leaders, who together may represent the entirety of the new class and may be able to bridge the gap in leadership after Tito's departure. Tito conveniently eliminates his prospective successors when they semed too threatening or too powerful, as with Djilas in 1954 and Rankovic in 1966. It is the Presidium's responsibility, however, to insure that no single member, and certainly nobody outside the group, becomes too powerful.

Now that Tito has halted the movement of the new class toward an intensified hierarchical bureaucracy and has allowed it to settle down as a ruling elite, the quality of new-class power is becoming more objectified. While subjective power was manifested earlier in the prominence of individual leaders, since 1967 the new class has been characterized increasingly by groups of leading personalities. At this point it is no longer important to continue the process of condensing power—it has already supersaturated the top of the new class; instead, the new class must adequately disseminate its power throughout society. The first obstacle in such a plan was the hierarchy of the Party which opposed the new class in order to rule by itself, not to help subordinate society. With self-management as the most favorable instrument of action, the method of the new class in achieving its goal is to infiltrate the minds of the people by means of the Party: its "aim is not a Communist Party, but a Communist society."[56] The Party is dangerous as a ruler, but it is needed as a tool. Communist itself, the new class will feel secure in its power when the whole of Yugoslav society becomes profoundly Communist.

7 *Yugoslav Economics*

THEORY

One difficulty in analyzing the Yugoslav economy is that it is measured in Yugoslavia by its own Communist yardstick. Failure from the point of view of a democratic economy may be considered an achievement by the Communists, and vice versa. While accepting economic laws as objective, the new class at the same time insisted that such laws are of a different nature when applied under socialist conditions. In other words, it is alleged that the objective quality of economic laws is relative and therefore not transferable from free to socialist economies; thus, one should evaluate the Yugoslav economy from the standpoint of those basic rules which are valid for the socialist society of the new class.

The task of evaluating the Yugoslav economy by its own yardstick is complicated, however, because a preliminary recognition is implied not only of Marxism but also of its elaboration by the new class. In addition, the elite adheres to economic theory less as an objective scientific system than as a flexible justification for its behavior. In other words, the current political views and needs of the new class shape economic theory according to political expediency and the given situation. It is interesting to note that economic theory is not the responsibility of scholars. The function of the economic theorist is performed primarily, if not exclusively, by the political leaders of the new class. Among the most active are Vlakhovic, Todorovic, Kardelj, and Milentiye Popovic, three of whom are members of the Party Presidium; Todorovic is the secretary of the Executive Committee of the Central Party Committee. Recently, however, the leading role in elaborating the economic theory of the new class has been played by Milentiye Popovic, who was elected chairman of the Federal National Assembly in 1967.

The focus of the economic theory of the new class is Marx's all-inclusive formula of economics and society:

$$P = C + V + M$$

P is the total product; C is capital in material form (machines, raw materials, fuel, power, installations); V is capital in the form of paid wages; and M is profit, the surplus value created in the processes of production. This formula also represents a price structure in which P is the market price; C is the material cost; V is the labor cost; while M is the net profit. According to the new class, this formula explains the economic, social, and political elements of the origin, implementation, and results of the processes of production, distribution, and consumption in a national economy. The formula also expresses the class conflict between capitalists (C) and workers (V). However, inasmuch as the capitalist class has been liquidated in Yugoslavia, capital (C) does not rule with labor (V); on the contrary, instead of capitalists, the Yugoslav laboring class (V), in the form of "workers' self-management," supposedly manages capital.

It is important to note that the new class concedes, as an objective social law, that, regardless of whether people exist under capitalism or socialism, they depend on and are determined by those material conditions in which they live: "We can begin only with those relations which are objectively contained in the price of production,"[1] which in simpler words means that each national economy is determined by the quantity and quality of its human and material resources. Thus the Yugoslav economy can be defined only within its own material frame of reference, limited by the availability of capital—finished products such as machines, materials, monetary reserves—and work. Capital and labor are combined in the economic process; they define each other and create the qualitative standards (productivity of work, technological levels, profitability) of economic enterprises. National production partly reproduces existing used values (material and labor), a process called "simple reproduction," but new values are created by what is called "extended reproduction." While simple reproduction determines the living standard, expanded reproduction determines economic growth. This is again expressed in the formula, $P = (C + V) + M$, but the total product (P) is now equal to the sum of simple reproduction, which includes material (C) and labor (V), plus extended reproduction (M), profits.

Profit (M) is divided into the formation of capital for economic growth and into raising the living standard. Although the transition from capitalism to socialism is considered a qualitative change which eliminates the antagonistic contradictions between the ruling capital (C) and exploited labor (V), the new class agrees that a valid framework of the given material basis remains. In other words, as Milentiye Popovic stated:

> . . . fundamental changes of production relations, as well as the growth of [socialist] self-management, does not mean that the basic

> laws of the price of production will cease to be applicable. This only means that in the expression, P = C + V + M . . . the position of labor (V), its relation to capital (C), and to net product (M) is qualitatively changed . . . because under self-management, labor (V) is not separated from capital (C), i.e., labor is not under the command of capital, but is its own direct manager.[2]

Here Milentiye Popovic wanted to underline the fact that the total product (P) in Marx's formula is the material expression of a given level of economic development and a given volume of production and costs. Therefore, the sum of capital (C), labor cost (V), and profits (M) cannot be greater than the total product (P). In other words, one cannot eat more than is available.

This also means that the values of capital (C), labor in form of wages (V), and profits (M) can change their volume only insofar as that what is added to one must be taken from another. According to Marx, capitalists tried to increase profits (M) when capital (C) was given by reducing wages (V). But the point is that a free entrepreneur could increase his profit (M) through other combinations: he could retain the same wage but increase working time to produce more and achieve a higher profit, or, retaining the same wage and working time, the work could be intensified. Most important, however, is the fact that still another way exists in which capital (C) is increased by investing to equip labor (V) better, thus raising its productivity and consequently increasing the profit (M). In this case there was no actual regrouping. The size of the entire formula was expanded because not only more capital (C) is used in the form of more machines, but more highly qualified labor is also better paid, thus increasing wages (V) and profits (M); the other side of the equation (P) is also greater by the sum of the increases in capital, wages, and profits. This expanding formula reflects the course of economic development.

Independent of Marx, but within his formula, it follows that the free entrepreneur always changes his role during the economic process. When an entrepreneur functions by combining his capital with labor (C + V), he does so to achieve higher profits (M); once he has realized his profit (M), he promptly invests it in new production process (C + V), but on a higher level. On the whole, entrepreneurs constantly tend to increase their profits and, for this reason, all three elements (capital, labor, profits) thus necessarily expanding the total product (P). Although the economic theory of the new class does not mention it, this is, nevertheless, the progressive and creative function of entrepreneurs throughout history; they cannot avoid developing and expanding.

The possession of capital is not a final objective which terminates an entrepreneur's activities. It is, rather, an intermediary means of realizing his responsibilities as an entrepreneur in the turnover of capital (C + V) so that each subsequent phase is greater than the preceding one. A free entrepreneur is like an alternating current, continually changing his nature, tending always to be the opposite of that which he is at the moment; when he is combining capital with labor (C + V), then he wants to produce a profit (M) as large as possible; when he realizes that profit (M), he wants to reinvest as soon and as much as possible in new production (C + V). This alternation of the entrepreneur's nature compels him, on the whole, to work always for the expansion of the total product (P).

In sum, the function of a free entrepreneur is never any one of the three factors, C, V, or M, separately, nor is it all three at once; it is, rather, the totality of their entire movement and sequence. That is why an entrepreneur's function cannot be evaluated and measured in only one part of the process, for example, as an owner of profit, because his task is primarily to make the turnover of capital possible. If any of the functions of a free entrepreneur become separated and independent of the others, he then ceases to be an entrepreneur, becoming instead a hoarder, if he acquires only profit, or a spendthrift, if he irrationally increases his material costs (C), wages (V), or both.

Entrepreneurs must always consider the entire process of capital turnover, searching for the best combination and use of the factors, C, V, and M, more precisely termed the rational functioning of the economy and its laws. Seeking the greatest profit, entrepreneurs have to combine all three factors in a way to secure maximum production at the lowest cost. The tendency to decrease labor costs (V), especially under modern conditions, is only the counterpart of raising the productivity of labor. To grasp this point, the function of entrepreneurs must be evaluated in the long run, not from the point of view of a single turnover of capital.

Since an entrepreneur does not think in terms of the quantitative relationships among capital, labor, and profit (C + V + M) as momentary situations, but as the totality of economic processes, he, as all entrepreneurs, is indeed interested in social overhead such as education and health as investments in greater labor productivity. An entrepreneur is not interested in reducing capital (C)—on the contrary, he is always trying to use it as much as possible—or labor (V), which he always wants to keep as busy as possible and at high levels of employment. In looking for higher profits (M) he is looking for higher profitability.

Under socialist conditions there are no more capitalists (C) in a commanding role (ownership) over capital and economic processes.

Socialism compensates for this through two media: through the state, which manages and plans the economy, and through workers' self-management. The former method is described in Yugoslavia today as bureaucratic statism, while the latter is hailed as the Yugoslav (new class) contribution to building a better kind of socialism. Conversely, statism is accused and condemned as a source of political distortions (Stalinism, Maoism) which pave the way for industrialization by suppressed standards of living and low wages for the laboring class. But at the same time that Stalinism is condemned as "technocratic statism" the other side of entrepreneurs and free markets, "bourgeois-democratic traditionalism," is attacked as being identical to Stalinism! "This is," as Kardelj said, "not a surprise since, after all, Stalinist statism itself represents only a consistently applied mechanism of the political system of the bourgeois state. [*sic*]"[3]

Mechanisms

Instead of choosing bureaucratic statism, the new class gradually (1952–62) established the system of "workers' self-management" by which capital (C) and socialized labor (V) are combined in the economic process. Consequently, the character of profit (M) was also changed from privately appropriated to directly social—a profit of the entire laboring class. Since there is no private ownership of capital, self-management, according to Yugoslav theories of socialism, replaces the former capitalist owner-entrepreneur or Stalinist plans of state economics, thus allegedly eliminating the "antagonistic contradiction" between capitalists or the state, on the one hand, and the laboring class on the other. The worker is supposed to operate the national economy by means of self-management on behalf of the entire society. The economic theory of the new class maintains that new values (M) in Yugoslavia belong to the laboring class who created them, as Marx postulated, but also that the laboring class, through self-management, implements processes of "social reproduction," i.e., manages the national economy.*

The establishment of self-management was touted to be the abolition of "state economic planning," but it in fact brought about a new type of

* "Because in our society the labor and hiring relations are being transformed, the category of personal income is to be understood as gross personal income, which reflects the change in the relationship between labor [V] and capital formation [M]. Personal income in our system is also quantitatively something different from hiring. It contains in itself a number of elements which mean general consumption. *Or put into everyday language: Social state services should be financed from personal income.*" M. Popovic, *loc. cit.* Our italics.

directed socialist society, a "consciously planned association" in which "social relations and movements are regulated by planning and coordination directly through self-management."[4]

The important factor is that the entire national product remains under the control of the regime which, through the social-economic plan and other devices, determines national monetary and fiscal policies and prices. In this manner the new class, even before workers' self-management was able to operate, had fixed the levels of national production (P) and employment. Other relevant ratios of the distribution and utilization of national production (P) and its component parts of capital (C), wages and employment (V), and profits (M) were also determined beforehand. Of particular importance are the budgets ascertaining the general consumption (GC), which consist of state (federal, republic, and local), military, social, and other overhead expenditures.* But, notwithstanding all the talk about a self-managed society, Kardelj confirmed that the state will have jurisdiction to determine spending in "the maintenance of society, its economic stability, and its culture and civilization . . . for a long time to come."[5]

By fixing the quantitative elements of national production (P) and its utilization (capital, wages, and capital formation, i.e., $C + V + M$) in general economic terms, the new class has done much more because it also determined the quality of possible social and economic relations. In other words, the new class alone sets the conditions which later result in low wages, thus depriving the economy of incentives. It still establishes or maintains high costs of production by regulating taxes and prices; it preserves the low productivity of labor, sanctions erroneous investment decisions, and causes losses in enterprises. These and similar factors and their interactions explain how economic crises are produced and why it is so difficult to find solutions.

Self-management, in the final analysis, means that the workers in Yugoslavia are expropriated by the regime, as Kardelj himself was forced to admit,[6] though all responsibilities are fixed on the self-management organs of the workers, and eventually on the workers themselves.

The workers' self-management bureaus are required to correctly implement the economic processes determined basically in advance by the new class. Since the new class has budgeted its own expenditures in the general consumption, and also those needed for economic growth, the enterprises can allocate the remainder through their workers' councils, the result being low wages. It superficially seems that the economic

* "Federal and republic provisions determine the budgets of communities . . . [but] what decisive voice do citizens have when 90 per cent of the budgets are fixed by the acts of federal and republic organs?" *Borba,* October 2, 1967.

processes as a whole are the aggregate functioning of self-management units. The conclusion, then, is that critical and unfavorable developments of the national economy are to be blamed on erroneous business decisions and incorrect behavior of enterprises, or the organs of self-management, but not on the state or the regime.

As a result of self-management and other devices in Yugoslavia, Marx's formula was modified. $P = C + V + M$ became $P = C + (PC + GC + M)$, in which P stands for the total product, C for material costs, PC for personal consumption, GC for general consumption, and M for capital formation. The important point is the consolidation of labor (V) and profits (M) into one group in which the components—personal and general consumption, capital formation—are mutually delineated by a specific procedure. Namely, the economic theory of the new class holds that drawing the line between wages (V) and profit (M) is the jurisdiction of self-management. Since that delineation is exactly the area of conflict between labor and capital in capitalism, Milentiye Popovic said, "Inevitably several political parties are created [in capitalism]; if, instead, there is only one political party, that means that there is no democracy,"[7] i.e. there is a dictatorship which alone decides the borderline between wages (V) and profit (M). It is different in Yugoslavia, however, because the one-party system there, according to Milentiye Popovic, does not necessarily mean a dictatorship. The distribution between wages (V) and profit (M) is supposed to be an internal matter of each self-managed unit in which "a special form of free political association, which we call direct democracy."[8] is established. Since—and one meets here again the idea of a corporate organization of society—the most important contradiction—the distribution of income between wages and profit—is contained within the self-managed units, the opportunity for essentially conflicting economic and political philosophies to erupt on the national level is precluded. The new class reasons, in consequence, that there is no need to express differences in the form of several political parties, but that "This in other words means that society can be democratic without a multi-party system,"[9] the implication being that since a one-party system "can be democratic," the new-class system *is* democratic.

Yet the fact remains that self-management relations necessarily "bring about inequalities among men, economic units, communities, and nations."[10] For this reason the Communist Party is needed to discover "forms of conflict between these contradictions . . . and to resolve them."[11] At this stage it is useful to return to the initial point, that in the Yugoslav system it is allegedly the jurisdiction of self-management to fix the line between wages (V) and profit (M), and to correlate that point with the fact that it is the duty of the Party, through "its uniform attitude and the activity of its members,"[12] to see that the dividing line is drawn exactly where it should be, as directed by those who control the Party—the new class. This was also one of the reasons that the Party underwent profound changes intended to make it, for all practical purposes, a tool of the new class, but at the same time to make self-management an instrument of the Party.

The advantage to Yugoslavia of the transformation of the Party is that self-management has freed its economy of the stigma of statism and bureaucratism. Even more important, the new class attained a kind of a permanent alibi: it would be very difficult to prove that the Party, much less the new class, legally has anything to do with the distribution of incomes or appropriation of profits created by the work of another person. Similarly, the new class cannot be viewed formally as the principal wielder of power. In other words, the new class believes to have succeeded in fully removing itself from the spotlight of Marx's formula.

There is a disadvantage for the new class which is indirectly decisive, however. The capitalist entrepreneur has not only made profit his goal, but has also established it as a criterion for his success. If he fails to make a profit he becomes bankrupt and is disqualified from participating in the economic process. The new class, on the contrary, sees profit (M), under the name of net product, as an integral part of labor compensation (V) because labor and its product are directly social. In so doing, the new class measures the extent to which an enterprise has met its obligations to society (the state and new class) by the yardstick of the net income of the enterprise. But, by merging V and M, neither the new class nor the workers' self-management (the enterprise) can calculate the real profit or loss of an enterprise. The new class has actually deprived itself—and the economy—of a measure of profitability. One of the main objectives of the economic reform (see Chapter 9) was an attempt to identify real profit.

In addition to eliminating the measure of profitability, the self-management scheme backfired by also befuddling the use of capital (C) in the economic process. A certain confusion resulted from the position of the new class in Marx's formula by emphasizing it as a co-creator, with the laboring class, of new values. (Another interpretation of Marx's formula, $P = C + V + M$, indicates the class struggle by taking C = capitalist, V = worker, and M = profit.) More importantly, labor, acting through self-management, began making decisions relating to the operative utilization of capital in the current economic process. The new class did not consider this development too risky since it assumed that the functioning of workers' self-management remained within the coordinates fixed by the new class—"economic plans," state economic policies, measures, and administrative regulations. The elite desired and intended that self-management be stimulated to increase the total product (P).

After determining the material limits within which self-management could operate, the new class made a political promise clothed in a generalized theoretical statement. "Wages [V] should continuously grow and should occupy a greater place in the product [P] than, all conditions being equal, in a capitalist or state bureaucratic system."[13] In Yugoslav reality, however, wages are very low, and "all conditions being equal" they are markedly lower than those in democratic economies, all because of the overriding priority given to the needs of the new class. Kardelj explained, "because of inequalities in distribution according to work rendered, . . . the worker is expropriated until the very end regarding the surplus product [profit], which, it is true, *is done on behalf of the entire society but, in reality, on behalf of the state authority.*"[14]

A tremendous strain of opposing and mutually competing pressures which, bound by the given total product (P), result in the suppression of wages and personal consumption has thus been built into the economic system. Pressures are intensified because Yugoslavia's national economy is relatively undeveloped and poor and, at the same time, has been exposed to a climate of artificially overheated economic expansion. The latter makes it necessary to utilize obsolete technological facilities, causing higher production costs and opening a vicious circle in which higher costs reduce the volume of profits so that economic development is decelerated and low labor productivity preserved. Low labor productivity has also been maintained by the policies of full employment and development which established a higher volume of production at the price of higher average costs. This type of economic growth is known as the extensive rise of production or "very extensive growth based on the simple multiplication of the producing capacities of the existing technical structure."[15]

Yet, workers' self-management bureaus are the heart of the economic process; they have been given the opportunity to manage, but are burdened with low wages. Under the circumstances described, workers become vitally interested in expanding or maintaining their wages when the cost of living rises and when high production costs depress profits. At this point an enormous degree of personal consumption breaks into the area of the material costs of production. While Marx used his formula to clarify his economic and political concepts, the new class wanted to use the same formula not to explain but to justify its concepts. Its formula, therefore, became a smoke screen intended to hide its grip on labor (V) and the parasitic appropriation of profits (M). The same screen, however, hides self-management's invasion by introducing personal consumption (PC) and wages in the material costs of production (C).

The contradictory interests of the new class and wage earners are one of the fundamental problems of Communist economics. Not only is the volume of production (P) lower when compared with needs, but because of it—and the lack of economic incentives—low labor productivity is preserved and economic development decelerated, each being at the same time the cause and the consequence of high production costs. Production is expensive and noncompetitive, and the economic process is wasteful and often unprofitable.

High costs of production, which partially constitute a hidden form of increased personal consumption, are seen in many cases typical of Yugoslavia's economic framework. This is further disguised by understated depreciation rates which siphon national wealth to current consumption in the form of overstated or inflated profits. Obsolete machines are operated more for the sake of employment than production; faulty investments and erroneous calculations* in current production (producing outdated or low-quality goods which, unsold, pile up in warehouses) add to the problem.

The daily wage, no longer compensation for work actually accomplished, became a vested right and the starting point for a series of concurrent advantages and facilities, all of which increase production costs. When employed, one's nominal wage remains low, frequently below the minimum for basic existence; yet, self-management connives to meet the worker's needs in various direct and, especially, indirect ways. The apartment of a man employed in a plant is probably subsidized through underrated rent; more than likely his lunch at the factory cafeteria costs less than the market price; summer is spent at a recreation center where the board bill is less than the actual expense; he also enjoys lowered railroad fares (along with huge railroad deficits). All employees, in addition, take advantage of guaranteed social insurance with full retirement benefits and free health service, free education, state recreational facilities, and sports. It was only in 1965, at the time of the economic reform, that practices overtaxing the national economic capacity were publicly de-

* One particular example of "erroneous calculations" is the case of the Velenye coal mines in Slovenia. Partly for the sake of political publicity, partly for the subsidizing of political connections, it was decided, without sufficient economic justification and by actually suppressing or distorting the facts, to build an ultra modern coal center, at the cost of $61 million. After $10 million had already been spent on the project, it was discovered that the project would be an outright loss, and the whole affair had to be cancelled. *Borba,* July 23, 1967.

nounced. Kiro Gligorov, Yugoslavia's Minister of Finance at the time, said, "When, however, we come into contact with countries abroad, the veil which obscures the actual situation is removed because exchange is conducted according to world prices and because in world markets the production costs of more developed producers are decisive."[16]

Socialist processes of production in Yugoslavia are hailed there as the creative use of capital (machines and materials) to produce new values, yet human work under these conditions becomes an erosion and misuse of national capital and wealth because of overly high production costs. Waste is not taken into account when natural resources are exploited (forests, mines, and the like) since they are free and not seen as an immediate value. The erosion of capital is given consideration, however, in cases when earlier capital investments have been neglected or over-exploited, as in frequent railroad accidents;[17] when unrepaired dams and canals cause disastrous floods, as in 1965; when mines, not properly maintained, contribute to frequent catastrophes.* But regardless of how the dissipation of national capital is accomplished, huge material wastes inevitably accumulate and cause unnecessary human suffering and loss.

The manner in which irrational spending in Yugoslavia's national economy is concealed reveals a new paradox: waste in production is presented as a gain in the national economy. The ceaseless investment of new capital increases fixed and working capital (C) engaged in the processes of production, resulting, under conditions of full employment and forced economic development, in the extensive growth of production so that high production costs are maintained or raised. The gist of the problem is that such production costs rise above the rational level, the difference being met by injecting capital from national capital formation (M), by using up previously accumulated national wealth and reserves, or by borrowing from abroad. The paradox remains that, just as the total product (P) appears to increase in volume on its side of Marx's equation, the costs of material production (C) on the other side increase above their normal rational level from the invasion of spending and consumption in the production costs.

* In the summer of 1967 many areas of Yugoslavia, particularly Serbia, Bosnia and Hercegovina, and Montenegro, were invaded by swarms of mice which destroyed wheat, hay, orchards, etc., and caused tremendous losses to producers of those crops. Organizations of experts and meetings of symposiums failed to produce a plan of action, but they agreed that the mice were indeed responsible for the losses. Few dared to point out that the mice had not dropped from the skies, but had been favored by many circumstances—no precautions against them, the extermination of foxes and hawks, upsetting nature's equilibrium. Instead of reacting promptly to correct earlier errors, the federal Secretariat for the National Economy decided to "consider the appearance of mice as a national disaster and behave accordingly," as reported in *Politika,* August 30, 1967; September 1 and 2, 1967.

Thus the problems become more serious as the Yugoslav economy reaches higher levels of production and development. By way of irrationally high costs (C), previously invested capital and national wealth flow simultaneously into the total product (P) and into more costs and consumption. Both sides of the formula increase by the same amount and therefore appear to be balanced. In this way the real situation of a degraded economy is not only hidden, but failures are presented as successes.

Unable to make ends meet or to compensate for the waste of national capital, the burden of loss to Yugoslavia's economy is shifted to the populace. Although it is certainly not in the political interest of the new class to antagonize the people, the new class is forced to lower the living standard or to slow down its rise. With the setbacks and poor functioning of the economic system, the slow-down in the rise of the standard of living is a result and at the same time a source of contradictions that strain the system internally.

The existence of the elite also caused a new kind of class struggle which can be explained in the theoretical arsenal of the new class itself. In addition to its economic aspect, Marx's formula, $P = C + V + M$, explains the class struggle between capitalists (C) and workers (V); the former appropriate profits produced by the latter. The new class theorizes that since the capitalist class no longer exists, capital (C) now represents only a mass of materialized values which are at present under the management of the working people in the form of workers' self-management. Since the workers are identified with society, the profits (M) created by them are considered as belonging to the entire nation. In this way the new class sought to modify Marx's formula of the class struggle into a formula of social harmony. Consequently, there allegedly was no longer a contradiction between profits and wages, and the new class sees profits and wages as merged categories. In the new formula the different uses of personal consumption (PC), general consumption (GC), and capital formation (M) are discernible, though there is some overlapping. Instead of Marx's $P = C + V + M$, the new class has set $P = C + (PC + GC + M)$. However, the distinction between PC and GC is essential because personal and general consumption fundamentally divide Yugoslav society into the exploiters and the exploited. Thus, though certainly against the intention or will of the new class, Marx's modified formula actually turns out to be the formula for the new-class conflict, but this time between the new and the working class.

These comments on the economic theorizing of the new class are not intended to enlighten the reader with Marxist semantics, nor are they intended to give a "scientific" clarification of the problem. The only purpose is to present, from those theoretical rules and positions, the economic and social issues that are alone recognized as valid in Yugoslavia today. The advantage of the new class in all this, evidently, is that it not only formulates these rules but can and does change and adapt them according to its needs.

Placing itself apart from the national economy, the new class differs from other exploiting classes. While capitalists are denounced for both managing economic processes and collecting profits, the new class, on the other hand, after charging the workers' self-management groups with responsibility for the economic process (Tito said, "Self-management means at the same time a strengthening of the personal responsibility of all the working people and its elected representatives in particular."[18]), dips freely into profits for its own needs. While a free entrepreneur must turn over capital to make a profit and then seek to reinvest it as fresh capital, the new class wants to retain the utilization of wealth as its function. Entrepreneurs have to measure their objectives in the light of necessity, i.e., of the price they must pay; the new class, conversely, does not consider the price, and it uses any means to achieve its objectives. Since an entrepreneur is not only identified with economic processes but is also personally responsible for their success, he has to search for the optimum conditions, wedding thrift to rationality so as to obtain the maximum result with the minimum outlay. On the other hand, not held at all responsible for the economic process—which is now the burden of self-management and perhaps the Party—the new class tends to go along with the irrationally high costs and indulges in deficit spending.

In the Yugoslav socialist system, the role of the entrepreneur is played by the director (manager) of the work organizations (firms). In addition to being the head of management in the firm, a director is charged with two other essential functions: On the one hand, he is the representative or trustee of the entire society, i.e., the state and the new class, taking care that his economic unit behaves in agreement with over-all social interests; on the other hand, a director represents the "work collective," i.e., the self-managed unit and its specific interests. Directors were supposed to occupy the key position not only by reconciling the general (national) and separate (firm) interests, but also by operating as a convenient instrument by which the new class can remotely control the national economy.

Matters developed differently in actual life. By self-management, the workers in enterprises have been given the opportunity to participate more directly in the firm's decision making. Giving primary consideration to narrow personal interests, workers strive to use self-management mechanisms to improve their own positions, wages, fringe benefits, and working conditions. In 1965, the economic reform began to exert pressure on employment and wages; firms, or their units of self-management, however, collided on a broad front with the general interests of society as embodied in the practices of the economic reform. Directors, previously the main channel through which the new class managed the national economy, were caught in the middle of the new situation. If a director supports the firm by agreeing to higher wages, he is then pressed by the state (the new class); if a director tries to implement the state's austerity policies, he is then thrown out of the firm by the self-managed workers' council. The result, by 1967, "66 per cent of all directors [in Yugoslavia] and 41 per cent of all business executives . . . [considered] abandoning their managing functions and finding new jobs in the same or other enterprises."[19]

In this manner the trend of estrangement between the individual and society has evolved into a new form in Yugoslavia. While the processes of alienation in general have penetrated deeply into the rank and file of the working people, new pressures have come to bear on management leaders, as well as the highly skilled workers. Managers are often criticized and fired, or they simply "desert" voluntarily; those who sincerely want to do their part are often rudely repulsed. According to an editorial in *Borba,* "Something very absurd is going on. At a time when it is very difficult, or almost impossible, to lay off a shirking worker, it is also quite possible to crush, mentally and morally, a good man and prominent worker."[20]

8 Background to the Crisis

The regime in Yugoslavia, as in other Communist countries, is vitally concerned with politics; the accrual of power is its criterion and main objective for being. For that reason economic behavior in Communist countries is subordinated to political considerations, and those who comprehend the political aspects of economic problems understand the essence and functioning of Communist economies. If politics is the use of power and the key to all locks, the people and their work, then, are the subject of power, the economy constituting, consequently, the physical content of power. While Lenin considered politics to be "concentrated economics," Djilas rightly extended and reversed this definition in his statement that "economy has become concentrated politics."[1]

The economy is important not only because material goods are created, but also because the work of the people within the national economy offers the new class a political criterion for evaluating the extent of their "socially useful" contributions. Ideally, the citizen is loyal and politically active; at the same time, he contributes the maximum to national production, in turn asking for a minimum as a consumer. The functioning of the national economy thereby exposes an inner dialectical contradiction in Communist countries: even though the Party (and the new class) is a closed social organization, the Communist society is open, since everyone is permitted and simultaneously required to participate in national activities in a loyal and productive manner.

The logics of economics and politics differ, however; the power of the state appears as a distorting factor in its enforcement of economically irrational decisions. Moreover, the mechanisms of state power (the new class, the Party, the police, the Army, the federal and local governments) account for heavy expenditures.* The result is waste, in the

* In 1964 there were 650,000 people employed outside the business bureaus and about 3–3.5 million in the economic service. Of the latter, "for every three, and in some places for every two, workers [in production] there is one official. . . . According to unofficial evaluations, these 'men of pen' in the economy cost around

literal meaning of the word, reflected in the unnecessarily high costs of production, low productivity, and large business losses common to all Communist countries. The basic contradiction is that power, while maintaining the regime, damages national economies which, in turn, eventually weaken the power and the regime.

The problem of waste in Yugoslavia's economy is complicated because the definition of *waste* still depends primarily on subjective, i.e., political, sets of criteria. It would be useless, therefore, to try to evaluate elements of the economy by applying the objective criteria of free market economies. The category of profit, it is true, is also recognized in Yugoslavia, though under the new name of *net income* and with a different socio-economic basis. Instead of profit created in production and realized by the market mechanism (which functions as an objective category), net income in the Yugoslav economy is considered to be the degree of fulfillment of an economic unit's obligation to society and the state. While profit in a market economy can be determined and monetarily quantified in a relatively direct manner, it is more difficult to evaluate that which is "socially useful" in the Yugoslav socialist economy. Besides, in Communist countries, the state (Party) represents society, and its actions contain their own justification. This is a well-known Stalinist principle, according to which the socialist economy has mastered the law of value and replaced it with the "law of planned economic development." The fact that the plan emanates from the government is sufficient certification of its economic correctness. Thus, though Yugoslavs departed from Stalinist forms, an evaluation of the Yugoslav economy is still a highly complex undertaking because the criteria of the new class are not directed toward an evaluation, but, rather, a justification of its existence and economic policies.

In Yugoslavia, as elsewhere, the economic process is based on the product of human activity by which material goods or services are created, distributed, and used. The issue there is more easily understood from the point of view of political objectives expressed in economic form, that is, of a Communist society in which the level of production would be high enough to satisfy all needs, personal and social, without restrictions. No enonomic problems would exist in such a society because there would be no need or possibility to measure value. Set against an

---

1,000 billion dinars yearly, which is almost one-quarter of the national income." This figure partly agrees with another even more significant one: "The total expenditures charged to the so-called general spending, that is to say, institutions that employ only around one-sixth of the total active labor force, climbed in 1964 to 2,263.3 billion dinars, which means that every second dinar of the national income ends up there." *Borba,* July 11, 1965.
P. 277

immensely high labor productivity would be the mass of valueless products, as seen by the new class in a future Communist society. Such an economy would include a kind of superproduction to be reached after the "barrier of productivity" had been broken. Customary standards of economics, of course, would not be valid. There could be no profit just as there could be no waste. Yet the hard fact remains that present needs, personal and social, are not only measurable but also enormously limited by the lack of products and services. Though the relation between need and availability (its satisfaction, including the costs of production) is not a tangible value, it becomes in a definite sense the measure of value, and also, therefore, the measure of economic success or failure. This point of measure explains in yet another way why all Communist regimes are vitally interested in economic growth.

Economic growth, namely, not only provides the regime with physical strength (national wealth and economic potential), but to the extent that production and productivity also rise, economic shortages that bother and restrict the power of the regime will be less important. Also, by eliminating shortages, which are a kind of imposed measurability, the objective yardstick for indicating failure or success is eliminated or at least reduced. While mistakes may be buried easily, successes become irrelevant. Such a situation would be true communism in which error would be impossible not only because the one who makes the decision is infallible, but also because mistakes cannot be measured, or would not count. Thus a higher degree of growth moves the economic base from politics, the relations among people, to technology, the manipulation of things. For the present, however, national economies are not sufficiently developed for a pure technological approach, and facts remain facts not only technically but socially and economically, too. For a long time to come, one must deal with the relations among people, that is to say, with the capacity of a human society to satisfy personal and social needs. Consequently, the disparities between need and satisfaction remain a measure of success and value, thus representing an objective economic criterion. Economic success or rationality is measured in the light of existing material relations between availability and need and between volume of production and consumption. The relevant factors include the volume of production and how, by whom, to whom, and the purpose for which a product is used. If waste does exist, then its existence must be considered—regardless of the supposed infallibility of the power (state or self-management) that caused the waste. A man without food is hungry; a man who has no shoes is barefoot.

Viewed in context, economic relations within the Yugoslav system are not flexible politics, as the new class would like to suggest, but are indeed defined by measurable material values. Unprofitability, waste, and loss are not theoretical or academic categories but the facts of existence which inevitably impose themselves as the criteria of economic success. The political goals of the future of a Communist society and the political practices of the present (the state and its role) which do not fit into given economic realities show a vital contradiction between high spending and low production. This contradiction and imbalance, which profoundly affect every Communist economic system, are the backbone of Yugoslavia's chronic economic crisis.

Of the numerous contradictions in the economic system, the most serious are those built into its very structure. The eventual outcome of such contradictions go far beyond economics and tend to result in a gradual alienation and consequent dehumanization of the producers as well as the rulers. Insofar as production does not meet existing needs and the productivity of labor is low, the economy is inevitably social and political, not technological. Adding to the dilemma of its previous mistakes, the Yugoslav system in manipulating economic processes cannot avoid treating people like objects and viewing social relations as techniques of applying power, as in Stalinist economic planning, or handling people, as in the workers' self-management units established by the new class.

Economic Development

The new class fails to comprehend the contradiction between its politics and objective economic laws. On the contrary, because it is the arbiter of the rational functioning of the economy, the new class identifies itself with progress and the attainment (in the future) of a Communist society of abundance and no economic laws. That is why the new class, as all other Communist regimes, believes that it has found the correct solution to its economic ills in a policy of hastened economic growth. The faster and more intense the growth, the nearer the regime approaches its objectives. But the new class fails to realize that it may be developing the national economy in the wrong manner or direction—what it builds on the one hand, it destroys on the other. Perhaps it should keep in mind the words of an old Chinese proverb: "All the while he piled soil into a heap, and only in the end did he see that instead of building a molehill he had dug a hole."

The regime's vital concern for national economic development has intensified because the Yugoslav economy still remains relatively undeveloped. Any increase in production appears as a means of stabilizing the regime; for this reason the new class seems to be a vehicle for effecting economic development. As in other developing countries, this façade is undoubtedly a valuable political advantage for the Communist movement, which presents itself as the standard-bearer of economic development at a time when economics is considered of first priority. Because of economic growth, the masses are tied politically to the Communist program. Even more important is the fact that economic development under present conditions has an emergency priority which carries a carte blanche for any political actions deemed necessary. If so required by the needs of economic development, democratic rights and institutions can be temporarily suspended and national and individual freedom can be limited or voided. The goal of economic development has provided the new class with a mandate to organize development, which means in practice that the new class arrogates the power monopoly, thus guaranteeing that economic development will be used primarily for the benefit of the elite. In other words, a more developed, more stable, and more wealthy national economy will constitute a broader and more reliable entrenchment of the new class.

When the new class found this nodal point at which political and economic advantages join, it geared its whole strength toward economic growth. The problem of postwar reconstruction in Yugoslavia was thoroughly tackled and apparently solved successfully; then an extensive and ambitious program of industrialization was started. Both undertakings were also intended to fulfill the expectations of the people, who indeed wanted growth at any price, regardless of the cost.

In the early postwar years, the people and the regime were sincerely devoted to their goals of economic development. The efforts invested and results achieved identified the new Communist regime as the dedicated progenitor and organizer of economic growth. The national economy, however, could not avoid an unbalanced and bumpy development because of its political superstructure. Paradoxically, the new class itself negated sound economic growth precisely when it wanted it most strongly, because in order to maintain great and radical efforts for economic development, it was impossible for the regime to avoid waste and imbalance in its practices. A deeper analysis of the much-publicized economic developments of Yugoslavia indicates, in addition, that their results failed to match similar efforts in democratic countries. Most important, however, is that what was achieved did not reveal fully the price the people paid in being deprived of freedom and prosperity. Living standards in Yugoslavia today are significantly lower than necessary, considering the level of development. The standard of living has not lagged because the regime so desired but because it could not avoid it.

Ever conscious of its political need, the preservation of power, the regime cannot foresee the economic ramifications of its decisions. When mistakes occur, economic losses and wastes follow, and somebody has to pay or to produce without being adequately paid. That somebody turns out to be the ordinary man who receives less than he gives, less than he deserves, less than he needs, and, finally, increasingly less than he wants.

In Communist countries it is not easy for economists to acknowledge their low standard of living. Believing that it has discovered the solution to economic limitations and an improved standard of living, the new class finds the harsh facts of reality difficult to accept. That is why the elite puts forth various explanations, produces scapegoats for failures, and chooses remedies which usually prove to be inefficient in the short and always in the long run. Consequently, national reserves are being spent, previously invested fixed capital is being overutilized, and the national wealth is being exploited. Huge debts, especially those incurred abroad, serve to transfer the economic burden to future generations. The elite is indifferent as to whether the loans from abroad are socialist, from the Soviet Union, or capitalist, from the United States of America. Nevertheless, these methods, separately and together, do not suffice to cover current waste and losses.

Finding strength in the policy of economic development and growth, the Yugoslav Communist Party, and later the new class, considered such action to be an optimum economic solution and at the same time, a matter of political necessity. After agreeing on these two basic issues, specific methods of procedure were worked out.

The policy of full employment was viewed as an all-inclusive model for achieving the two-fold goal of maximizing production and accelerating economic development. In fact, each part strengthened the other as higher current production speeded up economic development, while the latter increased production. The new class believed that a vigorous policy of full employment simply could not fail and that the only missing link was a temporary insufficiency of capital. This view seemed palatable since postwar economic rehabilitation had been successfully concluded by 1952, a favorable new starting point. Moreover, by 1952 the still-young Communist regime had become politically stable, and the apparatus of government had gained administrative experience. Also, Yugoslavia no longer needed to imitate Russian methods blindly; the Soviet system of economic planning and management was even seen as clumsy and inefficient.

The switch to the new policy of full employment had also been identified politically with the break with Stalin and with the effort to find new and better ways than the Russian for "building socialism." All past mistakes and difficulties could be blamed on either Stalinist methods or on remnants of Stalinist thinking—thus shifting emphasis from the present political responsibilities of the regime and insuring the position of the new class within the Communist Party. Besides, the elimination of unemployment and the decreased number of dissatisfied peasants who had moved into industrial centers enhanced the political authority of the regime. Increased national production enabled economic planners to squeeze extra capital from low wages by decelerating the rate of wage increase, while indebtedness to international organizations, foreign governments, and Western banks was increased to cover the growing national economic deficit. Meanwhile a moderate annual inflation of 5 to 10 per cent* was maintained, and everything seemed fine as the buoyant economy expanded and flourished.

Simultaneously, the organizational framework of Yugoslavia's economic system had been changed, and the government (the Party and the new class) declined direct responsibility for the functioning of the national economy. Although it is true that the essential decisions had been made by the top echelon of the new class, the responsibility for the bulk of economic decisions was moved to units in the field, either to local authorities or to business firms. Responsibility was relegated to lower echelons and explained in terms of self-management and liberalization. But the principle of first satisfying central "social" needs and then using the surplus for fixed or working capital, or for the payment of wages, was reasserted.†

By the summer of 1953, the policy of full employment had created an upsurge in the Yugoslav economy, supported by several hundred million dollars a year from the United States. Total industrial production increased by 355 per cent from 1952 to 1965, while the number of employed rose from 1,684,000 to 3,583,000.[2] Figures illustrating the rise in Yugoslav production are impressive, as seen in Table 3.[3] These

* "Kiro Gligorov emphasized that the rate of inflationary developments before the reform was about 7 per cent annually and considering retail prices and the cost of living, even more than 10 per cent." *Borba,* October 6, 1967.

† "Although the state has the legal power and means to intervene directly to carry out its objectives, and on some occasions does so, it has chosen as a matter of policy to rely increasingly on indirect financial and fiscal instruments to realize the objectives of federal plans. It retains control over production, the distribution of income, investment, and consumption largely through the system of taxation and contributions [obligatory] by enterprises, through allocations of investments and foreign exchange resources, by influencing the supply and direction of credit, and to a diminishing extent, by setting price ceilings and restrictions on foreign exchange and trade." Waterston, *Planning in Yugoslavia,* p. 88. Since 1962, substantial changes have been made in Yugoslavia's economic legal provisions; the above observations are basically valid still, though in somewhat different forms.

figures show that Yugoslavia did indeed manage a significant economic step forward, particularly after the new class took over in 1953 and almost removed Yugoslavia from the ranks of the underdeveloped. Marked economic improvements provided a favorable comparison with the low standard which prevailed in Yugoslavia before World War II and shortly thereafter.

TABLE 3
COMPARISON OF YUGOSLAV PRODUCTION

	1939	1952	1965
Coal (in 1000 tons)	7,032	12,098	29,257
Electricity (in million kw's)	1,173	2,700	15,523
Bauxite (in 1000 tons)	719	613	1,574
Steel (in 1000 tons)	235	442	1,769
Copper (in 1000 tons)	12.5	21.4	56.4
Glass (in square meters)	1,678	3,415	6,873
Electric bulbs (in 1000 pieces)	2,522	4,787	29,430
Calcium carbide (in tons)	54,920	39,684	105,250
Soap (in tons)	12,798	23,322	32,549
Bricks (in million pieces)	379.6	551	1,717.1
Cement (in 1000 tons)	894	1,313	3,104
Timber (in 1000 cubic meters)	1,922	2,112	2,677
Cotton fabrics (in 1000 sq. meters)	110,167	111,910	393,939
Socks (in 1000 pairs)	23,401	22,635	61,322
Leather shoes (in 1000 pairs)	4,208	5,756	29,987
Sugar (in tons)	107,599	57,560	333,566

The increase in production, however, was not adequately expressed in the rise of economic potential and labor productivity and in the reduction of production costs. Particularly, the raised standard of living of the masses was not in proportion to the growth of the national economy or the needs of the population. Neither were the results of economic development commensurate with the efforts invested. It was obvious that disturbing factors were interposed between consumption and national production—economically, high production costs and low labor productivity, socio-politically, the new-class burden of exploitation, each of which prevented the establishment of sounder and more stable economic conditions.

The policy and atmosphere of full employment, however, made it difficult to differentiate profit from loss or success from failure because Yugoslavia's actual economy was concealed under a veil of apparent growth. Unable to diagnose economic problems correctly, the new class could not undertake measures to deal with the troubles. Mistakes were sometimes acknowledged after a delay, but by the time they were brought to the public's attention the problems were already outdated. While former failures were used to prove that the regime's current policies were correct, contemporary successes were publicized as they took place. Thus the new class came to believe that the situation had improved substantially. Finally, when the seriousness of a deep economic crisis was officially and notoriously admitted at the beginning of the economic reform in 1965, *Borba,* nevertheless, brazenly stated, "It is not our economic situation, but our analysis, that is poor."[4]

The difficulties recognized were blamed on technical failures, personal deficiencies, or the lack of capital. Above all, the temporary character of the failures was stressed; everything would be set right with only a little more effort. Such an attitude explains why the new class, from 1953 to 1958, was almost inebriated with the success of the "Yugoslav economic miracle," becoming convinced that it could solve complex economic problems. Other Communist countries, for example, were often irritated by insistent references to the unique success and correctness of the "Yugoslav way to socialism." In the same vein, Yugoslavia's economic and political experts ventured to advise industrial economies on how to maintain full employment and to instruct the leaders of backward countries on how to develop their economies easily, rapidly, cheaply, and efficiently.

The Yugoslav economy, nonetheless, was constantly exposed to growing difficulties. Sound solutions for its problems were lacking because the new class treats the national economy as a subordinate category in which decisions must first be politically correct, and economic acumen is a secondary consideration. Political influence in economic policies was felt most deeply in the realm of investment decisions.

Under normal conditions, investments help to develop the national economy and to stabilize higher levels of production, productivity, and growth. Investments are a rational practice, however, only when they increase the volume of production and simultaneously reduce costs, a situation which too frequently is not the case in Yugoslavia. Investments there, rather, have increased an already excessive consumption, thus sustaining an overly high percentage of employment. Conversely, excessive consumption distorted the effects of investments. As a result, one could no longer clearly differentiate the cause and effect—consumption pushing investments or investments pushing consumption. The main idea was to invest, not to ask about profitability. Kardelj noted the phenomenon of "Investment-mania [which] has taken hold of a large number of Party functionaries . . . who are unable to see any other goal in our development but the building of factories . . . ,"[5] as did Tito, who said, "There are local units [firms] in which 100 to 200 billion dinars have been invested, without asking whether investments are profitable."[6]

The important fact, to which attention was not drawn, was that past investments were spilling over into current consumption in many ways, especially by an understated depreciation rate which falsely signaled an increased total net product. A seemingly high total product in turn sanctioned or rather hid irrationally high costs and created the illusion of higher profitability. On this basis, ever greater investments were deemed justified, but it was clear that the burden of high investment taxed the entire national economy since it was also one of the main sources of inflation.

Investments in Yugoslavia have assumed enormous proportions and become almost an end in themselves. The volume and rate of investments in 1965 alone amounted to levels that surpassed sound economic reasoning or ability. Gligorov, the minister of Finance at the time, spoke proudly to the Parliament on June 10, 1965, "Our current investments in the economy amount to more than one-sixth of all the means invested in the national economy up to now. Our investments at the end of the current five-year period will amount to more than one-third of the value of all the capacities we have now."[7]

Investments in Yugoslavia have fallen into a vicious circle; a project may be prolonged, of low quality, expensive, and sometimes unnecessarily luxurious, but more often useless; another is abandoned when completed; a third is simply dropped, while a fourth is revised before being finished.[8] In sum, vast investments, though increasing production, do not raise labor productivity sufficiently, nor do they lead to a corresponding lowering of costs. Since such investments expand national consumption beyond economically feasible levels, the Yugoslav economy is put under a serious additional strain. It is pressed both by the high spending of the new class and by the mass of wage earners who struggle for a better living standard. Investments have become one of the areas in which the entire society—led by the new class and the laboring class—contributes to the same economic ills.

Yugoslavia, in common with other Communist economies with high rates of investment, has focused on industrialization and has boasted a rapid rise in production figures. But for all Communist countries the catch remains that their production costs remain high by international standards. They succeed somehow in expanding production without adequately modernizing their techniques. To many observers of socialist economies it sometimes seems that built-in devices systematically inflate costs or at least interfere with their reduction to a desirable level which, under given conditions, is also necessary. Despite, perhaps because of, investment efforts, the Yugoslav economy moves from one crisis to another, accompanied by inflation, low labor productivity, low standards of living, and high production costs.

Crisis

A sequence of three devaluations (1952, 1961, and 1965) by which the official rate of the dinar was reduced by 96 per cent of its postwar value in only thirteen years indicated a chronic economic crisis. Even in 1961 an official statement held that the economy was sufficiently developed and production enough increased so that Yugoslavia could rely on itself. It was implied that the Yugoslav economy represented a successful blend of Marxist rules and capitalist business ability. It was further stressed that a system of "direct socialism," not Soviet "bureaucratic socialism," could be safely left to its own resourcefulness. The official position, therefore, was that only the negative residues of the past, both capitalist and bureaucratic-socialist, needed to be erased, for which purpose some 300 million dollars was obtained from abroad in 1961.

Yet, the new autonomy of economic laws "inherent in direct socialism" was unsuccessful and the money from abroad was soon spent; the government consequently decided to exert pressure on real wages in 1962, which was one of the reasons why living costs (consumer prices) were deliberately allowed to rise. But neither foreign money nor reduced personal consumption was enough to bridge the deficit gap. Evidently, affairs had already passed the point at which administrative measures could be effective. A sharp inflation occurred instead, increasing costs of production and living and preserving low labor productivity. The situation became even more difficult because Yugoslav statesmen did not evaluate their predicament correctly or in time; they trusted their instruments of power and hoped that problems could be settled simply by trimming excessively high spending. Basically, however, they wanted to retain an expanding economy. At the same time the entire national economy was pervaded with the spirit of the "good life" of leisurely work or idleness, all paid for by the society, colloquially termed *"sotziala"* (roughly, the abuse of welfare). The authorities had not yet realized the real depth of their economic predicament, so the almost exclusively monetary measures undertaken in consequence were both tardy and insufficient. Actually, instead of stabilizing the economy, they triggered a new sequence of critical developments. After reaching a plateau in 1962, prices continued to soar. Several increases, particularly in the cost of bread, cut substantially into real wages, depressing the position of wage earners.

Even in 1963, when it was evident that the economy was maladjusted, the new class failed to evaluate correctly the ominous signs of more serious troubles. Instead, it sidetracked the main issues, blaming its difficulties on the irregularities of individuals, corruption, lack of economic discipline, or natural causes (floods, blizzards, droughts, and earthquakes). Even though the national economy was already unbalanced, overemployment was maintained, and almost every worker requesting employment had to be hired. Simultaneously, the surplus workers in the factories could not be laid off. On the whole, a hypertrophy of labor insured quantitative production growth and hid absenteeism. Subsidized personal expenditures became a definite part of production costs, health insurance was misused, and the practice of collecting a salary while not working was tolerated, even admired. Under such circumstances inflation compromised the devaluation of 1961, which, instead of steadying the national economy, now encouraged further low labor productivity, high-cost production, malpractices, and waste. Inflation, naturally, was a major economic crisis.

Efforts after 1963 to stabilize the economy showed that Yugoslav leaders were gambling that pressure could be relieved not by cutting expenditures but by further expansion and more employment. These views were determined by political considerations. Therefore, with the hope of increasing the general level of production and thereby sustaining a politically desirable full employment, intensified investments were allowed. Support was given to the theory that labor productivity could be raised more easily in a booming than in a contracting economy. But, as discussed above, the increase in investment only aggravated the situation because investment in Yugoslavia is conducted in calculated darkness. Prices became so disproportionate, exchange rates so confused, tax and depreciation rates so contradictory, and the income of enterprises so complex, with a rash of subsidies and premiums, that the situation defied any analysis. One could not determine what was unprofitable or, if so, to what extent. Unproductive investments further distorted an already broken economic picture. In sum, the total mass of investments merely complicated the problem instead of correcting the situation through strengthened or healthier growth of the national economy.

The economic crisis increased, however, bringing about an over-all deterioration of the entire national economy. At the same time, specific unfavorable developments originating in separate parts of the national economy caused further diffusion of the general crisis. Critical developments in all sectors of the economy increased in intensity. Domestic trade continued to decline: in 1965, there was, on the average, one shop for every 419 Yugoslavs; in 1945 this ratio was one to 374.[9] Agriculture and transportation specifically affected the entire national economy.

Agriculture in Yugoslavia has been a critical area from the very beginning. An insufficient volume of food production put pressures on the supply of staples and raw materials which had to be imported and resulted in chronic balance-of-payments deficits, while low productivity and high production costs in agriculture elevated the average cost structure of the national economy in a preponderantly agricultural country. Since the agricultural crisis was fundamentally determined by the social and technological backwardness of the peasants, agriculture became the bottleneck of economic development, jeopardizing advances reached in other sectors, particularly manufacturing. As the new class saw it, the only solution was an accelerated development in agriculture. For that reason substantial amounts of capital were invested in the "socialist" sector of agriculture—state farms and cooperatives. In 1964 alone, for example, 85 billion dinars were apportioned from the federal budget as a direct subsidy to agriculture for its current production: mechanization, 44 billion; fertilizers, 36 billion; machinery repair, 5 billion, etc.[10] In addition, agriculture benefited from many other subsidies of milk, meat, sugar, tobacco, wine, etc., from export premiums, tax and depreciation facilities, and discounts. Above this aid, the "socialized" sector of agriculture was credited with 353 billion dinars.[11]

Thus the price-cost pattern of the entire economy, not only agriculture, was further confused, and intensified pressures increased inflation in order to achieve a new balance on higher levels of prices and costs.

Contrary developments, but with similar results, occurred in transportation. While efforts were made to modernize agriculture, the transportation system, which formerly had been relatively well developed, was now utilized to improve or embellish the national cost structure. In maintaining low passenger fares and freight rates, both national production costs and the cost of living were made to appear lower than they actually were. "Last year," stated *Borba,* on September 25, 1963, "about 30 per cent of the passengers in the municipal public transportation systems were transported free or with a discount. . . . In Zagreb such passengers made up 44 per cent of the total." A similar situation existed in the railways.[12]

When capital depreciation was disregarded or kept below the level of actual utilization of fixed capital, previously invested capital, the national wealth, that is, was then channeled into current consumption.

Not only was transportation *not* modernized, but the entire system, particularly inland river shipping and railways, also reached lower levels of obsolescence than in 1939, and this was after more than twenty years of socialization. In this case the solution seemed to be a general and substantial increase in transportation rates which, in turn, only added a new series of inflationary pressures.

Parallel to developments in agriculture and transportation were inflationary measures in internal and foreign trade, the result of a chronic scarcity of trade commodities and price instability. Inflation in the construction business was based on an overheated expansion in investing and building. Eventually each practice neutralized efforts to control the monetary side of inflation. Also, the industrial sector stubbornly resisted efforts to tighten the unbalanced economy, particularly by means of credit restrictions. One of the leading principles of Yugoslavia's economic policy was that in no case could insufficient credit be allowed to restrict increases in production. That meant simply that a bank could not refuse to extend new credit, nor could it refuse to prolong repayment of the existing credit. Thus by 1964, instead of restricting credit to control inflation, a large-scale increase in the quantity of money took place, an increase which seriously exceeded the volume of national production. Short-term credits granted by banks increased sharply from 2,528.6 billion dinars in January, 1964, to 3,550.2 billion in April, 1966.[13]

Inflationary developments clearly indicated that one part of the problem was the growing gap between high spending and the scarcity of available goods. In theory, that gap could be eliminated if production outpaced consumption, but the new class was unable to curb its appetites, afraid to weaken its security, and incapable of organizing production rationally. Instead, it took the easy road by increasing purchasing power. Currency in circulation increased from 193.1 billion dinars in December, 1960, to 536.5 billion dinars in May, 1966, an increase of 178 per cent. During the same period sight deposits in banks increased from 802.0 to 2,276.3 billion, or 184 per cent.[14] Inflation actually became a vested right, a direct consequence of the inability of the new class to comprehend that one cannot spend more than one has, that real purchasing power cannot be created merely by governmental fiat, and that quick and easy profits are not reliable.

It was not by chance that inflation was used. It was a convenient and seemingly painless method of covering deficits and concealing deficiencies. A policy of cheap money and abundant credit to finance expansion of current production, investment, or consumption was a popular technique. But the money injected into the national economy was not offset by corresponding increases in production. The money issued was just an advance on future production.

At the beginning of the inflationary process, the national economy appeared exhilaratingly expansive, especially to those who looked at it from above. But in truth, a downgraded economy gave only the appearance of prosperity. Incomes rose, economic mistakes were obscured, failings were hidden, and old debts were reduced because of the decreased value of money. Then the clever "socialist businessmen" began to compete for credit because an investment loan, particularly a long-term one, made building possible. What one built was not important since money was available and there was income to be earned. When the building was finished or stopped or delayed, extra capital could be nibbled on. Meanwhile the national debt had shrunk because the currency had been concurrently devalued; smaller real capital expressed in new, but devalued, currency would appear bigger than before. Thus, the economy seemed to improve at the very moment when it became worse. The more spent, the higher the figures on the balance sheet; the greater the loss, the higher the compensating bank credit; the bigger the debt, the less indebtedness, since the vanishing capital seemed to grow because of current reevaluations.

The inflationary boom in Yugoslavia became so feverish that "every 100 dinars invested into business last year [1964] brought 42.9 dinars of gross profit,"[15] and, nonetheless, every third enterprise (socialist business firm) showed a loss. The analysis of the annual statements of all Yugoslav enterprises for 1964 showed that "of every 100 dinars [of gross profit] enterprises received 52 and the community and the state received 48." Inflation twisted economic relations so much that, according to the same statements, "production was around 16 per cent higher than in 1963, while gross profits increased by 25 per cent, and the net profits of enterprises by 34 per cent."*

Regardless of whether the profits were real or apparent, they spilled over into personal consumption in the form of wages, salaries, facilities, and fringe benefits. During 1963, nominal personal incomes increased, as compared with 1962, by 25 per cent, and in 1964 by an additional 42 per cent.[16] The much faster rise of prices,† however, forced wage

* Expressed in numbers, the gross profits of all enterprises were increased in 1964 by 1,065 billion (from 3,133 to 4,198 billion) dinars. The principal forms through which the state received its 2,015 billion were: interest on capital (330.8 billion), the turnover tax (442.2 billion), the corporate tax (212.5 billion), and the income tax (891 billion). *Borba,* May 30, 1965.

† The retail price index (1965 = 100) rose from 71 in 1963 to 123 in June, 1966, i.e., by about 75 per cent in three years. *Indeks,* No. 7, 1966.

earners to moonlight with the result that "income from extra work was almost the same as from one's principal occupation."[17] The position of wage earners was also aggravated by the push for *uravnilovka* (equal compensation wages), which was initially intended to achieve socialist equality for the majority of workers by a higher level of real wages. Owing to the inflation since 1961, however, the elimination of wage disparities by *uravnilovka* actually became an instrument for discrimination against the better and more productive workers. According to newspaper reports, "The *uravnilovka* appeared as a form in which nominal minimum wages were pushed upwards. Consequently, *uravnilovka* is not really what it seems, namely wage equalization, but instead represents a method by which the living standard [real income] of the majority of the population is reduced."[18]

The economic paradox of the system is that as the national economy grows and production increases, equality among the majority of the people increases—but on a lower level. As conditions seem to approach the well-known objective, "to everyone according to his needs," the objective retreats; instead of initiating greater production to strengthen the country, that is, to make it less limited by material shortages, the regime in Yugoslavia is faced with ever increasing conflicts because of the intensified limitations imposed on it by the economy.

Immediately preceding the economic crisis of 1965, wages and salaries in Yugoslavia, according to the official report,[19] averaged 40,400 dinars monthly ($53.87) within a fairly wide range, as shown in Table 4.[20]

TABLE 4
AVERAGE EARNINGS, AUGUST, 1964

Earnings	Percentage of Wage Earners
Under 25,000 dinars ($ 33.33)	24.4%
to 40,000 dinars ($ 53.33)	42.7%
to 50,000 dinars ($ 66.67)	15.4%
to 60,000 dinars ($ 80.00)	8.2%
to 80,000 dinars ($106.67)	6.3%
to 100,000 dinars ($133.33)	1.9%
Over 100,000 dinars ($133.33)	1.1%

(The 1965 exchange rate was 750 dinars per dollar; the next year the rate was 1,250 dinars per dollar)

The entire wage situation was further complicated by the income discrepancy among the Yugoslav republics. This added a new economic factor to already overheated nationalistic frictions. Table 5[21] shows the wage situation geographically.

TABLE 5
GEOGRAPHIC DISTRIBUTION OF WAGES
AND PER CAPITA INCOME, 1964–65

Republic	Average Monthly Earnings
All of Yugoslavia	40,400 dinars ($53.87)
Slovenia	52,800 dinars (70.40)
Croatia	41,800 dinars (55.73)
Bosnia and Hercegovina	38,300 dinars (51.07)
Serbia	37,500 dinars (50.00)
Montenegro	35,300 dinars (47.06)
Macedonia	34,000 dinars (45.33)

Low wages in general, particularly in the less developed republics, could not be improved by a nominal increase because of the faster inflationary price rise. When material means, that is, goods, are limited, an expansion in the volume of currency does not increase purchasing power but instead raises prices.* Objective economic laws, even as recognized in Marx's formula, establish an equilibrium by automatically restricting excessive consumption through increasing prices. Nonetheless, the new class, by virtue of its commanding status, adjusted its position by promptly issuing new money to compensate for price increases. Thus the burden of deficit spending had to be shifted to personal consumption, i.e., to the mass of wage earners (and also retired people), thereby causing widespread poverty. Subsistence-level real wages rose nominally to affect an ever greater number of Yugoslavs.[22]

The surprising feature of the critical economic situation was that despite an inflationary boom many businesses operated at a loss. According to an official analysis of the composite annual balance sheets of all business enterprises, the aggregate of losses in 1963 was 77.6 billion dinars, and the next year it was 76.2 billion. "Every seventh Yugoslav business ended 1964 with a net loss. Every fifth employed Yugoslav, about 580,000 of them, belonged to such a business."[23] Businesses operating at a loss were automatically granted bank credits to cover their deficits and to enable them to pay wages. In addition, incomes were computed not on the basis of realized net profit but on the volume of goods produced, even when the latter were stockpiled and possibly unsaleable. By this practice business losses actually became a major source of, rather than a brake on, new inflationary pressures, and though operating at a loss, businesses increased wages.[24] The net result was

* The wholesale price index (1965 = 100) for manufactured goods increased from 76 in 1957 to 110 in June, 1966, while that of agricultural products rose in the same period from 37 to 128. *Indeks,* No. 7, 1966.

that personal consumption (wages), social services financed from business profits, and state taxes were not covered fully by actual income but by the creation of new money by printing it or granting credit.[25]

The state (the new class) became the recipient of by far the greatest income; it also became the biggest spender, a fact which caused the workers to lose interest in production and the management of business. The producers, consequently, tend to feel estranged from their work, creating a broad basis for alienation from the economy and also from the society. Big profits could be made without working simply by manipulating money and business and trade transactions and by completely denying Marx's concept that only work creates new values. *Borba* stated, "The returns in trade are larger than those in industry by 300 dinars per employee, and they are twice as large as in agriculture or construction. That is why, as the saying goes, it pays more to be in business than to produce, and it is more profitable to divide income than to create it."[26]

Yugoslavia's entire national economy experienced many such contradictions, and the press brought them increasingly to the attention of the general public, appearing to discredit the regime and creating both confusion and a widespread abdication of responsibility. The titles of a few articles from *Borba* illustrate the situation: "Hens Are Laying Deficit Eggs" (September 16, 1964); "More Expensive Meat Produced on Modern Farms" (December 18, 1964); "Doubled Number of Cows, Halved Production of Milk" (December 18, 1964); "Halved Coal Production because of Lack of Construction Wood" (May 22, 1965); "Fear from a Good Tobacco Crop" (May 27, 1965). Public debates on economic difficulties increased at the beginning of 1965, and many in Yugoslavia were puzzled when they recalled that the regime usually allowed only favorable topics to be openly discussed. Public discussion, of course, was oriented primarily toward interpreting difficulties as the result of personal deficiencies and technical bottlenecks, but this time, however, the new class was forced to admit that serious defects existed in the organization and functioning of the entire economic system.

It is remarkable that criticism was not only accepted but also reiterated with astounding aggressiveness by the new class, almost as if it held no connection with or responsibility for the situation. Washing its hands, the new class accused the bureaucracy of the state and the workers' self-management units and at the same time reserved for itself the right to put matters in order. Increasingly aware of the critical situation, the new class first decided to intervene with radical administrative measures, among the most important of which was a general price freeze enacted in February, 1965. The price freeze was too late and too little because the economy stubbornly continued to deteriorate and threatened to dissolve into chaos, which would subsequently endanger the political supremacy of the new class.

Tito rang the alarm bells in May, 1965. "Now, at this moment, the essential task is to put our economy in order."[27] His call was followed promptly by a campaign in which leaders of the new class enthusiastically participated, especially those in charge of economic matters—Kardelj, Todorovic, and the minister of finance at the time, Gligorov. Each attacked the extensive but costly production, low labor productivity, the poor quality of products, and bad organization, both of businesses and the entire national economy. They were highly critical of excessive and very often unproductive investments, of prolonged construction work, and of idle capacities; they have been disgusted that those economic branches into which the greatest amount of national capital had been invested were in fact unprofitable. The subsidies, premiums, high financial losses, deficits, price disparities, tangled financial and banking regulations, and confused multiple exchange rates were seen as disastrous. They were particularly outraged that the national currency had ceased to be a measure of value and that there was no way to make reliable calculations of value. But most important was the concession of the leaders of the new class that the economy was spending more than it produced and that it was actually supported from abroad through credits by which the balance-of-payments deficit was financed. There was also an important admission that because of all the mistakes and malfunctionings, somebody in Yugoslavia had to be paid less and have an even lower standard of living.[28]

Measures which the new class proposed and developed were long overdue; they were designed to improve an economic situation nearly out of control. Thus the most salient question: Is the regime capable of rationally organizing the Yugoslav economy? Admittedly, the Yugoslav economy faced many of the difficulties found in relatively undeveloped countries. Its productive capacity is small, labor productivity is low, capital is lacking, and natural resources are not overly abundant. The task of getting the economy to stand on its own feet is not easy. This fact can serve as explanation for the troubles but not, however, as a justification for mistakes. The main point to remember is that the new class does not give primary consideration to its economy; rather, it subordinates the economy to politics. But objective economic laws which disregard boundaries and political philosophies do not permit their basic principles of rationality to be violated with impunity. Thus one cannot spend more than one has. That is why Communist economies, Yugoslavia among them, find themselves in a chronic crisis.

9 *A New Economic Reform*

In the summer of 1965 a new economic reform was instituted in Yugoslavia, indicating a search for a way out of the economic crisis. Earlier economic crises had somehow been overcome, but since every successive crisis was more severe than its predecessor, evidence pointed to some profoundly disrupting factors built into the Yugoslav socialist economic system. Although a broad foreign-exchange reform attempted to stabilize the national economy as recently as 1961, by 1965 a new crisis had occurred more severe in volume and depth than those before. After 1965 it was no longer a matter of foreign exchange or dislocations in a given sector of the economy, but, as described in the preceding chapter, the entire Yugoslav economic and political system was shaken.

At this time a series of radical measures and reorganizations was formulated to solve a complex of varied issues. Using the Constitution of 1963 and workers' self-management as an administrative-political framework, the new class, threatened, undertook the task of bringing the national economy into order.

The economic reform proposed specific and basically sound measures consisting of: (a) searching for a balance between available resources and consumption in order to remove the gap of deficit spending; (b) establishing stability, if necessary, at a lower level of national employment and with a definite decrease in investments; (c) eliminating or reducing waste when possible, thus emphasizing higher business profitability; and (d) reducing costs of production to measure and adapt them to average international levels so that Yugoslav goods could compete in the world market. In executing the reform, the regime retained control of essential factors such as prices, wages, credits, and the like, but at the same time it endeavored to employ as many indirect methods of the market mechanism as possible. Particularly important was the workers' self-management, which was allowed to function on the basis of the residuum principle by the prior satisfaction of obligations to the state.

PRECARIOUS STABILITY

Since July, 1965, the reform has manifested itself in various laws, decrees, and measures which *in toto* made a fairly well-rounded package. The pivotal position in the economic reform was given to a new devaluation of the domestic currency from 750 to 1,250 dinars to the dollar (in 1952 the dinar had been devalued from 50 to 300 per dollar; in 1961, it had been further devalued to 750 per dollar). The new rate of exchange was far more realistic than the former, making it possible for the national currency to become, at least partly, a measure of value. Taking 1,250 dinars for the dollar as a fixed limit of orientation, domestic prices were to be aligned into more rational mutual parities. Actually, alignment became evident in sizable but not linear increases in prices, which were frozen immediately thereafter. The purpose of aligning prices was to smooth out substantial disparities, the residua of various interferences in the economy, some of which were as old as the Communist regime in Yugoslavia itself. Further, especially as related to personal consumption, the raising of prices purported to reduce real wages and to absorb the excessive purchasing power of consumers as much as possible.

Within the guidelines set by devaluation and price alignment, the reform endeavored to decrease significantly the total mass of national consumption and simultaneously, if possible, to avoid affecting national production negatively. Consumption was slowed down in all aspects. Real wages and salaries were reduced since even the somewhat increased nominal level of wages was more than offset by the rise in prices. The number of wage earners was reduced, and budgets (federal and local) were sharply tightened. Taxes, levies, fees, and other fiscal measures affected personal incomes and at the same time decreased that part of business profits which could be used to pay wages. Significant decreases were achieved by political directives on the basis of which workers' councils and business managers, "through their own initiative," decided to lower daily wages, to fire laborers, and to increase those parts of business profits which had been frozen and sunk into reserves. Personal consumption was further lowered through substantial, though staggered, rent increases of about 100 per cent; the prices of transportation services, as those of public utilities, were raised significantly.

The reform introduced radical measures which tightened control of the volume of investments and at the same time improved their structure in favor of production. Also, the government intended to economize by shifting to the relatively less expensive modernization of existing production capacities instead of carrying out new construction. Other aspects of the reform included definite efforts to reduce imports and stimulate exports in general in order to decrease the balance-of-payments deficit. Various other explicit and implicit measures concerned the elimination of subsidies, regresses, discounts, premiums, and compensations, as well as multiple exchange rates and prices; monopolistic practices were prohibited, and restrictions hampering the flow of goods on the internal market were canceled. A systematic cutback of surplus workers in business was undertaken, as well as the removal of obvious or covert stratagems by which, legally or semi-legally, personal and general consumption filtered into the national costs of production. The basic plan of the reform was to maintain high production with lowered employment, so that exports could be increased to the extent that domestic consumption was reduced, and to eliminate internal inflation. The goal was to stabilize the national economy by raising labor productivity, thus lowering the costs of production.

Even though the reform measures were healthy and desperately needed, important obstacles soon arose for both objective and subjective reasons. The first serious hindrance arose in generating additional inflationary pressures in an already highly inflationary situation. Exports, for instance, were increased, thus draining goods from the domestic market, bringing in money, and intensifying the inflationary disproportion between insufficient commodity supply and an overabundant monetary demand. It is true that devaluation of the dinar made Yugoslav goods cheaper and more competitive abroad, but at the same time imported raw materials became more expensive. The net result was an inflationary upward pressure on material production costs. Again, the price freeze in the domestic market partially prevented an increase in the costs of production, but, on the other hand, it acted simultaneously as a brake on the lowering of costs, one of the cardinal aims of the reform. Moreover, frozen prices gave the impression of lower costs of production; amortization was incalculable since a revaluation of the existing fixed capital did not coincide with the devaluation of the currency.

An insufficiently developed economy, an obsolete capacity for production, previous investment errors, and unrealistically low amortization, as well as excessively high production costs, were obstacles in the path of economic reform. Extra-economic measures were therefore applied, and, in March of 1966, a political directive ordered businesses to use "internal reserves," such as savings, unused supplies, and stocks, as a cushion to reduce the costs of production on their own. This approach was unsuccessful. Officials soon saw that when reserves were most needed there were none to be found and that the economy was incapable of creating them.[1] In other words, the national economy lacked alternatives of action for the reform. For example, the reduction of personal consumption was considered the most important means to bridge the inflationary gap and to attain stability. Yet, the level of personal consumption was already so low that further depression of living standards would create a new set of political difficulties.

When the reform was initiated in the summer of 1965 the new class expected that the beginnings would be troublesome but that subsequent development would proceed smoothly. Although it was clear that a thorough reform would take time, it was also evident that the reform was long overdue and that its urgency required decisive successes in the first year to enable its further implementation. Results during 1965–66, though on the whole moderately favorable, fell far short of necessary goals. In an over-employed economy with inefficient use of the labor force, the number of employed was reduced by only 3 per cent. In the meantime, the price of manufactured goods rose 19 per cent, and that of agricultural produce rose 41 per cent, backed by a 15 per cent credit expansion and 20 per cent increase in the volume of currency in circulation.[2] It was already evident by 1966 that the economic reform was marking time, a situation which was officially labeled as dangerous.[3]

Neither was the next year, 1967, evaluated as an improvement; it was likened, rather, to sailing between Scylla and Charybdis, or, as stated in one newspaper's editorial, "The year 1967, the second year of the reform, is also the most difficult."[4] Tito added his estimate, "This year of 1967 will be rather difficult."[5]

The initial mistakes and overly optimistic estimates of achieving the economic reform quickly led the Yugoslav government to freeze prices at the very outset of the reform, supposedly as a brief, temporary, and extraordinary measure. In practice, however, it was considered a great success when the prices of "only" 60 per cent of all manufactured goods remained frozen in the summer of 1967.[6] Thus, instead of stabilizing the economy by means of free price developments, prices by themselves became one of the crucial hindrances to the reform's success. The possibility of free price formation was obliterated by controls which in their intensity surpassed those of the preceding fifteen years. On the one hand it was "clear" that prices ought to be freed, on the other was the awareness, or fear, that such action "would constitute a great danger" because "obstacles to reform" might appear which would "lead to a chain reaction,"[7] as explained by Tito. Actually, frozen prices exert substantial upward pressure.[8] The most probable outcome will be a compromise, with the prices of more important items frozen and others more or less free—in other words by maintaining the word but breaking the spirit of the reform. *Borba* conceded that "The new law relating to price formation and control uses, in its opening articles, the slogan that economic units are free to form prices for their commodities and services; in following articles this freedom in reality is transformed into the freedom of state officials to fix prices."[9]

Because of contradictory pressures, the economic reform decelerated in direct proportion to the amount of publicity it received. After several interim optimistic evaluations,[10] reports began filtering to the public of a Yugoslav economic development which was becoming worse as time went by. After two years of the reform, the Yugoslav Minister of Finance revealed many doubts and weaknesses of it in a television interview. He admitted that

> criticisms are often heard regarding the basic concept of the reform, . . . [which] surpasses our capacity. . . . We implement our tasks under the conditions of an undeveloped economy. . . . Personal consumption bears the brunt of the reform . . . real personal incomes, indeed, have been in advance of labor productivity. . . . Our over-all consumption is maintained within our possibilities but this does not mean that everything is well since here and there are pressures to expand consumption . . . [etc.][11]

While in 1965 no one was allowed even to whisper that a "crisis" existed in Yugoslavia, in 1967 one of the Croat leaders stressed the need to seek the "way out of the crisis" since "a more difficult phase in the implementation of the reform has now arrived."[12]

Various reports indicate that domestic consumption was consistently suppressed while living costs increased by 32.8 per cent in the first year of the reform,[13] bringing additional pressures on the living standard. In January, 1967, alone, rents increased by 25.6 per cent, the cost of services by 6.6 per cent, food by 2.8 per cent, and manufactured products by 1.5 per cent.[14] Production was reported to be in difficulties caused by a shortage of raw materials. Goods became scarce because producers kept them in warehouses (for which bank credits were granted almost automatically), waiting for prices to "thaw" in the promised free market. Investments were statistically stagnant, yet "construction [was] everywhere" on a wide front.[15] Banks were issuing credit for the current financing of the federal and local government, for social organizations, and also for social insurance, which alone had run a daily deficit of 200 million dinars at the beginning of 1966. Budgets, already tightly squeezed, were further trimmed by 20 per cent—and no one respected the cutbacks. Local governments in particular tried to extricate themselves by introducing various disguised taxes (water fees, land-use taxes, etc.) placing additional burden on the production cost structure.

Basic assumptions of the reform included the limiting of demand, but in the meantime the market supply of goods deteriorated because of enforced exports, controlled imports, immobilized commodities, and above all, stagnated domestic production. Thus the reform, after its most intensive opening performance, left the "costs of production high . . . because they are tolerated by a protected domestic market, so that despite all measures, the [Yugoslav] businesses" are stimulated to "produce more new income, not more commodities."[16]

Among the many problems exposed by the reform, some loom so large that any one of them might jeopardize the entire plan. For instance, difficulties are created even by such favorable developments as the rich 1966 harvest, which happened to have been accompanied by substantially increased prices in agriculture. Many state farms which had previously operated on a deficit were thus made less unprofitable or, in some cases, profitable; mostly, however, the reform supplied peasants with sizable volumes of cash. Peasants would normally invest such windfall incomes into their holdings and expand production. But individual peasants in Yugoslavia cannot increase their land holdings (private ownership of more than 25 acres is prohibited); besides, until recently, peasants were not allowed to buy tractors and modern farm machinery. Yet, when the latter restriction was lifted in 1966—and peasants had the money—there were no tractors or machinery on the market. Private agricultural producers were forced in this way to divert their swollen incomes into personal consumption instead of production. Such developments markedly enhanced the current pressures of inflation.

Another problem resulting from the reform concerned the stores of manufactured products. Unsold commodities have been stockpiled, providing the basis on which banks have granted credit to businesses. According to previous Yugoslav regulations, credit could be issued to an enterprise which merely produced commodities and stored them without selling, since the products of such enterprises automatically qualified as income. Instead of striving to sell their products to earn an income, firms were more interested—because it was easier—in storing them to receive credits from which they paid their wages and met other obligations. In this manner the producing units concerned themselves with abstract production (of stocks) in general, regardless of the costs of production and even less of the demands of the market. Disinterested in and independent of the market and consumers, and having simultaneously increased the fictitious bookkeeping value of assets by inflating the costs, the Yugoslav economy became overburdened with enormous reserves of manufactured commodities, which, for all practical purposes, were solidly frozen. By 1967, the nominal value of such unsold, and most probably unsaleable, stock was officially estimated at about 8,000 billion "old" dinars,[17] which at the 1967 exchange rate would equal about 6.4 billion dollars.

The paper value of national assets became dangerously inflated while the actual value was much lower. Business firms were not only unable, but decidedly unwilling, to absorb the losses which they would have to incur if they wanted to sell their stocks or to devaluate them to the level of the real value. The vested interests of the socialist self-managed businesses violently opposed and persistently obstructed any solution to reduce prices and costs along the guidelines of the reform. In this way the businesses collided directly with the reform and the policies of the state. Firms simply decided to sit tight and wait for the thaw and rise of prices. Then, instead of suffering the losses (and low wages), they would pluck substantial gains (and higher wages). The Yugoslav Minister of Finance attempted to refute the expectation that "we are going to give in and approve the rise of prices," and he threatened that the government was going to insist on price reductions.[18] In fact, in the spring of 1967 the government offered a seeming compromise. The plan foresaw that the firms would be granted tied credits for "two, perhaps three, years" to cover the losses resulting from the price reductions.[19] Sacrificing the time already spent in implementing the reform, the new class definitely intended to shift the losses to enterprises and their self-managing workers and to penalize them for the previously incurred high costs of production. The economic reform, then, instead of establishing a rational, sustainable, and flexible low-cost production, would push the national economy into deeper and more rigid indebtedness to keep self-managed enterprises financially in bondage for a long time to come.

However, the enterprises in the meantime were not quite idle. They found it easier, and more profitable, to stymie the government's intention of burdening them with eternal debts by simply going further and deeper into debt by themselves. In only one year (1966), all Yugoslav firms increased their total debt by 40 per cent. According to a newspaper editorial, "Debts grew faster than the total product of the national economy," and "at the moment, the insolvency of the Yugoslav economy is equal to that of 1962."[20]

Under these and similar circumstances, the economic reform was in the process of changing both its character and its direction. Even some of the greatest Yugoslav firms, the Zenica Iron and Steel Works, for example, dared to distance themselves from the reform, cynically stating, "In fact, the reform has not improved our situation. We gained nothing in particular, but neither did our position deteriorate."[21] At the same time a representative of the new class conceded that "the slow growth of production [it actually stagnated; see later] can be explained by the fact that a part of the national economy is unable to adapt itself [to the reform]."[22] As a matter of fact, "talks about the implementation of the reform are becoming more violent," as a *Borba* editorial of July 17, 1967, "Government and the National Economy," put it; "Businessmen are baring their teeth at the government. They are resisting. . . . Just a bit more [resistance] and one could say that they are of the opposition."

The implementation of the reform and the state of the national economy deteriorated so far that newspaper editorials had the courage to write, "For certain politicians and businessmen this [stagnation of national production] represents one more proof that the reform . . . is too big a chunk to be digested in such a short time. For others it is proof that the national economy has entered brackish stagnant waters where it has not been since the war."[23] A representative in the Federal Economic Assembly said bluntly, "A situation has been created in which the people openly ask, 'Do we really need the economic reform if we are going to live [under] worse [conditions] than before?' "[24]

From the data available it is evident that the economic reform in Yugoslavia was a great and fairly constructive effort in the right direction. Although achieving several goals, the new reform, as earlier ones, failed in its basic and strategic economic objectives, but this time on a much broader basis.* Postponing the solution of difficulties, the present reform sets the scene for the next economic crisis—and reform—which will be more complex in nature and wider in scope. Summarizing the economic situation in an article in *Borba,* October 5, 1967, Milentiye Popovic explained the difficulties in implementing the reform as ". . . the consequence of failing to introduce all measures necessary for the reform. I mean the revaluation [of fixed capital], the introduction of a new depreciation rate, the establishment of new credit, foreign trade and foreign exchange systems, etc. All these have created an inaccurate picture of the real income of business firms." The present economic reform has entered a new stage: as its efforts become frustrated and distorted, and as they fail or bog down, the old familiar pressures and problems come to the surface. Those problems are a part of the core of the Communist economic system and consist mainly of high costs of production, low productivity, waste, and now creeping then rampaging inflation.

Reform difficulties were also reflected in deviations from the current five-year plan in Yugoslavia, confirmed by the announcement of the need to "readjust" or, rather, to change the plan, which in Communist

* "The financial situation of our national economy—we must not close our eyes—is extremely disquieting and unfavorable. The only question is: How long can this situation last?" *Politika,* September 27, 1967.

terminology means failure. "Since it has been shown that all the intentions of the current five-year plan are not being realized in their entirety, it is necessary to reconsider this plan . . . and to adjust it."[25] Others who discussed the course of the economic reform in the Yugoslav Parliament, on June 4, 1967, wondered "where, actually, is the borderline between economic stabilization and stagnation?"[26] Gligorov, the new vice-prime minister, again gave a reassuring report on the implementation of the reform and the development of the national economy.[27] But even the docile Yugoslav national assemblies did not hesitate to brand Gligorov's report as "too optimistic," and an attempt to "win the approval of business by singing chansons."[28] His statements were denied only a week later in an official announcement that Yugoslav industrial production during the first nine months of 1967 did not increase at all compared with the same period of 1966, but went down by 0.2 per cent.[29] Also, publicized successes in the expansion of foreign trade were qualified by the unpleasant fact that the trade deficit gap increased* by 25.5 per cent compared with the same period of 1966.[30]

The core of Yugoslavia's difficulties is a deficit economy of high-cost production which consumes more than it produces. Three factors particularly characterize the Yugoslav national economy: (1) a low standard of living and personal consumption which eliminates incentives and alienates producers because the deficit is shifted to the population; (2) inflation, which disrupts the national economy and by which fictitious purchasing power is created; and (3) financial aid (loans and credit) from abroad which sets right the new-class errors. The economic reform should have limited excessive spending and costs. Instead, hidden or disguised in new forms, the old practices are being continued. Production costs remain high, spending is limited mainly within the ranks of the working class, while inflation hovers impatiently and waits to move in openly. This is the reason that after two years of reform, solutions from abroad are again sought to cover the domestic deficit.

In the decade following World War II, the Yugoslav economy was substantially assisted by loans and aid from abroad. Since the middle 1950's, when decentralization measures were introduced, the main form of foreign financing has been commercial credits granted to Yugoslav enterprises. Thus the Yugoslav economy became one of the seven most indebted developing countries in the world, according to a member of the Yugoslav government.[31] Since the debts incurred surpassed the credit

* According to the Yugoslav Federal Statistical Institute, exports in 1967 amounted to 15,600 million dinars (2 per cent more than in 1966), while imports increased by 8.4 per cent to 21,345 million in 1967. The total trade deficit in 1967 rose to 5,745 million dinars.

capacity of both the government and the enterprises, new convenient methods were sought by which foreign means could be utilized. One of the latest solutions is in the "cooperation of our economy with foreign capital," that is, inducing the investment of private foreign capital in Yugoslav enterprises.

Because of ideological and constitutional obstacles the evolution of such ideas was not easy. In Yugoslavia's socialist economy any private, particularly foreign, capital is legitimately and automatically expropriated; it cannot exist legally in Yugoslavia. Since the new class knows that there is no point in inviting foreign capital to Yugoslavia only to be expropriated, its economists attempted to devise forms which on the one hand would meet ideological and legal requirements and on the other hand would simultaneously attract foreign capital. When, after long and puzzling discussions, regulations regarding foreign investments were published in July, 1967, the solutions were highly pragmatic, flexible, and ambiguous.

According to these new rules it is Yugoslavia's sovereign jurisdiction to state in which kind of businesses foreign investments are allowed or forbidden (as, for instance, in banking) in order to insure that foreign investments will not move only to the most profitable ventures or key positions. Direct foreign investments, including equity participation, are prohibited. In no case may foreign capital constitute more than 49 per cent of an enterprise; the ambiguous point, however, is that neither does the first 49 per cent give any property rights to the foreign investor. Finally, the socialist and self-managed Yugoslav enterprise is the exclusive channel of foreign capital entering Yugoslavia.

Yugoslav enterprises thus enjoy a position of monopoly in dealing with foreign firms. Their self-managing character both excuses and excludes the state, which does not appear formally but is in fact close behind each arrangement. Of particular interest is the fact that the entire responsibility in dealing with foreign capital is put squarely on the enterprises themselves. The "economic enterprise *enters into contractual obligations on the basis of its own decision, and it is the enterprise itself which limits its own freedom of action* when dealing [with foreign firms]."[32] Each enterprise, within legal limits of course, is free to conduct business with foreign firms, provided such business is advantageous to Yugoslavia. If not, then self-management must accept the consequences both economically and politically. The new class generally assures that the state and the Party apparatus do not exert decisive influence in an enterprise; when foreign capital involves a Yugoslav firm in the whirlpools of international finance, however, the new class then magnanimously directs the enterprise to make its own decisions, even at the price of losing one part of its "freedom" to foreign capitalists.

Many reasons explain Yugoslavia's desire for foreign capital. In addition to bridging the domestic deficit gap, foreign capital helps to modernize the Yugoslav economy: "Reconstruction and modernization of the national economy are the main motives for attracting foreign capital."[33] The new regulations do not allow "mixed societies," which are an undesirable side effect of foreign capital and a natural result of property rights acquired by foreign investors. To avoid direct foreign control, but to insure its own best interests, the new class devises contracts between the foreign and Yugoslav firms as instruments of "equal rights in cooperation." By contracts, mutual rights and obligations are foreseen but can be suspended or terminated if the need should arise. Thus the official Yugoslav theses on dealing with foreign capital stated that "There is no need for the foreign partner to place its representative in the self-managing organs of the [Yugoslav] enterprise."[34] Since foreign firms can be represented legally in Yugoslavia only by a self-managed "incorporated" domestic enterprise, they can function only as absent partners of Yugoslav enterprises or be represented by another Yugoslav enterprise. The "special business committee" is viewed as a solution to the possible impasse of conflicts of interest. A consultative and parity body with equal representation, the committee would actually be in a stalemate in cases of disagreement. To solve *this* problem, a third party, namely, a representative of the Yugoslav state, would have to intervene by means of regular, commercial, or arbitration courts.

The foreign partner may share the net profits of the domestic enterprise according to the intended provisions of the contract, but payment can be made only after the enterprise has met all of its internal (Yugoslav) obligations, particularly taxes and wages. Rather liberal degrees of foreign participation are possible because the Yugoslav interest as a whole is not so much in limiting profit as in attracting foreign capital. Any net earnings which appeared could be transferred outside Yugoslavia only in accordance with the domestic foreign exchange regulations valid at the time of transfer (but not of the contract).[35]

This means that the Yugoslav state regulates the transfer of profits, commissions, and other interests. Regulations may change or even arise any time after the contract is signed since the Yugoslav enterprise, of course, does not have the right to make decisions for the state. Thus the Yugoslav side may change even the essential conditions of the contract. The state has already decided that a percentage of foreign earnings must remain in Yugoslavia, but such nontransferable funds are "free" for further investment in Yugoslavia: the foreign investor "will be obliged to unconditionally reinvest at least 20 per cent of his annual profit in the Yugoslav economy." He is assured, however, of freedom to "reinvest in any other Yugoslav enterprise he wants."[36]

The last point surpasses prima facie economic or financial considerations, revealing the entire scheme as a plan to use foreign financing not only to cover the domestic deficit gap and modernize Yugoslavia's technology, but also to lure foreign capital and then force foreign private investors to increase their financial stake in Yugoslavia by reinvesting. Foreign investors would have no alternative, if they wished to recover their capital, but to try to keep themselves in good standing with the Yugoslav government. In this way, economic difficulties ironically effected the political coup of binding and, if need be, even forcing big foreign businesses to maintain and support the regime in Yugoslavia—because of their financial involvement.

Political Character

In time we shall see whether the devices of the new class, such as the use of foreign capital, are indeed a solution to Yugoslavia's problems or are simply an added failure. Regarding the relations between Yugoslav socialism and international capitalists, the new class is less concerned with the prospect of foreign capital penetrating into Yugoslav socialist enterprises than the danger of the self-managed enterprises turning into socialist capitalists *sui generis*. A quasi-capitalist peril has appeared in the tendency of Yugoslav self-managing enterprises to appropriate "social" capital and use it to their own advantage. The new class has already perceived this threat, and the Secretary of the Party's Central Committee pointed out that self-management opens the "possibility of creating monopolies of the means of production [capital], the possibility of making the work organization [enterprises] *autonomous and private and of divorcing them from the entire complex of social work. . . .* [It] generally *tends to usurp social property in favor of more narrow and more particular interests and to transform social property into group property.*"[37]

"To usurp social property" is not the formal expropriation of social means; rather, self-managed enterprises assume for themselves the right to use capital to their own advantage. The interests of self-managed collectives, consequently, are often in direct opposition to the goals and methods of the economic reform. For example, one clearly established aim of the reform is the reduction of production costs. A corollary to this goal is the modernization of production techniques, which saves on labor and has a negative effect on the working collectives because they must fire surplus labor and then deal with unemployment. Therefore, contrary to the guidelines of the reform, self-managed enterprises and workers' councils have elected "to remain with the old machines and the same number of workers. . . . The workers do it because of their mutual solidarity, because of their business shortsightedness, but mostly because they feel insecure."[38] As a matter of fact, workers simply decided to defend their own interests.

A battle rages between self-managed enterprises, composed of workers who avoid unilateral exploitation by the socialist society, and the new class, whose fundamental interests require a stable national economy. Having thus evolved into a social conflict, the economic reform is manipulated by the new class to prevent the political situation from getting worse. The defensive strategy now is to see by whom and how the past, present, and future losses will be paid. Basically, the whole problem has turned into a political struggle between the working class and the new class. The problem of the reform became identified with various political ferments such as the struggle between the Party apparatus and the new class, the nationalities issue, and maneuverings of the "bureaucratic" faction.

At first glance the economic reform seemed to be a radical turnabout from former political interference with objective economic laws. This was true partly because the new class recognized that political instability resulted from the unbalanced national economy. Further, political issues would normally have been resolved within the Party, but the Party's monopoly excludes any deviation from the official political "line." Since the Party, controlled by the new class, is ideally united in a monolithic structure, it has to operate through uniform and obligatory "platforms," pushing actual political struggles and currents underground. Thus political life is carried on in the otherwise nonpolitical sectors of social life—science, literature, philosophy, art, and so on, but above all in the national economy. The economy, the material basis and framework of the lives of the people, is the most natural field for the expression of political unrest. Political life in Yugoslavia, therefore, manifests itself less in election statistics or parliamentary proceedings than in economic activities such as the reform, the drive for industrialization, and the struggle for higher productivity and lower costs or, vice versa, for higher wages—eventually in growing unemployment. Consequently, from its very inception the economic reform has had a definite political character. As the new class strives for a healthier economy through reform, it also moves to strengthen the material basis of its power. The economic crisis, however, in an unexpected way and according to its own logic, has separated the economy from the main body of the Yugoslav socialist system, and the new class has been forced to bow to economic laws through the reform. It attempts a compromise with reality, as did Lenin with the NEP in the Soviet Union.* Fighting for time, the new class wields the economic reform in strengthening its political regime. In this process the leadership of the new class purges its own ranks, removing competing factions that struggle for supremacy in the Party and the new class by labeling their activities as resistance to the economic reform. This ploy clarifies Tito's statement that the reform was not only economic but at the same time profoundly social, "a step forward in the development of our revolution."[39]

At the seventh Plenary Meeting of the Party in 1967, two years after the beginning of the reform, Todorovic said, "It is necessary to clarify basic trends in reorganizing the Party and developing society by the economic reform. Thus shall we achieve *a more unified, ideologically stronger, and politically more militant and effective* organization."[40] Probably President Tito best explained the situation when he equated the reform with the war in which the enemies of the revolution were destroyed by armed struggle. "We Communists have to wake up and realize clearly that we are confronted by that which we fought with guns, that which still shows some signs of life and must be finished off."[41] This time the guns were aimed not at reactionaries, but at close associates in the Party.

In its political movements the new class pragmatically resorts to compromises and retreats temporarily when necessary.[42] The explanation for such conduct can be found in the critical condition of the national economy which requires treatment according to its own laws if it is to be cured. The new class, however, cannot respect economic laws because such concern would entail a weakening of its hold on power.

Thus, when almost every economic measure was permeated with political considerations, the economic reform reached an impasse. For example, one of the most important aims of the reform was to establish free price formation on the market; instead, the reform "temporarily," but actually sine die, froze them. Although the new class knows that prices should be free for economic health, it freezes them for political reasons. It realizes that prices are the key to the entire economy and does not dare lose control over them, fearing that prices could affect the

* NEP, the New Economic Policy, was a set of temporary adjustments initiated in 1921 in the Soviet Union. Strict state interference was abandoned or modified, and a limited system of market economy and private enterprise was restored. After achieving its purpose, a system of rigid economic state planning (five-year plans) was introduced in 1928.

whole political system through their own logic, "like a chain reaction,"[43] as Tito has said. Yet a meeting of the Labor Union of Service Workers in 1967 modified Tito's words: "The present system of price formation and social control of prices has not done away with administrative measures and has prevented work organizations from adapting themselves to the new situation."[44] Or, as a *Borba* editorial commented, "The liberalization of prices was discussed; prices were kept at a level established by the reform, which practically means their freezing."[45]

The contradiction between economic need and political expediency is illustrated also by the hesitating and unsatisfactory monetary devaluation. The new rate of exchange for the dinar (1,250 dinars to the dollar*) is obviously still overvalued and does not offer sufficient basis for economic stabilization. Yet that rate is retained for political reasons because any additional devaluations right after the establishment of the "final" rate could discredit the reputation of the entire reform.

While the new class conceded partial measures of devaluation to meet economic needs, it was forced to initiate radical changes in the case of widespread unemployment created by the reform, a problem which the government was unable to handle and afraid to face. Two politically unfavorable solutions had to be accepted: the unemployed were allowed to return indignantly to their villages and there increase the number of already dissatisfied peasants; and the unemployed were permitted to work in Western Europe. The political delicacy of mass unemployment was accentuated by the fact that the problem appeared a few months after the adoption of the new Constitution, in which the right and the opportunity to work was guaranteed to all citizens.[46] Moreover, by the summer of 1966 there were about 300,000 Yugoslavs working in Western Europe;[47] in 1967 that number rose obviously, but no one dared to express it in figures. One enigmatic report was "Nobody knows how many are employed abroad."[48] The new class also has no choice but to accept the political risk that those working abroad might not return or, if they did return, would bring with them democratic criteria for evaluating conditions in Yugoslavia. The political risk, of course, is conveniently balanced by the economic advantage of exporting the unemployed and importing indispensable foreign money in the form of wages sent home by emigrant workers to their families.

Once forced to allow labor emigration, the new class tried to make the best of it by taking the whole matter into its own hands in "guiding

* In the meantime, a "new" dinar was established to replace 100 "old" dinars, so the present official rate expressed in "new" dinars is 12.5 dinars to the dollar.

the migratory movements of Yugoslavs abroad so as to protect social interests."[49] The new class decided to make a virtue of this necessity: it changed the provisions relating to travel abroad instead of being maneuvered into intensifying the border control, shooting the escapees, installing electrical wires and mine fields, and, particularly, dealing with the harmful publicity of an iron curtain. Emigration rules and exit permits were relaxed substantially in 1966–67.[50] The new class readily conceded whatever it considered unessential for the core of the regime. Ducking criticism and exporting the unemployed, Yugoslavia distanced itself from other less flexible Communist countries. Instead of forcing citizens to be idle at home and to nurse the political ferment, the regime saw to it that emigrants sent their earnings home and received supervision abroad. In agreements with Western European countries, Yugoslavia seeks to arrange departure, travel, and residence of its citizens abroad and to control job placement, conditions of work, social and health insurance, legal protection, and the cultural life of Yugoslav workers. Through such agreements the government discourages and often makes it practically impossible for individuals to travel abroad on their own.[51] Belgrade is not pleased with those foreign governments allowing direct "unorganized" hiring without the mediation of Yugoslav authorities. "Employment abroad is conducted officially only through Yugoslav employment agencies."[52]

Yugoslav authorities continue to expand services connected with foreign employment. Since the families of workers remain at home as a rule, Yugoslav diplomatic representatives in the foreign countries have adapted themselves to new assignments on the emigrant workers. Clubs, homes, posts, institutes, and similar recreation centers have been established to keep the workers together and expose them to official Yugoslav propaganda. Emigrants are also supervised politically by an infiltration of police and Party members directed from diplomatic centers. Party member-emigrants, of course, are organized abroad in Party units whose range of activities and alertness supposedly permeate all aspects of the lives of Yugoslavs there, as at home.

Despite attempts of the new class to handle the problem of surplus manpower, Yugoslav workers abroad cannot be selectively controlled. Thus unskilled workers are forced to remain in Yugoslavia where they cannot find work, while many experts and skilled workers go abroad when they are needed at home and when it is vital to increase labor productivity in Yugoslavia. Even though the intellectuals are economically affected by low wages, their departure also reveals definite elements of political dissatisfaction. It is not by chance that "in Paris alone several hundred Yugoslav architects work as ordinary draftsmen, that mechanical engineers are working as dishwashers in Swedish restaurants, and doctors of medicine are employed as ordinary laborers in German breweries, or auto mechanics became street sweepers."[53] Obviously, the readiness of Yugoslavs to work abroad (also below their qualifications) rather than at home indicates that they are not content with political conditions or economic exploitation in Yugoslavia. It is interesting to note Tito's complaint that Yugoslavs work better when they are abroad. "If our worker were working here in our country as he does, e.g., in Germany, he would have earned a car even here. *But it is different over there.*"[54] It must be clear to Tito that better work results from better incentives, which in this case are both political and economic.

While the reform provided a convenient boost to further concentration of the regime's power, political resistance expressed itself by confusing, disrupting, and delaying the reform. Insofar as the reform reflects a cross section of Yugoslav political and social developments, it can be viewed as an indication of general unrest. Various types of opposition to the reform, even though overlapping, can be identified politically as anti-Communist, Party bureaucratic, nationalist, localist, or finally as democratic-socialist.

The Yugoslav regime has been preoccupied with its opponents since 1945, ringing the bells of alarm to mobilize the populace against "the class enemy," which is always described as lurking just around the corner, ready to attack and create chaos. The new class brought its campaign to a higher pitch by placing the economic reform at the very center of domestic political developments, allowing it to become both a measure of loyalty and a test of adversaries of the regime, "the class enemies." Opponents of the reform were declared traitors and collaborators with enemies abroad, or as Tito said, "the class enemy . . . has ties with all possible forms of the class enemy abroad and has support from abroad."[55]

President Tito dramatized the increased resistance to the reform and emphasized the seriousness of the situation by saying that "the class enemy uses various approaches in his work, and in the course of the last two years the favorable conditions for his work have greatly increased."[56] A year later the President was forced to repeat his exhortation. "We have not yet finished off our class enemies. . . . They only withdrew to wait for the first opportunity of our weakened alertness. The class enemy appears in the form of all those who attempt to foil the realization of the economic reform."[57] These implications were taken so seriously that even economic investments which turned unprofitable were categorized as political opposition; those frustrated investment projects were described as "fortresses from which the economic reform is being bombarded."[58]

One can hardly say that anti-Communist resistance in Yugoslavia today has assumed an open form of the class struggle. The social groups which could lead the resistance referred to by the new class are the *bourgeoisie,* which is practically nonexistent in Yugoslavia now, and the peasantry, which has been totally pulverized and weakened. Anti-Communist resistance to the economic reform, therefore, is unorganized and expressed more in the views and actions of individuals, every one of whom in his own way resists the regime through a negative attitude toward the reform. One worker quipped, for example, "Nobody can pay me an amount so small that it can match how little I can work."[59] Individuals are not dangerous, but a band of them could significantly threaten the tempo and character of the reform. The regime exaggerates the importance of this type of anti-Communist resistance, however, in order to divert attention from the much more pressing nationalities question and intra-Party ferment. The regime believes that generalized anti-Communist opposition can be compromised more easily by identifying it with the restoration of the reactionary past or with enemies abroad.[60] Or, as Tito himself put it, "The class enemy in the person of the imperialist and capitalist *bourgeoisie* is now on the offensive on all fronts. Somewhere he advances with money or rebellions, elsewhere with the gradual infiltration of his ideology."[61]

The nationalities question, apparently solved in 1945 through the introduction of federalism, but always simmering, boiled to the surface as the reform fanned nationalist aspirations or dissatisfactions of the separate Yugoslav peoples and provided material content for sharp conflicts. No longer was it a mere discussion, as in the fifties, of whether Belgrade, Serbia, would have a large commercial exhibition because Zagreb, Croatia, had one, or whether the Belgrade-Bar railroad line would be finished, connecting Serbia with the Adriatic through Montenegro and providing competition for seaports in Croatia and Slovenia, and so on. The economic reform unavoidably penetrated the economic relations of nationalities by abolishing or introducing advantages for one group or another. For example, the parity of prices was changed by the reform, with the result that the privileged position of industrialized Slovenia and Croatia was partially curtailed while the agricultural producers in Serbia or Macedonia hoped to fare better; or, in turn, more modern producers in industrialized republics tended to take relative advantage of and compete with the producers in the less productive, economically backward areas.

Regardless of which republic gained the advantage of price relations or something else established or changed by the reform, it was evident that, after twenty years of highly publicized efforts at economic progress, Yugoslavia remained unevenly developed, with some regions like Slovenia and Croatia fairly industrialized, and others more backward, like Macedonia and Montenegro. The geographic areas delineated by industrialization coincide with the borders between various Yugoslav nationalities, and the gap between the developed and the underdeveloped, the rich and the poor, lends additional gravity to an already complicated nationalities problem. Under such conditions, the socialist principle of distribution according to work cannot be applied because a uniform economic criterion does not exist; in result, a worker from industrialized Slovenia is far better rewarded for the same work than a Serb, a Macedonian, or a Montenegrin.[62]

Contrariwise, the effort to match an unequal level of growth with equal remuneration according to the work rendered discriminates automatically against the more developed, stifling their incentive to work and aggravating the nationalities problem. Communist functionaries and especially new-class leaders, as representatives of their immediate environments, perforce tend to evaluate problems in light of the interests of their own particular nationality. For that reason the leaders of the elite are motivated by narrow nationalist positions, and the economic reform thus became an embittered battlefield with national and political overtones. Borko Temelkovski, a Macedonian member of the Party's Central Committee, demanded more intensive implementation of the reform's price relations, which happened to suit Macedonia; Norbert Weber, on the other hand, a Croatian member, stated flatly, "It [should] be more definitely affirmed that [in investment policies] the *modernizing of existing productive capacities must have priority in further investments,*"[63] an attitude which in practice would conserve existing unevenness in various parts of Yugoslavia. Representatives of underdeveloped areas of Yugoslavia reacted to the situation by daring to describe inequalities of development as a "form of exploitation . . . which . . . some persons would like to perpetuate and promote as an ideal of socialism."[64]

The less developed Yugoslav nationalities underscored their need for economic aid. Accepting this in principle, the more developed nationalities pointed out that "to make themselves capable of rendering such aid, . . . they would have to strengthen self-rule on the republic level, which, in the case of Slovenia, means on the national level."[65] The request was a bold Slovene move for more national identity and autonomy.

All Yugoslav nationalities are competing among themselves for more investment advantages and higher living standards. As the Croats and

Slovenes boasted of their greater contributions to the community, the Serbs and Montenegrins pointed to their contributions during the war and the revolution. The Slovenes complained, "The oldest working class in Yugoslavia, the Slovene, is in the most unfavorable position,"[66] while Macedonians, in turn, alluded to Slovenes by bitterly criticizing "the appearance of express aristocratism and egoism in parts of the [Yugoslav] working class. . . . Group interests are frequently presented as eminent interests of socialism itself."[67] Such discussions are conducted not only among ordinary citizens but even among Party members and officials, especially at the very top of the new class. Acting in the name of socialism, according to the leader of the new class in Croatia, Vladimir Bakaric, representatives of the various nationality groups actively introduce extremely dangerous "disintegrating processes" into Party unity,[68] i.e., into the new class.

Just as nationalist resistance was initiated outside the Party and the new class but later penetrated both, so intra-Party conflicts spilled over into the life of the entire nation through the economic reform. One side of the reform developed into a political arena in which the local Party apparatus faced the domination of the new class, which, in turn, intended to transform that apparatus into an obedient instrument. The Party and the new class collide with each other over the economic reform in the name of the same principles—socialism and self-management—and even while using identical terminology. The new class claims that the local Party apparatus has "interfered as an element of power in the rights of self-management,"[69] characterizing it as a "bureaucratic usurpation" committed by the local Party organs, or more precisely by the "Party organizations and committees."[70]

For their part, Party functionaries in the field decelerated, distorted, misinterpreted, or implemented reform measures to their advantage—in the county, commune, factory, or association—disregarding the interests of the new class and the country in general as much as possible. Ignoring the criticism of the new class as if it were directed at somebody else, the local leaders, the so-called *vrkhushkas,* tried wherever possible to take over. In the summer of 1966, when the new class opened the campaign against the secret police, the implementation of various measures was left to the local Party organizations which, however, as stated by Miyalko Todorovic, began "little by little to occupy the positions of the U.D.B. [secret police], which we wanted to eliminate, and from those positions they [the local Party functionaries] opened the political fight."[71] Veljko Vlakhovic, in a Belgrade television broadcast on January 6, 1966, stated that in the field "things are being taken into the hands [of the local Party functionaries]" representing "really small coups, *putsches*."[72]

Centralist by nature, the new class needs to become an integrating force to eliminate particularist and centrifugal tendencies; thus, the broad all-Yugoslav character of the economic reform inevitably clashed with the local and parochial interests personified in the *vrkhushkas* of enterprises, territorial units, etc. The *vrhkushka* in this manner became a channel through which Communists, in linking themselves to the local interests of self-managed units, break away from the Party, now controlled by the new class, and from the new class itself.[73] The new class consequently refuses to allow social and political functions of lower levels to become the "acquired rights" of local functionaries.[74] Sensitive when these "acquired rights" are transferred to the economic field, the new class charges the local apparatus with irresponsible spending. Insisting on discipline and directives which exclude from the Party all who do not "implement decisions,"[75] the new class utilizes economic transgressions to morally compromise its intra-Party opponents. But the new class is less disturbed by economic aberrations than by signs of the growing political independence of the local Party apparatus, and it also attempts to identify signs of independence with the inertia of public opinion. Thus, regretting the losses and waste of many frustrated projects, the official analysis dulls political alertness in stating, "The barriers of prejudices and opinions are much stronger than economic losses."[76]

Since the Party apparatus usually does not openly resist, it is difficult to locate opposition to the new class and its economic reform.* Moreover, Party communication channels are still controlled by the restive apparatus itself, so that directives from the elite reach the apparatus first for processing. Thus lower-echelon Party expulsions involve, as Tito said, "those men who were defending a just cause while their punishments were pronounced by the very persons who are guilty."[77]

Party crosscurrents were reflected quite openly for the first time in the meetings of the Central Committee in February and March, 1966. Although convened to debate the implementation of the economic reform, the meetings mainly criticized the Party organizations. The conclusions of the Central Committee regarding economic reform were general; precise instructions, however, were formulated to intensify Party discipline, to replace erring functionaries, and to force the deprofessionalization of personnel in the Party apparatus. Only a few days later, on April 5, 1966, the Republic of Serbia's Central Committee met and "recommended" that nonprofessionals "be considered" for "election" as new secretaries of local Party committees. This was a blow to the middle and lower professional Party cadres who were to be replaced by temporary, unpaid amateurs.[78]

Even though it is a basic rule that intra-Party frictions are dealt with

* Approving the reform in principle is actually a way of working against it." Todorovic, in *Borba,* October 8, 1967.

in secrecy, this time the whole matter was made public—obviously a deliberate dramatization of the situation. In a note reminiscent of 1948, when Tito liquidated his intra-Party Stalinists by the support of the people, the new class appealed to the citizens, working men, and patriots to join against the "enemy of socialism and self-management" entrenched within the Party apparatus itself.

The opinion of the new class, however, is not united, and differences exist not only among individuals but also in definite groups and factions. One group centered about Alexandar Rankovic, a pragmatic Party apparatus man who wanted to stabilize the already conquered positions of the new class in an all-embracing dictatorship of the Party. For Rankovic, the Party represented the safest organizational form for the new class. As far as the economic area was concerned, this group considered it something almost alien, responsibility for the proper functioning of which should be left to experts, economists, theoreticians, ideologists, managers, administrators, activitists, and especially to the "working people"; in the meantime it wanted a strong and efficient security force topped by the secret police.

Around Tito formed another group from the mainstream of the new class. This group realized that it constituted only the commanding core of the Party, not the entire Party, and it was particularly irritated by the control of the secret police, even though, for instance, "The Executive Committee of the Central Committee of Montenegro specifically stressed in 1958 that it [the secret police] was not allowed to check on and shadow the high leadership and functionaries [the new class]."[79] Disagreements between both factions, however, did not in fact relate to the supreme power, its character, or its aims; the factions clashed over methods and the implementation of power. In this sense, the reform was the latest edition of a blueprint for dealing with economic and particularly political difficulties. Within such coordinates the new class lost whatever unity it once had. Thus Tito demanded, "One cannot leave the meeting of the Central Committee . . . and then disagree around corners and oppose the execution of our decisions made by the majority."[80]

It was natural that differences between the groups became sharpest in discussions of the Party's role, so Vlakhovic attacked Party members, saying, "outside the Party we have a large number of people who are really Communists . . . better than some who are members."[81] In contrast to this statement, Rankovic, at the time vice-president of Yugoslavia, defended the Party and its apparatus. In one of his last public appearances, Rankovic addressed members of the Party directly, praising and exhorting them to be prepared to fight for their rights. He appealed to "Communists, organizations, and leaders" to create "new conditions for realizing the leading role of the Party. . . . We Communists have to be aware of the opportunities created by the economic reform for the Party . . . because we are bound to guarantee the continuity of the revolution."[82]

After colliding with Rankovic and throwing him out, the new class became increasingly conscious that the growing resistance to the economic reform was of a political and even "ideological" nature.[83] There is no doubt that the many strikes, or "work stoppages" as they are called in Yugoslavia, as well as numerous individual resignations from various functions are clear signs of growing political opposition.[84] There is even less doubt when the entire Party or local government bodies, committees, or groups tender their collective resignations.[85]

More serious are cases in which entire Party units have been "disbanded," which means not only cancellation of Party functions but also automatic expulsion of all members in such units from the Party.[86] In 1966, about 7,500 Party members voluntarily withdrew their membership, and Party discipline was intensified. The number of Party punishments in 1966 increased 11 per cent over 1965, while the number of Party expulsions increased at the same time by 27 per cent.[87] These and similar cases certainly represent a transition to a new stage of political development which can at least be diagnosed as critical.

Thus the economic reform was no longer economic but definitely a complex political and social process identifying itself with the continuation of the revolution. The reform asserted itself as a catalyst which further accelerated but also complicated the political ferment, deepened the economic troubles, resurrected and intensified the nationalities question in a more difficult form, and opened a new series of other disintegrating forces. Among them is the conspicuous fact of the split in the top stratum of the new class, manifested in the Tito-Rankovic confrontation and continued struggle. It all began as a reform to stabilize the shaken national economy, but it continued as a purge of the Party to stabilize the new class. The main point of these complex developments is that, despite twenty years of building and cementing a "monolithic Communist unity," there is no such unity in either the ranks of the Communist Party or the new class itself.

10 *The Golden Coach*

Although the process of new-class self-disclosure is relatively slow and complex, it shows that present-day Yugoslav reality is far removed from what communism once promised to the world in general or to Yugoslavia in particular. It has been of no avail to Yugoslavia or other Communist countries to have proceeded through supposedly progressive "proletarian," "social," and "democratic" revolutions, through liberation, industrialization, collectivization, decentralization, and liberalization, to have fought fascism and colonialism, to have created popular fronts and supported revolutionary movements while clamoring for world peace. Despite frenzied efforts to take the lead in progressive social movements, communism, though materially strengthened, is losing the world-wide battle; the loss may be faster here and slower there, but the current is clear. Widespread disillusionment with communism is certainly contributing to the weakening of Communist strength in Yugoslavia.

Yugoslav Communists, compressed into a special type of a new class, seem to have sensed the trend of discontent and have moved aside, almost for an alibi. Since the Yugoslav variant of communism has strayed considerably from Soviet orthodoxy, many outside observers and some Yugoslavs have reached the curious conclusion that, though Communists do exist in Yugoslavia, they are somehow unlike those in other countries. Thus the viewpoint that everything that is evil in communism, or at least in the Stalinist or Chinese forms, is somehow transformed in Yugoslavia to be less evil, perhaps even acceptable. Consequently, Yugoslav communism is pictured as nationalistic, democratic, and nonaligned, or simply a mutation—all with the implication that democratic, or at least anti-Communist, "Titoist," heresies are possible.

Yet the facts indicate that developments in Yugoslavia actually further enhanced and entrenched qualities which, to coin a phrase, make communism even more communistic. Power has been concentrated in a separate social group—the new class—which is vitally interested in preserving its dominating and privileged position. From its own point of view, the new class has succeeded in rationalizing its hold on power, making it more flexible, deeper, and temporarily capable of averting the processes of disillusionment. The system of the new class has thereby provided Yugoslavia's Communist regime with the opportunity of developing with and adjusting to changing conditions. However, the new class is so sincerely concerned with its struggle for survival that it is capable, if necessary, of abandoning world communism to safeguard its own.

It is not coincidental that the Yugoslav regime is also concerned with further ideological justification of its system, because it considers the latter to represent the "continuity of the revolution" and seeks to win ever greater control over the human mind. Preservation of the regime thus depends not only on material conditions; the decisive battle is to be fought over the minds of men. For these reasons, the otherwise materialistically oriented regime has directed its attention to the realm of ideas. Today the regime is no longer satisfied with merely loyal co-operation, but it demands voluntary, self-managed, devoted, and free participation, based on firm personal conviction identical with the Party "line." This is one-way freedom where everyone is obliged to be "free" in the prescribed manner. Failure to accept this kind of freedom is considered dangerous and is branded a political crime because it might conjure up another sort of freedom. The new class is conscious of this threat, and, for this reason, the motive behind its constant reorganizations and reforms is an intense desire to add a complete monopoly of ideas to its already firm physical hold on the power structure.

In the interplay of two great forces, one material and the other ideological, the latter, though apparently less important in materialistic Marxist ideology, tends to become decisive. Heavy indeed is the material burden which the people bear because of the new class and its privileges, spending, waste, and blunders, but even more grievous and irreplaceable is that suffering which Yugoslavs endure by living under conditions which erode morality and dehumanize the individual. This moral decomposition affects those who rule, those who support that rule, those who are ruled, and even those who believe themselves to be neutral. Regardless of a man's station in life, he is compelled to make a compromise with his own conscience to maintain power, to hold a job or to advance in it, or, in most cases, simply to survive.[1] The ethical confusion is greater because communism negated the earlier values of national traditions and respect for cultural heritages, thereby creating a moral vacuum convenient for its takeover. Yet the new class remains unable to fill the vacuum with positive, and progressive values. Taking power as a measure of value, the only moral code the new class knows is exploitation and subordination of the nation.

Because it cannot create new ethical values, communism must revert, especially in moments of great crisis, to traditional values such as patriotism, nationalism, local traditions, and the like, which it otherwise seeks to destroy. Yugoslav Communists seized an existing national liberation movement and usurped leadership of the patriotic defensive war; thus they degraded it from the heights of moral idealism to the depths of power politics. Even today the new class continues to identify itself with national values, and on that basis, it labels dissenters as traitors or renegades. The regime still embeds itself in the soul of the people, leaning on Communist ideology but borrowing heavily from the national ethical treasure. Although founded on and established in a national framework, the ideology of the new class nevertheless appears to be supra- and extra-national. Class unity is not patriotic but is based primarily on the mutual identity of interests of the elite, whose members are in power. It matters little if one is from Serbia, Croatia, Slovenia, or a national minority group—perhaps Czech, Hungarian, or Albanian—all participate and are represented in the new class. Yet it is indeed important how one aligns himself in the common game. That is why the new class as a whole, in connection with the nationalities question, favors Yugoslav unity, which is in turn considered only an intermediary stage in the movement toward broader "proletarian internationalism." Thus does the new class undermine the very foundation of those "old" national and patriotic standards of ethics on which it leans so heavily today.

It was unavoidable that, under such conditions, the processes of demoralization made deep marks in the ranks of the new class and undermined its strength. On the one hand is the moral frustration of people who struggled in the revolution in search of progress, freedom, and improved standards of living; on the other hand is an increasing awareness that developments in Yugoslavia are generally either misdirected or failures. That such disillusionment has already moved beyond individual or sporadic manifestations and has become a widespread problem was confirmed by Kardelj, who was motivated or forced to say, "Even among Communists are those who are disappointed and surprised, asking themselves: Why have we, who during and after the revolution worked toward ideals of the future society of camaraderie and brotherhood, lost our way, entangling ourselves in such conflicts and problems? The question is also whether or not the contradictions and issues we face today discredit many things we have been fighting for."[2]

Not only have its ideological difficulties deepened, but because the crisis is growing, the new class is losing the advantage of initiative and the ability to dictate the subject, timing, place, and form of the struggle, as well as the arms to be used. Neither can the new class lean on its apparatus: the government and party bureaucracies proved themselves potentially dangerous, tending toward establishing independent authority rather than serving the new class. That is why the new class chose the course toward "liberalization" and "self-management" as the means of reshaping the Party from a position of power, for example, to that of an instrument for remote control and propaganda. The new class thereby deprives itself, at least theoretically, of the advantage of central administrative measures, and is forced, at least on the surface, to operate more by consensus than commands. This happened right at the time when the new class was compelled, for other reasons, to shift the center of the power struggle to the ideological field, using the Party for "ideological-political" activities (cultural, political, scientific, economic, etc.). During his tour of Slovenia in September, 1966, Tito said, "The role of the Party is not diminishing, as some people abroad say, or as the class enemy in our country says. On the contrary, its role is growing, and will increase for a long time to come. Withering away is a long process and does not mean the withering of the Communist ideology: it means the growth of the citizens' Communist consciousness."[3]

This also means that the battle for the minds of men must be fought with ideological weapons which are gained by knowledge and education but not easily controlled or understood. In this subtle battle the new class sorely needs the intellectuals, who are at home in the realm of ideology where they possess both strategic and tactical advantages. Yet, while the intellectuals sided predominantly with the Communist movement in the course of the revolutionary war, they are increasingly turning against the Communist regime today. Their views sometimes leak into public, projecting a dark and negative picture, as, for instance, "Deprived of personality, this mutilated and impoverished world [of ours] deserves total destruction, but an individual, being alone, does not have the strength for it. Therefore he is unavoidably lost in the darkness of each day."[4] Or, "The reality around us [in Yugoslavia] is dark and we are its victims."[5] These and similar testimonies of the new anti-Communist intellectual orientation are met now by open threats from the new class. Tito said, "They [the intellectuals] say that the Party is obsolete and that it has lost the political battle. It seems that they have not yet felt us strongly enough. But I think that from now on they will feel us and will look differently at the Party."[6]

The present course against the intellectuals disregards the historical and vital role they have always played in promoting communism, having, in fact, been its pioneers from Marx and Lenin to date.* But after the new class assumed power, intellectuals found themselves pushed out while the reins fell into the hands of dictators like Stalin, Tito, and Mao. In the same way they once created fronts against tsarism, feudalism, or capitalism, so today intellectuals are turning anti-Communist. When the "third revolution" is mentioned, one must consider the growing influence of the intellectuals in the countries of Central and Eastern Europe.

It is not surprising that Yugoslav intellectuals are turning against Communism and "new classism," and that many of them do so exactly as proponents and defenders of the ideals of socialism. It is unimportant whether this intellectual approach to socialism is called democratic socialism or socialist democracy; it *is* important that it rejects the totalitarian and undemocratic socialism of communism as seen in the various forms of dictatorship—the Party, Tito, Stalin, Mao, or the new class. For this reason, the Yugoslav new class found itself faced with a twofold political handicap: It was compelled, first, to shift political emphasis to ideology, where the growing number of opposing intellectuals are more adept than the new class in matters of theory. Second, the intellectuals argue, persuasively, from the very positions considered to be the sacrosanct monopoly of the new class. The socialist orientation of the majority of intellectuals removes the halo of the "builders of the future"

* As an educated social avant-garde, intellectuals influence their surroundings out of the proportion suggested by their numbers or economic and political strength. This is particularly true of the intellectual strata of Central and Eastern Europe. They are always the sentient medium that experiences, observes, studies, and processes the reality of their environment. In one sense the intellectuals are detectors, transmitters, and amplifiers of their time and milieu. Because of these attributes, intellectuals do not react as a homogeneous social group, but rather as the vehicles and catalysts of the various and sundry contradictions which already exist in a society. Consequently, intellectuals take part in all social upheavals in Central and Eastern Europe, where they usually are called the intelligentsia; they are represented in all movements and factions, on the one hand forming the ruling apparatus, on the other leading the revolutionaries. Thus, before 1945 Yugoslav intellectuals led bourgeois, socialist, and agrarian movements (as integralists, federalists, nationalists, separatists, etc.), and while some strongly supported the military dictatorship, others fought against it with even greater ferocity. But the kaleidoscopic excursions of Yugoslav intellectuals, which ran the gamut from romanticism through communism to surrealism, were not of their making. The trouble stemmed from the confusion that permeated the relations, forces, and trends in Yugoslavia itself, disrupting its society, politics, and economics. The disunited intellectuals merely reflected the turmoil that prevailed in all horizontals and verticals of Yugoslav society. That is why before World War II the intelligentsia appeared at the same time as the bearers of the Yugoslav nationalist platform and of the socialist-Communist ideology. Within these coordinates the intellectuals were the leading force in the establishment of Communist power so that a new Yugoslavia could be federally organized and dedicated to economic growth which, in turn, was expected to promote more social and personal freedom.

from the new class, while the anti-dictatorial stand of the intellectuals threatens its power directly.

A deep social, political, and economic crisis, after twenty years of Communist rule, was bound to find expression in the reaction of an intelligentsia which had collaborated in the building of that rule. Even though many issues in Yugoslavia were solved after a fashion, one cannot ignore the evidence that the royal-military dictatorship was replaced by a dictatorial republic, that the old exploiting class was replaced by a new one, that federalism became a mask for greater centralism, and that, though the national economy has developed considerably, the people for the most part continue to live at a minimum level of existence, or even below it.

Whether they participated actively in the Communist metamorphoses or watched from the sidelines, Yugoslav intellectuals could not avoid the reality of the new class, and now, after an incubation period, they are reassessing it. The intelligentsia's mounting anti-communism is not the result of a fad but is determined by the class character of the society,[7] especially when the system persistently excludes intellectuals from participating in it. In fact, Yugoslavia's intelligentsia has become relatively depressed economically. Differing from the workers and their self-management, it does not have the opportunity or authority to manipulate wages, fringe benefits, and retirement benefits in order to increase personal income. The work of the intelligentsia increasingly receives substandard pay, and members of this group are particularly suppressed when they approach retirement age. "A woman messenger without any education who had been employed by a foreign-trade firm received higher benefits when she retired than a scholar who had gained world renown as a professor of the medical sciences."[8]

In addition, the new class frequently weeds out those intellectuals arising within its own ranks. In representing subjective and personalized total power, that is, in ruthlessly eliminating any opposition, the new class collides in principle and in practice with the scientific objectivity and ethical strivings which intellectuals recognize and seek to apply in their views on society. Thus the new class needs to control the reasoning of the intellectuals, eliminate their objective approach to problems, and corrode their moral integrity. In its "Communist society" the new class prefers a "socialist man," the reactions of whom can be completely manipulated. In Tito's words, "It is indispensable to mold a socialist man and to permeate the minds of the people with socialist ideas."[9]

In order to achieve such objectives, Stalinist methods were applied earlier by simply prohibiting intellectual endeavor outside the officially prescribed limits (*postanovka*), much as art was directed in the socialist realism of the Soviet Union, or official science was controlled by Lysenko's conceptions of genetics. The new class, however, understood that such a nonintellectual method of struggle against intellectuals is frustrating and impractical, and therefore searched for other means. Instead of commanding, the new class is trying to "guide" intellectuals toward loyalty and cooperation, even at the price of some sort of compromise. Such compromise frequently creates a split personality in intellectuals in which one part pays the price with active political cooperation in order to enable the other part to live independently, and probably even creatively. According to one opinion, "A man can be politically and ideologically progressive, but that progressiveness does not have to conflict with questions of his aesthetic taste and education."[10] One can conceive the example of a scientist who for the sake of his work will see nothing wrong in signing a protest sponsored by the regime or an appeal dealing with some distant international problem. From this apparently innocent and even humanely motivated signature, the slide begins toward gradually greater concessions, greater involvements, and eventually deeper subordination. The new class accepts the compromise with intellectuals as a necessary but temporary evil from which it will eventually derive benefit, first by involving the intellectual in closer association, then by compromising him, and finally by binding him to itself in permanent collaboration. So long as the intellectual remains faithful to his ideals, the new class allows an occasional liberty—but on the condition that it take place within the limits of, at most, a benevolent political neutrality. The advantage for the new class is that an impression is thus created, in Yugoslavia and abroad, of a liberal intellectual life. If the intellectual threatens to express himself "mistakenly" or "incorrectly," however, the regime quickly applies different rules. One method is that of establishing taboos and voluntary intellectual paralysis; for example, any discussion of Yugoslav problems in the presence of strangers is considered a national disgrace, equal to betrayal. Mihaylo Mihaylov, a former university teacher at Zadar, Dalmatia, spoke of this in his article "Why We Are Silent," when he said, "the Socialist intellectual who expresses himself freely before the Western public begins to feel, somehow, like a traitor."[11]

When it cannot uproot the opinions of intellectuals, the new class tries to localize and control the heresies; as the Soviet Union dealt with Pasternak, so—in fact much worse—did Yugoslavia deal with Djilas. In the first place it is impossible for dissenters to publish anything against the system of the new class because it has total control, directly or indirectly, of the press, publishing houses, radio, television, and other media of communication. In addition, the Party has a tight grip on public forums, lectures, conferences, symposia, and the like. Even though preventive censorship does not exist in Yugoslavia, the results are nonetheless efficient. The situation was well summed up by Tito:

> I am against administrative measures. I would like the collectives [employees] in this press to know what they print, what they should *and should not print.* . . . I would like to see our comrades . . . *be good journalists following the socialist line. If* in this way negative activities are not eliminated, then *necessary* administrative *measures are to be undertaken.* Naturally, we are a revolutionary Party . . . *and we have the right to apply all means necessary* . . . *to protect the correct line of our socialist development.*[12]

If some undesirable criticism slips by and becomes public knowledge, then the writer and publisher, and even the printer, are fully aware that appropriate political and other measures await them, with consequences ranging from the loss of privileges or employment to long-term imprisonment and social ostracism. Mihaylo Mihaylov was sentenced by a court and lost his academic position for writing an article in 1965 criticizing the Stalinist concentration camps in the Soviet Union. It is worth noting that at the time both Soviet and Yugoslav opinions on the subject did not differ much from Mihaylov's, but, while the Soviet Union tolerated some vagaries in its writers (Solzhenitsyn, author of *One Day in the Life of Ivan Denisovich*), the new class did not want to antagonize the Russians.

Having chosen the role of a martyr, Mihaylov became a symbol for Yugoslav intellectuals and a danger to the regime. Determining to frustrate any future attempt at self-immolation by the intellectuals, the new class conveniently found Mihaylov to be a "psychopathic personality insufficiently prepared for social adjustment," according to *Politika*'s report of October 17, 1967. This diagnosis was made by the new class through experts at the Neuropsychiatric Hospital of Belgrade's Medical School. The regime perpetrated the image of a clement ruler by reducing Mihaylov's prison term from four and one half to three and one half years; yet the above medical opinion represents a clear warning of the measures that could be taken against intellectuals who are unwilling or unable to "adjust" themselves to the social environment created by the new class.

In this regard it is interesting to note the banning of *The Dictionary of the Contemporary Serbo-Croatian Literary Language,* by Dr. Milos S. Moskovlyevic, a professor and scientific associate at the Serbian Academy of Arts and Sciences. Printed in Belgrade in March, 1966, the entire edition was confiscated and destroyed after a court decision, with the justification that it "brought out statements that tend to provoke unrest among the citizens."[13] The new class, through the Belgrade City Party Committee, also punished all those who were involved in any capacity in the publishing of the *Dictionary,* from the General Director on down, because of their "lack of political alertness." On April 14, 1966, Prvoslav Traykovic, director of the Technical Book publishing house, and Zhivoyin Yeremic, chief editor, were punished by expulsion from the Party; Sava Lazarevic, general manager of the printing firm *Nolit,* and Vasco Popa, a writer and editor, were given a reprimand and "last warning prior to expulsion." The City Committee also decreed that "Worker's councils of the respective enterprises should consider the consequences which resulted and determine personal responsibilities."[14] But when someone such as Djilas succeeds in publishing abroad, he is then sentenced as a criminal and sent to prison.

Less dramatic but more far reaching is the elite's deft transformation of the field of education into a vehicle for propaganda. Here the new class approached the problem of the intellectuals at its very root, the place where their minds are shaped. The traditional European humanistic practice, in which schools and education in general primarily developed independent reasoning, has been replaced by indoctrination. The schools, instead of teaching a student *how* to think, now teach him *what* to think. Knowing this, one can easily understand the incessant reorganization of the Yugoslav educational system, the ultimate goal of which is the political conditioning of the entire populace. Also, by persistent agitation, people are brainwashed and conditioned with terms of technical reference, established semantic or connotative values, and obligatory slogans, all of which comprise a rounded system of clichéd questions and answers.

Degrading the national values and eroding the character of the people on whom it has forced itself, the new class is unable to understand that it is thus accelerating its own downfall; it has effected a chronic crisis in economics; it has produced a mutiliated, servile, and pliable pseudodemocracy in its politics; it has formed a moral vacuum everywhere. Obsessed with the maintenance of power, the new class is incapable of extricating itself from a bad situation which is growing worse. If the new class is unable to lead Yugoslavia out of its deep crisis, however, other social forces already in existence are capable of assuming this responsibility.

It is idle to predict the future development of social processes, and it is impossible to guess the sequence of coming events. Nevertheless, as things stand today, the intelligentsia seems to be the social force most capable of initiating change and showing the paths of future social trends. This was indirectly confirmed by Tito in his Lichki Osik speech of October, 1967, "There are, in our country, among intellectuals and in certain circles, some people who would like to present this [situation] as a withering away of the Party and as a reduction of the role of Communists in our social system. . . . I believe, however, that they are very much mistaken. We have given them enough opportunity to behave like this, but now it is high time to deny them the possibilities for such activities."[15] The intelligentsia, however, is neither numerous enough nor sufficiently homogeneous to become an independent political movement with the power to transform its ethical and political views into the direct political action of a "third revolution." The significance of the intelligentsia lies in its ability not only to analyze the regime but also to formulate programs that will mobilize the people against communism. The programs will succeed to the degree that they recognize and give shape to national and social aspirations, correlating them with economic realities and needs and integrating them in a unified progressive political movement. The programs will be even more successful if they are based on the rich traditions of the Yugoslav past and oriented toward democratic practices offering greater freedom and abundance.

Yet democratic programs and moral condemnations are not sufficient to negate communism; behind them must be vital social forces interested and strong enough to transform Yugoslavia. These forces exist today, in the first instance, in an expanding Yugoslav working class which is ever more conscious of itself, though still young.[16] The process of awakening the working class is, of course, slow and uncertain. The new class, however, attempts to identify itself with the working class by saying, "We . . . are not some kind of special class or socio-economic interest group outside the working class."[17] It seeks to fully permeate the working class and the people, "to truly reform our [the people's] minds and to adopt and enliven the basic tenets as well as the essence [of Communist ideology] . . . we must adopt them in our activities. Only a real political activity will reform our minds and our participation in the ideological and political struggle."[18] Besides, the new class controls all social organizations and forms through which it exists and functions, such as the Party, the labor unions, the Socialist Alliance, and the workers' councils. On the other hand, the regime systematically indoctrinates the workers with Marxist ideology which, in turn, teaches them the mechanisms of class exploitation and revolutionary solutions. Until 1958 such radical implications were not dangerous for the new class since the policies of economic growth (industrialization) and full employment transformed peasants into workers, thus improving their economic position and social status. Nevertheless, the regime brought about a chronic economic crisis.

The new class has no alternative but to try to alleviate it through reform and other measures by shifting the burden of a deficit economy to widespread personal consumption. But an unemployed and poorly paid worker—in contrast to a peasant—cannot withdraw to his small holding to await the arrival of better days. The worker feels economic pressures immediately and directly and at a time when his expectations are greater than ever. His natural propensity for class-consciousness increases acutely.* The decrease of his standard of living is tangible evidence to a worker that he is exploited, and since he has been indoctrinated with Marxism, he cannot but seek the class pattern and become even more class conscious and ripe for political action.

The Yugoslav working class has already begun to maneuver with strikes, the classical weapon of organized labor. When strikes appeared in Yugoslavia they were first hushed up, then conveniently termed "work stoppages" and ignored by the new class, as with the numerous strikes of 1965–66. It was only in the spring of 1967 that some official commentators in Yugoslavia started to wonder about "the ideological aspects of work stoppages."

In a surprising move, the new class even began to prepare the ground for a different pattern of relations with the working class, should it prove necessary. Thus Crvenkovski, one of the outstanding builders of the new class, observed in an interview that "The working class, which is otherwise the moving force of progress, appears sometimes as a hindrance."[19] Behind such a statement, the new class prepares for a possible direct confrontation with the Yugoslav working class. Tito himself formulated the same threat to that class in a more indirect way when he proclaimed at the plenary meeting of the Central Committee, "We ought to respect the rights of the working man. But *we must make the working man understand his responsibilities, too, and his obligations.* Communists should explain all this to the working people."[20] In this connection it is interesting to note the recent, persistent trend in the decreased percentage of workers in the Party's membership. In 1964 workers represented 36 per cent of the Party, in 1965, 35 per cent, while in 1966 the figure went down to 33.9 per cent.[21]

* One of the implicit aims of the reform of 1965 was the reduction of real incomes. As of August 1, 1964, 58.7 per cent of the Yugoslav population earned above $40.00 a month; by August 1, 1965, that percentage had dropped to 43.4, according to *Borba,* December 18, 1965, calculated by the exchange rates of the time.

During one year of the reform (July, 1965–July, 1966), the cost of living had risen by 32.8 per cent; retail prices by 32.3 per cent; the price of food by 30.7 per cent; bread by 53 per cent; clothing by 35 per cent; heating and light by 49.4 per cent; rent by 65 per cent; health services by 47 per cent; and transportation by 34.2 per cent, all according to *Borba,* September 14, 1966.

In its theoretical and political behavior the new class took the Marxist concept of dictatorship seriously, but not that of the proletariat. More important was the awareness that, after all, the workers work, and the rulers—namely the members of the new class—rule. Publicly and officially, therefore, lip service is paid to the authority of the Yugoslav working class; yet, the real props of the regime have been mainly the Party and military and security networks. Socially, however, the new class endeavored to encompass all who became involved with its regime during and after the war. Policies of consistent care for workers, war veterans, and retired military and security personnel were implemented. Benefits and housing priorities for war veterans were not overly generous, but they were just a bit more than other people received. Small privileges made them feel favored, as if they belonged to the regime which they were ready to support always and unconditionally. A known proponent of organized care for war veterans was Rankovic, who served for many years as the chairman of the Yugoslav War Veteran Organization.

Looking backward, it is clear that war veterans and retired military and security personnel even saw themselves as an integral part of the new class and its regime; a great majority of them had also been Party members, occupying minor Party functions as a rule. But the split between the new class and the Party in 1966, the subsequent ouster of Rankovic, and especially the economic reform, which tried to cut down unessential privileges and subsidies, created quite a new situation in 1967 for all associates of the new class. The already small veteran and retirement benefits were cut back sharply or eaten away by inflation. Thus the new class faced new resistance in the area in which it had until then considered itself most secure: politics. Widespread dissatisfaction of fired policemen, prematurely retired officers, impoverished war veterans, ignored Party members, and politically castrated Party secretaries, etc., added to the general discontent. A slowly accumulating mass resentment, gradually becoming hostile opposition, is directed toward the top leadership.

In the spring of 1967, conflict over the old issue of privileges intensified to such proportions that it drew the entire public into a heated controversy expressed in the metaphor of the Golden Coach. According to an old Yugoslav folk tale, Fortune traveled about from door to door in her golden coach, driven by white horses, and invited people to come along with her. The point of the tale is that those invited by Fortune usually had some reason to delay, or they simply missed the opportunity, which never returned. Under the conditions of Yugoslav communism, the Golden Coach was identified with those privileges and benefits which are publicly enjoyed by the elite. The new class frustrated the ambitions of those just on the border line who considered themselves entitled to privileges too. In this way the people of Yugoslavia were able to witness the open clash between the new class and those who were once its closest allies—security officials, army officers, war veterans, Party functionaries and similar people, all trying to catch the running board at least. But the Golden Coach threw them off, and the new class kept the golden privileges exclusively for itself.

Because the new class failed to guard its privileged status alertly, it was thrust into the spotlight of publicity, showing both the way in which it was created and, even more, the increasing political distance between the former revolutionary rank and file and itself. An error or omission on the part of the complicated informal press censorship of the new class, which was then preoccupied with its internal crisis and foreign political difficulties, revealed the affair at a time when the regime was marking a new phase in its development, when it had to separate itself from its hangers-on. Although this entire process—part of the general economic reform—is a stage in the shaping of the new class, it inevitably disturbs the previous political equilibrium or, rather, the preponderance of the new class. In this way, too, the process of change gave vent to a new force of opposition in Yugoslavia's political arena, from the former wing of the new class in the Party.

The grave qualitative deepening of the political crisis was caused directly by the privileged position of the elite. Hopelessly striving to deceive the people by words, programs, and promises, the new class tried to hide behind the screen of "direct democracy" and self-management. Political crises had erupted frequently because of trivial motives; similarly, this one appeared unexpectedly. In the spring of 1967 the Belgrade city administration made a clumsy though well-intentioned move to create part-time jobs for retired military and security personnel. Jobs were offered in various city departments, as in positions of night guards and in parking lots. Some eagerly accepted the possibility of increasing their meager incomes, but the majority exploded in an emotional outburst of dissatisfaction and insulted dignity. Fuel was added to the fire by a *Borba* editorial, "The Golden Coach,"[22] expressing the official attitude and reminding those who "forgot that each job is good" that no man has the right to "cut dividend coupons his entire life" simply because he was a Partisan fighter during the war. While the top of the new class failed to realize that the editorial evoked a picture of them with the right to privileges for their "entire life," the war veterans became enraged. In a flood of open letters to newspapers they expressed their disgust with the scandal. The formerly staunch supporters of the regime were especially irritated by the editorial statement blaming the war veterans and pensioners for bungling the opportunities offered to them. The editorial also implied that each Yugoslav had been given his chance to succeed. "How many times has this Republic given valuable opportunities to those who fought for it? The Golden Coach has been waiting in front of our gates, leaving and returning all over again. Those who were stronger, abler, or simply smarter and nimbler got inside. Those who did not get in have now either to accept the offered jobs or to humbly receive what they are given in their exile from social life."[23]

This blow was too much for the rejected builders of Yugoslav socialism. The editorial further inflamed passions and established the whole issue as a political problem of the highest importance when it both inadvertently and impertinently explained the creation of the new class: "Those of merit had been given the chance to soar to dizzy heights, provided, of course, that they were able or smart enough to take advantage of their chance." The Golden Coach parable of chance was turned into that of the Golden Apple of Discord; today it is both a slogan about burning discontent and thirst for dizzy heights and a symbol of fulfillment for some, failure for others. While those in the new class are riding merrily in the Golden Coach of affluence and power, those rejected are well aware that they also provided their share of sacrifices; yet, disregarding their former war and political merits, they suffer today because insult has been added to injury. What have they been doing for the last twenty-five years? There were not too many answers published, but some told the whole story, "In each tempest, in full military preparedness, heavily armed, we have been shunted from one border to another . . . we spent years separated from our families, and without housing." Or another, "In maturity we are pushed out into the streets to wander aimlessly and ashamed." Or, "Others own two houses and two cars in addition to fat salaries. They did not smell the gunpowder, but they nevertheless soared to dizzy heights . . . while we fought continually and kept annihilating our class enemies."[24] In the flood of protests some of the claimants did not hesitate to state sincerely that they "did not fight in the revolution for the sake of an abstract freedom," and they openly requested their share of the spoils.

Under these turbulent conditions, even without definite intention or special organization (such as a political party), the role of the intellectual is to incite the citizenry, particularly the working masses, to political mobility. Lenin was acquainted with this role of the intellectuals, "Class consciousness can be brought to the worker only from the outside."[25] Aware of the intellectual menace, Yugoslavia's new class becomes worried and tells the workers through Tito that "Views like these, however, do not come from the working class but are forced to the surface by various intellectuals. We must be careful! We cannot allow such views to take root."[26]

The resistance to communism in Yugoslavia has gone through several phases. At the outset, when communism was dynamic and revolutionary, destroying everything in its path, resistance was expressed in opportunistic subservience to the regime. With the maturing of the new class, and concomitant with its efforts to stabilize itself, the people have become alienated from the regime and its system, and the functionaries and workers feel increasingly estranged from their responsibilities.*

Each Communist regime, by its past experience, should be aware that the reification (dehumanization) of human and social relations is only one aspect of widespread alienation. Namely, all such regimes have passed through a stage of state-planned economy, with its basic assumption that economic processes are mainly a technique of handling objects. In almost all decisive policy switches, from Lenin's NEP and Khrushchev's de-Stalinization to the present Yugoslav economic reform, the dominant feature has been the realization that it is impossible to manipulate human beings by economic laws, as if people were inanimate things of limitless endurance. Communist economic failures invariably appear as social and political problems, although they may well be neatly covered in financial balance sheets. The new class, in its "Yugoslav way" to communism, attempted to disengage itself from Stalinistic bureaucratic measures. It endeavored to establish—by self-managed firms and in a limited-market mechanism—a self-regulating economic functioning motivated by shifting the responsibility for economic processes from the state to the direct producers (workers' councils). But in precisely this manner the economic reform was instantly transformed into a political struggle.

As shown by current reports from Yugoslavia, the main issue is in deciding which social group is to bear the burden of waste and economic mismanagement. Thus material economic deficits and high costs are directly reflected in human relations in the form of growing unemployment, suppressed personal consumption, low real incomes, and other examples of want.

The predicament of the new class is that its present variant of Communist economics is deadlocked between the subjectivized totalitarian

* "The theory of man's alienation from society and from himself was central to Marx's entire philosophy," said Gayo Petrovic, a professor at Zagreb University and a Yugoslav Marxist philosopher. "The transformation of private property into state property (be it capitalist or socialist property) does not introduce an essential change in the situation of the working men, the producers," *New York Times,* April 27, 1966.

power of the Party or of a dictator, on the one side, and the objectively functioning market, based on commodity-money relations, on the other. The new class sought to introduce the latter by the present economic reform; yet, in this attempt to avoid alienation between the producer (the worker) and the means of production (the socialist economy), the new class is warned, by its own domestic Marxist intellectuals and Party members, that it is pushing the entire society into the abyss of ever deepening alienation. Defending Marx and citing his works to oppose the new class, Yugoslav intellectuals state that "the essential feature of commodity-money economics [the economic reform] is to reify relations among people, and in the last instance, to reify all human creativity."[27] In fact, Yugoslav intellectuals assert that the processes of estrangement have not only penetrated economic relations, but have come to encompass spiritual values, too, by "a spectacular commercialization of education, science, and culture."[28]

Examples of the processes of alienation in all dimensions of Yugoslav society would constitute a sizable book, but they do not seem to have affected the new class. When the manager of the gold and lead mine, "Lece," in Serbia, went to check the night shift, he found the "entire shift sleeping . . . machines were still. . . . The night guard in the control room also slept beside a warm stove behind the locked door. The electrician on duty, in charge of all equipment, could not be located for more than an hour."[29] In other cases irresponsible attitudes regarding material objects were recorded. "Let it burn; the insurance will pay."[30] Yet, the worst form of alienation is the one that distorts the relations between men. On June 25, 1964, *Borba* reported, for example, that on June 22, 1964, a group of teenagers raised an alarm in the public swimming pool at Mostar because one of them, thirteen-year-old Husniya Feriz, had vanished and was feared to have drowned. The guard agreed only to call Husniya on the loudspeaker, without explaining why. That was supposedly the end of it. But the teenagers ran to Husniya's home and told his parents, who then hurried to the swimming pool; "officials at the entrance did not let them in, requiring first the 50-dinar entrance fee. . . . While the parents were seeking their son, the crowd was swimming and loudspeakers played music." When Husniya's father requested that the water be drained from the pool to find the drowned boy, he was told that he must first pay 50,000 dinars. All this happened around 2 P.M. At about 6 P.M. divers were let in, and after a short search the body of the drowned boy was found.

The regime of the new class dehumanizes less by calculated premeditation than by a spontaneous lowering of the status of the human being to that of an instrument whose values are measured by his degree of social usefulness. The whole society and economy are permeated with mutual estrangements, stratifications, separate interests or disinterests, needs and ideals, demands and resistances. For example, it is illuminating to note the departure from the common interest of Yugoslavs for a sound economy in the reaction of self-managed bodies (workers' councils) to the economic reform. While the reform attempted to reduce personal consumption by eliminating economically unnecessary employment, many enterprises disregarded common interests and protected those individuals soon to be fired by simply refusing to do so, or by retiring them and shifting the burden of their support to the bureaus of social insurance. Thus, "retirement . . . has become the Yugoslav method of solving the problem of unemployment."[31]

Finally, the behavior of the new class itself changed. As it became more powerful it also grew more cynically insolent, acquiring a kind of *hubris.* When privileges were criticized in the late 1940's, the Party apologetically tried to hide them; when Djilas denounced the privileges of the new class in the 1950's, he was promptly punished, while privileges were not mentioned at all. It was quite different in 1966, when, after Rankovic's ouster, Yugoslavs thought that they could freely criticize both the police and privileges, and a wave of public indignation arose. Even *Borba* published such vitriolic comments regarding privileges as "if one is a meritorious revolutionary, it does not, certainly, mean that he is predestined to be given more than he earns by his work. . . . Privileges, absolutely disregarding who enjoys them [*sic*], may be sanctioned only by those depraved individuals who were trampled by the times, who withdrew into their own shells, unable to tell morality from immorality, honesty from dishonesty, and responsibility from irresponsibility."[32]

But this time the new class did not hesitate to answer. In the same issue of *Borba,* Miyalko Todorovic, the new secretary of the Party's Executive Committee, reacted against any and all criticism of privileges, branding it "*petit bourgeois* hysteria," and stated, "it is with revulsion that I use the word 'failing,' because this same word is frequently used by some people to criticize. . . . I do not think that the Party and its members should not criticize. However, if it becomes their main occupation, then we do not need such a Communist Party at all."[33]

Tito, as usual, personally condemned and concluded the discussion relating to privileges. "Oh no, comrades, this is a matter of cheap demagogy, and also an attempt to compromise our best comrades. It is *necessary to put an end to this* [criticism of privileges] *at once and for all.*"[34] Then he volunteered to explain and, perhaps, justify the position of the new class by saying, *"I am against privileges that have not been earned.*" This statement made the new class feel better, but it did not avert general and growing discontent with the regime.

It was not by chance that Tito so openly defended the otherwise unpopular and odious privileges. Tito has not only decisively molded Yugoslav development since 1941, but he has sought social expression for his regime in deliberately creating a new class. Tito was favored by circumstances in this undertaking, but he shrewdly knew how to select, read, interpret, and manipulate people and events to his advantage. For instance, his regime received, among other things, more than $3 billion from the United States of America—by various means but never on the false pretence that he was not a staunch Communist.

The magnitude of Tito's personality is reflected too in his seizure and stabilization of power in Yugoslavia. He was able to appraise political, social, and economic developments on both the domestic and international level. By his outstanding perception, Tito understood that the spontaneous growth of Communist power leads unavoidably to its bureaucratic degeneration. Consequently, his efforts were directed to the creation of a Communist class of a quite new type—a class which does not own capital but instead controls power—which he could use to give his personal authority a more stable and reliable social basis. As a dictator, more specifically as a Communist dictator, Tito will be categorized by history as one among many. But as the founder of a Communist new class he was the first and, it appears thus far, the only one. The new class is the highest and most distinctive of Tito's achievements.

The surprising aspect of Tito's work is that the new class was created in Yugoslavia almost against its will, and certainly without its immediate understanding. Tito's closest followers are accustomed to finding themselves puzzled, from time to time, by his decisions, which are first applauded and enthusiasticlly accepted—the safest recourse—and only later really comprehended.

Learning partially from the mistakes and experiences of other dictators, Tito endeavors to transform Communist power into something more durable than a succession of the Party's supreme leaders. In fact, not only to insure future stability but also to strengthen his present rule, Tito is bent on infusing a firm, close-knit, and committed social identification into the marrow of the Yugoslav Communist system. The issue for Tito is that of establishing a solid platform of common merit and guilt, of interests and fears for his followers and collaborators, the new class. Under Communist conditions, however, neither interests nor fears can create unity automatically; rather, they bring a uniformity to the new class, whose ranks are increasingly filled with lonely individuals whose attitudes are more monomaniacal than monolithic. Communist unity is but a mechanical aggregate of individuals whose value to the system is commensurate with their lack of personal identity. Thus they have no choice but to follow or to second-guess directives from above, always helplessly exposed to a possible exercise of power by their superiors. For this reason Communists tend, willy-nilly, to structure and shield themselves in the form of a Party hierarchy. Eventually, without fail, they create dictators of the Stalin or Mao type. In other words, a "normal" Communist hierarchy cannot avoid, indeed does not want to avoid, transforming itself into a bureaucracy. But that is exactly what Tito decided to avert.

The price paid by Tito and the new class for their common endeavor is recurrent conflict with the classic, Leninist, or Stalinist elements of the Party and its apparatus and functionaries. This explains why Tito collided with Stalin in 1948, why he excluded the rank and file of the Party from power in 1952, and why in 1966 he had to oust his second in command, Rankovic, who represented one part of the high Party structure. In maneuvering to reshape the Party, breaking down its hierarchical participation in power, and stabilizing his power and that of the new class, Tito elected to centralize authority and decentralize responsibilities by means of self-management.

Such critical developments will of necessity lead to the breakdown of the new-class system in Yugoslavia. However, despite the economic crisis, suppressed political freedom, and class stratification, all conditions together will not necessarily force the immediate overthrow of the Communist regime. Perhaps one day it may seem to have come about spontaneously, but it must be planned. Much work is needed to overcome the barrier of taboos, inertia, fear, and prejudices, as well as the hypnotic, nearly traumatic, impact of Tito's dictatorship on the general populace of Yugoslavia.

Finally, one must remember that the new class believes itself to be stronger than ever. In its view, the Yugoslav socialist system of "direct democracy," has achieved complete harmony of both practice and ideology in which cause and effect, action and reaction have been welded into one dialectic unity of dynamic growth.

Although the path of historical movements is always circuitous and frequently violent, the new class believes that it cannot be dislodged. But the group does not realize that in identifying itself with power it has become an obstacle to progress and a "counterrevolutionary" force in Marxist terms. Even Tito seems, at least subconsciously, to have been aware of this when he said, "It is clear that today Marx would add many things to his conceptions and categories because at his time it was not possible to foresee what we have today."[35]

The result is a general inversion in which the new class, unable and unwilling to understand that it is only a phase in history, tries to manipulate history as a dimension of its own power. The regime intensifies frictions which increase internal strains in Yugoslavia—conditions for the downfall of the new class and its Communist system. The prelude to this is the great drama of present-day Yugoslavia; each citizen participates in it in one way or another by either maintaining the regime or resisting it. The new class has insured that, after more than two decades of rule, almost everyone has become more or less involved with it. If struggle against communism develops through revenge or by retaliation, however, a pattern not uncommon in Yugoslav history, wholesale mutual extermination would result, and that would be just as wrong as the motive of justice is right. Instead of a philosophy of formal purism, a great deal of understanding will be necessary, an understanding in which the dominant concerns should be love of country and human beings.

The processes of ferment in Yugoslavia have been operating for a long time, though hidden beneath the surface. They have been taking shape in a specifically Yugoslav form, though dealing with the problem of communism in general, which is international. It is true that the regime of the new class sees democracy and freedom anywhere in the world as a challenge, but it would be an error of judgment to expect that intervention from abroad could resolve the problem. Intervention from outside, in the long run, would only make the building of democracy in Yugoslavia more difficult, and the new class could turn the people again to its favor under the guise of patriotism.

But this does not mean, on the other hand, that help and support could not be given to Yugoslavia's democratic forces. The isolation of Yugoslavia from the outside world, as with any other Communist country, is a great loss for domestic democratic forces because the Communist monopoly is thus strengthened. Coexistence in an international framework is a positive goal because contacts with the world at large help Yugoslavs to interpret their own position more objectively and to reevaluate their traditions and legacies critically in order to formulate a better stand at the present.

Throughout history, the transition to a new social-political form usually begins unexpectedly. The lines for change are already set by the fact that the new class has condensed power in itself. The effect of this power condensation is not less pressure on, but more subordination of, the people. Under such conditions, change could be initiated by some insignificant event or incident, historical developments often being a question of chance, and though the basis of its theory is the historical necessity of change, the new class always hopes for favorable conditions which would maintain its position. On the one hand, the new class expects its opponents to be frustrated somehow; on the other, it believes that by behaving pragmatically it can escape difficult situations. Thus the new class reveals a gambling tendency in its already exploitative nature.

Fundamental social changes in Yugoslavia cannot be achieved merely by an abstract idea, a practical motive, or a vigorous fighting force. An idea can be formulated by intellectuals, the motive will appear by itself, while opposition forces grow among the people, especially in the working class. Politically aggressive leadership against the new class, however, has not yet developed in the Yugoslav intelligentsia, not to speak of the working class or peasantry. But history provides a pattern, and it should come as no surprise if the first leaders to fight for the overthrow of the new class come in fact from its own ranks.

When one scratches the surface of the new class and the Party a little, it becomes obvious that beneath is a strange company of essentially homogeneous, but varied and often sharply opposed, mutual interests joined in some sort of dynamic equilibrium. All are united today by common fears and desires under the supreme authority of Tito, who himself is growing very old. Within the realm of subjectivized and personalized power, every change in leadership personnel is delicate and perilous. At any moment the balance of forces could be upset, exploding into an internal maelstrom which, when it breaks to the surface, can create a revolutionary tidal wave that will swamp the regime of the new class.

It was not a complete surprise that Djilas, one of the outstanding leaders of the Yugoslav Communist Party, was the one who bravely rebelled against communism and the new class. It was even less an accident of history that Rankovic, for different reasons, also turned rebel. That is why future events could conceivably summon forth new leaders from those who today are "monolithically" united at the top of the Party and the new class.

Both the Party and the new class are composed of a fascinating and strange mixture of lonely individuals suspended amorphously in various groupings. Each of course has his own personal ambitions and anxieties, but the political environment determines his actions. That is why all are caught in a bizarre whirlpool of dialectics, "collective leadership," united only to be divided into mutual contradictions, rivalries, and interests. They calculate, speculate, make factions and clash in bitter skirmishes that are often fought without a sound. All is invisible except the casualties for whom there is no mourning. The paradox of the conflict of personalities and groups is that each individual is nothing more than an instrument of broader and stronger social forces. Thus the struggle is more dramatic and, in the classic sense of the word, even more tragic: men destroy and are destroyed by that which they created and to which they belong.

When the time is ripe in Yugoslavia, events will follow in the direction set by today's situation. In the same way that Djilas rose against communism, Rankovic against the new class, and Tito against the classical Party, so can the new class supply the revolt against itself with capable and passionate leaders. If one reads the list of members of the Party's Central Committee, and especially the new Presidium, he will probably find the names of future leaders. They will begin but not end the destruction of the new class; other leaders will be born and continue the struggle. It is idle to guess their names because unexpected individuals often appear at crucial moments as the executors of major historical assignments. Great men are endowed not only with uncommon personal abilities but also with an understanding of the needs and currents of their time. The new class, however, suspects that right in its own center, on the membership lists of the Presidium and the Central Committee, are the names which presage its fall. For this reason it frequently and hurriedly changes those lists, corrects them, increases and shortens them, always reexamines them. The new class constantly rotates people and revises its lists and policies, not knowing that the more accurate and complete the breadth and depth of that list, and the more up to date it is, the more certain that the right name is there.

Appendixes

A. *Selected Biographical Notes*

(Prepared by the Author)

Bakaric, Vladimir (1912–), Croat. LL.D., Zagreb University (1935). Leading Communist in Croatia; has been the highest Party and state official there since the war. Member of the Party's Presidium and the Council of the Federation. Known as a Marxist theorist, especially in the field of agriculture and nationalities questions. Medal of the *People's Hero.*

Broz, Joseph "Tito" (1892–), Croat. Became a Communist while a prisoner of war in Russia, 1915–20. Tito was put in control of the Yugoslav Communist Party in 1937 by Stalin. Has become its most prominent leader since then. After 1945, he succeeded in uniting the highest Party, state, and military functions in himself. Widely known by his conflict with Stalin in 1948, Tito is President of Yugoslavia, Commander-in-Chief of the Armed Forces, Chairman of the Communist Party, and Chairman of the Council of the Federation. Medal of the *People's Hero.*

Cetinic, Marin (1915–), Croat. High-school education. Party member since 1936; involved in various duties in Dalmatia and Croatia after World War II. Member of the federal government since 1965, mainly in the field of economics.

Crvenkovski, Krste (1921–), Macedonian. Studied law at Skoplye University. Party member since 1939; member of the federal government, 1958–62; in charge of the Macedonian Communist Party apparatus since 1963. Member of the Party's Presidium and the Council of the Federation. Medal of the *People's Hero.*

Dugonyic, Rato (1916–), LL.B., Belgrade University; Party member since 1937. High functions in the federal apparatus of the Communist youth organizations, 1941–49. In charge of the committee for the local economy, 1949, then appointed ambassador to Poland, the UAR; eventually became chairman of the parliament of Bosnia and Hercegovina; later was moved into the Socialist Alliance for Bosnia and Hercegovina, from there transferred to the chairmanship of the federal Socialist Alliance. Member of the Party's Presidium and the Council of the Federation. Medal of the *People's Hero.*

Gligorov, Kiro (1917–), Macedonian. Law degree, Belgrade University; Party member since 1944. Subsequently occupied different high functions in the federal state apparatus. Became a member of the federal government in 1963 and designed the economic reform of 1965. In 1967 he became vice-prime minister of Yugoslavia.

Grlichkov, Alexandar (1923–), Macedonian. Graduate of the School of Economics, Belgrade University. Member of the Macedonian government (planning commission, later chairman) until 1964, when he became a member of the federal government; concerned primarily with economic matters. Member of the Party's Central Committee.

Kaleb, Vyekoslav (1905–), Croat. Teacher before the war; has asserted himself since the war as a prominent writer and also has occupied leading positions in Croatian cultural institutions. Involved in political difficulties with the regime because of his support for the creation of an independent Croatian language. He has published many books, short stories, and novels.

Kardelj, Eduard (1910–), Slovene. School teacher before the war; joined the Communist Party in the late twenties. After Tito took over the Party in 1937, Kardelj became the leading Communist of Slovenia. Always close to Tito, he distinguished himself by his theoretical work in applied Marxism; one of the main designers of the Yugoslav socialist system, and has occupied various high functions in the Party and the state. Member of the Party's Presidium and the Council of the Federation (and its top Organizational Committee). Medal of the *People's Hero.*

Kavcic, Stane (1919–), Slovene. Party member since 1941. After 1962, he became a prominent party leader in Slovenia; has been a member of the federal Party's executive committee since 1966. Considered an economic expert.

Kraigher, Boris (1914–1966), Slovene. Killed in auto accident. Party member since 1934; engaged mainly in the Slovenian Party and state apparatus after the war. Appointed to the federal government in 1958; later became prominent as one of the designers of the economic reform of 1965. He was a member of the Party's Presidium and the Council of the Federation. Medal of the *People's Hero.*

Krleza, Miroslav (1893–), Croat. Closely connected with the Communist movement since 1917. One of the most prominent Yugoslav writers, outstanding intellectual, and a thorough Marxist. A member of the Central Committee for Croatia until 1967, when he resigned because he approved the action to make the Croatian language independent. Very prolific writer, especially between the two world wars. Widely known outside Yugoslavia, particularly in Central and Eastern Europe, he was a candidate for the Nobel Prize in Literature in 1962.

Nikezic, Marko (1921–), Serb. Studied architecture at Belgrade University; became the secretary of the Party's committee for Belgrade after the war. In diplomatic service, 1952–62, as ambassador to Czechoslovakia, UAR, and USA, he has been Yugoslavia's minister of foreign affairs since 1963.

Peshic, Branko (1922–), Serb. Party member since 1942. Attended the high Party political school after the war; later occupied minor and local Party apparatus positions. Appointed mayor of Belgrade in 1964.

Popovic, Milentiye (1913–), Serb. Architecture graduate, Belgrade University, before the war; a member of the Serbian government (planning commission); member of the federal government (foreign trade, finance) since 1947; secretary-general of the Socialist Alliance since 1963; elected chairman of the federal National Assembly in 1967. Member of the Party's Presidium and the Council of the Federation; has published many studies on contemporary Marxist theory.

Radosavlyevic, Dobrivoye "Bobby" (1915–), Serb. Holds a degree in agricultural technology from Belgrade University; Party member since 1933. Secretary of the Belgrade Party committee after the war. Member of the federal government, 1949–63. After Rankovic's ouster, Radosavlyevic became the head of Serbia's Party apparatus.

Rankovic, Alexandar "Leka" or "Marko" (1910–), Serb. Joined the Party in 1928. When Tito took over control of the Party in 1937, Rankovic was put in charge of the Party's security and, after the war, of the state security also. Generally considered Tito's successor; vice-prime minister of Yugoslavia, 1963–66. On behalf of the Party apparatus, Rankovic openly opposed the growing power of the new class. He was consequently ousted in 1966, accused of plotting, and expelled from the Party. Rankovic was a member of the Council of the Federation. Medal of the *People's Hero.*

Shegedin, Petar (1909–), Croat. Philosophy degree, Zagreb University; served as a high-school teacher after the war. He later published several novels. Came into disgrace with the regime in 1967 because of his participation in the movement to make the Croatian language independent.

Stanovnik, Yanez (1922–), Slovene. Studied law; Party member since 1944; personal secretary to Kardelj, 1945–51. He was in the diplomatic service until 1958, and then became director of the International Politics and Economics Institute. Professor at Lyublyana University since 1962. Appointed a member of the federal government in 1967; considered an expert in international economic relations.

Todorovic, Miyalko "Plavi" (1913–), Serb. Graduated from school of engineering, Belgrade University; since the war he has participated mainly in federal high economic functions; vice-prime minister in charge of the Yugoslav economy, 1958–64. After the ouster of Rankovic, Todorovic was shifted to the position of secretary-general of the Party's executive committee, i.e., the head of the entire Party apparatus. Member of the Council of the Federation; medal of the *People's Hero.*

Tripalo, Miko (1926–), Croat. Studied law in Zagreb. Mainly a provincial leader of Communist youth organizations after the war, he has become a prominent Party leader in Croatia since the economic reform of 1965.

Vlakhovic, Veljko (1914–), Montenegrin. Studied technology in Belgrade, Prague, Paris, and Moscow; later participated in the Spanish Civil

War. In Moscow during World War II. Primarily occupied with high functions in the propaganda apparatus of the Party. Has staunchly supported Tito since the beginning of the sixties. Member of the Presidium and the Council of the Federation (and its top Organizational Committee). Medal of the *People's Hero.*

Vukmanovic, Svetozar "Tempo" (1912–), Montenegrin. Law degree, Belgrade University, before the war. During the war he rose to the highest Party and state positions. Vice-prime minister in charge of the national economy, 1953–58. Head of the Yugoslav labor unions until 1967. Member of the Presidium and the Council of the Federation (and its top Organizational Committee). Medal of the *People's Hero.*

B. *Statistical Notes*

Yugoslavia was created in 1918 after World War I by the union of Serbia and Montenegro and by the incorporation of those parts of the Austro-Hungarian Empire which were predominantly populated by south ("Yugo") Slavs. Economically undeveloped, politically unsettled, and with potential for profound social change, Yugoslavia went through a series of crises until it was overrun by Nazi Germany in 1941. After a bitter and stubborn liberation and simultaneous civil war, Yugoslavia was reestablished in 1945 as the Communist dictatorship of Joseph Broz, known as Tito.

Yugoslavia, called the kingdom of Serbs, Croats, and Slovenes, in 1918, was renamed the Kingdom of Yugoslavia in 1930; in 1945 the name was changed to Democratic Federal Yugoslavia; in 1946 it became the Federal People's Republic of Yugoslavia, and finally, in 1963, the Federal Socialist Republic of Yugoslavia.

Area, population. Yugoslavia covers an area of 255,804 sq. km. (98,725 sq. miles) and had a population of about 20 million in September, 1967. Yugoslavia consists of six socialist republics:

	Capital	Area (sq. km.)	Population (1966)	Population Density Per Sq. Km.
Serbia	Belgrade	88,361	8.0 mil.	86.5
Croatia	Zagreb	56,538	4.3 mil.	73.6
Bosnia and Hercegovina	Sarajevo	51,129	3.6 mil.	64.4
Slovenia	Lyublyana	20,251	1.7 mil.	78.6
Macedonia	Skoplye	25,713	1.5 mil.	54.7
Montenegro	Titograd	13,812	0.5 mil.	34.2
Yugoslavia	Belgrade	255,804	19.6 mil.	72.5

Serbia contains two autonomous provinces: Voyvodina in the north, with a land area of 21,506 sq. km. and a population of about 2 million, including a substantial Hungarian national minority; Kossovo-Metokhiya in the south, with a land area of 10,887 sq. km. and a population of about 1 million, mainly Albanians.

Yugoslavia is situated along the northeast Adriatic coast, bordering Italy, Austria, Greece, and four other Communist countries: Hungary, Rumania, Bulgaria, and Albania.

The capital of Yugoslavia is Belgrade (pop. 678,000); other important cities are Zagreb (pop. 491,000), Skoplye (pop. 212,000), Sarajevo (218,000), and Novi Sad (100,000).

The inland *climate* of Yugoslavia is continental, with hot dry summers, cold winters, and rainy spring and fall seasons. Along the seacoast and in Macedonia the mild Mediterranean climate prevails.

The *language* of Yugoslavia is Serbo-Croatian, which is spoken in Serbia, Croatia, Montenegro, and Bosnia and Hercegovina; Slovenian is spoken in Slovenia, Macedonian in Macedonia. The Cyrillic alphabet is used predominantly by Eastern Orthodox Serbs, Montenegrins, and Macedonians, while the Latin alphabet is used mainly by Roman Catholic Croats and Slovenes. There are substantial Moslem groups in Bosnia and Hercegovina and Kossovo-Metokhiya.

Education. Elementary schools are free and compulsory for eight years. In 1964–65 there were 14,317 elementary schools with 100,456 teachers and about 3 million pupils. The 370 senior secondary schools have 8,215 teachers and 161,000 students. In addition there are 90 teachers' colleges with 29,000 students and 1,644 faculty members, and 1,260 vocational schools with 15,500 teachers and 380,000 students. There are six national universities composed of 263 schools with a faculty of 15,750 and a student body of 171,000.

Transportation and communication. Yugoslavia's maritime fleet consists of twenty-six relatively modern ocean-going ships with a tonnage of 250,000. The length of railroads is about 12,000 km. (7,500 miles), tracks and rolling stock being, by and large, obsolete. In 1966 railways transported 213.2 million passengers and 71.6 million tons of freight. The highway network is 55,000 km. (34,400 miles) long, of which, however, only about 5,000 km. (3,400 miles) are near to modern standards.

There is a good network of modern airports—at Belgrade, Zagreb, Dubrovnik, Lyublyana, Pula, Sarajevo—with a well-functioning domestic airline, Yat. (Total number of air passengers in 1966 was 0.6 million.)

By 1964 there were only about 370,000 telephones in Yugoslavia. Eight radio broadcasting stations are strengthened by six TV stations, all of which have the same program.

Economy. Yugoslavia uses the metric system of weights and measures. The currency unit is the ("new") dinar, made up of 100 para; the official exchange rate at the present is 12.5 "new" dinars for one U.S. dollar. Yet, "old" dinars, one hundred of which make one "new" dinar are still in common usage.

Yugoslav exports in 1966 amounted to $1,220 million, and imports $1,576 million, the trade deficit being $355 million. The chronic and growing trade deficit is covered, however, by large invisible receipts (tourism, workers' remittances from abroad, maritime shipping) which were estimated in 1967 at about $500 million.

The working population of Yugoslavia is estimated at about 8.34 million, of which 3.5 million were included in the "socialist" sector in 1966. The following chart shows the breakdown of the working population.

Industry, mining	1.358 million
Agriculture, forestry	.371 million
Construction	.305 million
Transport, communications	.246 million
Trade	.349 million
Crafts	.200 million
Public utilities	.067 million
Education, health, social services	.423 million
Administration	.168 million

Those employed in the "private" sector work mainly in agriculture and crafts. (Data based on *Statistichki Godishnyak SFRY* 1966, *Indeks,* and reports in the Yugoslav press.)

Notes

Notes to Chapter 1

1. *Borba,* April 20, 1967.
2. Karl Marx and Friedrich Engels, *The German Ideology,* p. 75.
3. Vladimir Ilyich Lenin, *Collected Works,* VII, pp. 265–66.
4. Marx and Engels, *op. cit.,* p. 23.

Notes to Chapter 2

1. Marx and Engels, *The German Ideology,* p. 49.
2. "Answers of Kardelj to *Nova Makedoniya,*" *Politika,* May 30, 1965.
3. Milovan Djilas, "The Anatomy of a Moral," *Nova Misao,* January, 1954.
4. The name of the Yugoslav Communist Party (CPY) was changed to the Union of Yugoslav Communists (often translated into English simply as the Union) in November, 1952, under the influence of Djilas. He had hoped that the Communist Party would be replaced by a loose union of persons with similar political views.
5. *Borba,* December 20, 1966.
6. The Socialist Alliance of the Working People of Yugoslavia (SSRNY), i.e., the prewar Popular Front, is a broad national political organization led and controlled by the Communist Party.
7. According to "Rights Pertaining to the Highest Decorations," *Politika,* March 2, 1965, there were at the time 1,080 National Heroes in Yugoslavia.
8. "Annual Vacations Pertaining to the Memorial of 1941," *Borba,* December 23, 1963; November 11, 1963; April 13, 1967.
9. *Enciklopedija Jugoslavije,* VI, p. 370.
10. *Ilustrovana Politika,* March 23, 1965.
11. "Even the youngest are evaluated according to the behavior of their families during the war," *Borba,* October 19, 1966; "even more important: one's activities, or who is from what family," *Borba,* November 14, 1964.
12. Cartoon by M. Ciric, *Borba,* March 3, 1967.
13. *Borba,* November 27, 1963; April 11, 1964; October 29, 1964; February 12, 1965; March 5, 10, 12, 17, 22, 1965; April 2, 1965; April 12, 1967; *Politika,* March 5, 1965.
14. "Interview with Marshal Tito," *Narodna Armiya,* October 8, 1965.

15. This Russian word is still used in Party jargon to denote those who deal specifically with personnel matters.
16. "Law is Written by the Man for the Man"; "Why so to Edhem Shkoric?" *Borba,* August 14, 1964; "The Tears of Joy of Edhem Shkoric," *Borba,* October 14, 1964.
17. Under the pressure of hidden, but nevertheless very bitter, popular resentment against high and multiple salaries, some rectifications were promised in the autumn of 1966.
18. "Rotation is Not Dogma," *Borba,* March 12, 1967; "Safer Status of Functionaries," *Borba,* March 18, 1967.
19. "The Law on Employment and Rights of the Federal Representatives and Functionaries," *Borba,* April 8, 1967. The corresponding laws for republics were enacted separately, e.g., in Croatia, *Borba,* April 12, 1967.
20. *Borba,* April 12, 1967.
21. "Federal Chamber Passed Constitutional Changes," *Borba,* April 8, 1967.
22. *Ibid.,* our italics.
23. *Politika,* September 21, 1965, reported that the railways were forced to cancel fifty-six passenger trains, to scrap 600 obsolete carriages, and to reduce daily passenger facilities by 14,800 seats.
24. "Budgetary State Spending," *Borba,* September 30, 1966; *Politika,* September 30, 1966; October 1 and 3, 1966.
25. "A Communist in Power," *Politika,* September 5, 1966.
26. "Kardelj's Speech in the Federal Assembly," *Borba,* March 13, 1966.

Notes to Chapter 3

1. Information from a private source.
2. Personal experience.
3. *Borba,* July 18, 1967.
4. Personal experience.
5. "A Million Members in the Party," *Borba,* November 23, 1964.
6. *New York Times,* September 25, 1966.
7. *Tanyug,* official Yugoslav news agency, August 11, 1966.
8. Name withheld.

Notes to Chapter 4

1. *Borba,* January 26, 1963; November 11, 1964.
2. "Eight Million Members," *Borba,* June 6, 1966.
3. *Borba,* January 27, 1965.
4. "Theses for the Reorganization of the Party," *Borba,* April 27, 1967.
5. Lenin, *Collected Works,* VI, p. 248.
6. *Borba,* March 30, 1967.
7. "Theses for the Reorganization of the Party," *loc. cit.*
8. *Ibid.*
9. "Speech at Bileca," *Politika,* August 23, 1966.
10. Tito, speaking to the Belgrade Communists, *Borba,* April 18, 1967.

11. *Ibid.*
12. *Ibid.*
13. *Ibid.*
14. Djilas, *Conversations with Stalin,* pp. 180–84.
15. *New York Times,* July 2, 1966.
16. Krste Crvenkovski, speaking at the seminar on the Party reorganization, *Politika,* June 7, 1967.
17. *Politika,* September 8, 1966.
18. *Politika,* September 9, 1966.
19. *Borba,* September 24, 1966.
20. *Ibid.*
21. Speeches at Belgrade and Kossovo, *Borba,* March 30 and April 19, 1967.
22. The declaration was signed by the Matica (Association) of Croatian writers; the PEN Club of Croatia; the Croatian Philological Society; the Department of Sociology of the Yugoslav Academy of Sciences and Arts (YASA); the Institute of Languages, Institute of Literature and Theatrology, and the Department of Modern Literatures of YASA; the Department for Modern Croato-Serbian Language at the Universities of Zadar and Zagreb; the Departments of the History of the Croatian Language and Dialectology, New Croatian Literature, and Old Croatian Literature, the Institute for Literary Science, and the Old Slavonic Institute—all of the University of Zagreb; and the Association of Literary Translators of Croatia. Also among the signers were such prominent Croatian writers as Miroslav Krleza (also a member of the Central Committee of the Communist Party of Croatia), Gustav Krklec, Petar Shegedin, and Vyekoslav Kaleb. The Serbian proposal was signed by forty-eight writers, among them Aleksa Isakovic (a member of the Serbian Party's Central Committee) and the well-known cartoonist, Zuko Djumhur. See all Yugoslav newspapers, March-April, 1967.
23. *Borba,* March 27, 1967.
24. *Borba,* March 29, 1967.
25. *Borba,* April 5, 1967.
26. *New York Times,* March 25, 1967.
27. "Theses for the Reorganization of the Party," *loc. cit.*
28. *Ibid.*
29. *Borba,* April 18, 1967.
30. "Theses for the Reorganization of the Party," *loc. cit.*
31. *Politika,* June 18, 1966.
32. "Theses for the Reorganization of the Party," *loc. cit.*
33. *Ibid.*
34. Eduard Kardelj, speaking at the seminar on the Party reorganization, *Politika,* June 7, 1967.
35. "Theses for the Reorganization of the Party," *loc. cit.*
36. *Ibid.*
37. "Caricature Instead of a Party Meeting," *Borba,* February 27, 1965.
38. According to *Borba,* March 30, 1967, this suggestion had been introduced in the fourth territorial organization, Titograd, Montenegro. See also "Retired Communists," *Borba,* April 1, 1967.
39. "Theses for the Reorganization of the Party," *loc. cit.*
40. *Ibid.*
41. *Ibid.*
42. *Ibid.*
43. *Borba,* March 25, 1967.

44. *Ibid.*

45. Discussion by Latinka Perovic at the seminar on the Party reorganization, *Politika,* June 7, 1967.

46. *Ibid.*

47. "Theses for the Reorganization of the Party," *loc. cit.*

48. *Borba,* July 3, 1967.

49. "The Party Today," *Borba,* July 24, 1966.

50. Crvenkovski, speaking at the Montenegrin seminar on the Party reorganization, *Politika,* June 28, 1967. Our italics.

51. Bakaric, in *Borba,* August 14, 1966.

52. Milentiye Popovic, speaking at the seminar on the Party reorganization, *Politika,* June 8, 1967.

53. *Borba,* April 17, 1967.

54. *Politika,* September 5, 1966.

55. *Borba,* July 3, 1967. Our italics.

56. Rato Dugonyic, speaking to local committee Party secretaries of Bosnia and Hercegovina, *Borba,* October 24, 1964.

57. Tito, speaking to the Belgrade Communists, *loc. cit.*

58. "Underground Election Campaigning in Nis," *Borba,* April 1, 1967; "Request for Recall of Federal Representation Nomination," *Borba,* April 4, 1967; "Severe Criticism of the Irregularities Committed by the Chukarica Election Commission," *Politika,* March 25, 1967; "Intrigues Under the Cloak of the Struggle for Democracy," *Borba,* December 20, 1965.

59. "Theses for the Reorganization of the Party," *loc. cit.*

60. *Ibid.*

61. *Ibid.*

62. "The *Vrkhushka* Exposed," *Politika,* March 12, 1965.

63. *Borba,* January 1, 1966.

64. "The Serbian Central Committee Plenary Meeting," *Politika,* April 22, 1967.

65. Veljko Vlakhovic, speaking at the seminar on the Party reorganization, *Politika,* June 10, 1967. Our italics.

Notes to Chapter 5

1. "Statement of Marko Nikezic," *Politika,* May 21, 1967. Our italics.

2. *Ibid.*

3. "Seminar on the Reorganization of the Party" and "Speech of Veljko Vlakhovic," *Politika,* June 6, 1967.

4. "Statement of Marko Nikezic," *loc. cit.*

5. *Ibid.*

6. All Yugoslav newspapers, October, 1967. Our italics.

7. "Kardelj's Statement on the Eve of the Trip to India," *Borba, Politika,* December 6, 1962.

8. "Seminar on the Reorganization of the Party," *loc. cit.*

9. Speaking in Alexandria, Egypt, *Politika,* May 7, 1966.

10. *Borba* and *Politika,* December, 1962. Our italics.

11. "Eduard Kardelj's Speech in Moscow," *Politika,* October 30, 1966. Our italics.

12. "Speech of Veljko Vlakhovic," *loc. cit.*

13. "Statement of President Tito," *Politika,* June 6, 1967.
14. "Yugoslavs Break Ties with Israel," *New York Times,* June 14, 1967.
15. "Serbian Central Committee Meeting," *Borba,* June 15, 1967.
16. "President Tito's Speech at Prishtina," *Politika,* March 27, 1967.
17. *Ibid.*
18. "Statement of Marko Nikezic," *loc. cit.*
19. *Ibid.*
20. *Ibid.*
21. *New York Times,* September 5, 1964.
22. *Ibid.*
23. V. V. Zagladin, "The World Communist Movement in the Struggle for Unity," *Voprosiy istorii KPSSR* [Questions on the history of the Communist Party of the Soviet Union], a report of the Institute of Marxism-Leninism of the Central Committee of the CPSU, published by *Pravda,* June, 1966. It is important to note that the article was accompanied by the remark: "it [the report] may be useful for the analysis and processing of the CPSU's 23rd Congress materials."
24. *Pravda,* March 28, 1967, as cited in "Moscow Chronicle," *Borba,* March 29, 1967. Our italics.
25. Boris N. Ponomarov, *New York Times,* September 28, 1964.
26. "Unity under the Condition of Respecting the Autonomy of Each Party," *Politika,* April 24, 1967.
27. Crvenkovski, "Communist Parties and New Social Phenomena," *Borba,* April 16, 1967.
28. *Ibid.*
29. Tito, speaking to the Belgrade Communists, *Borba,* April 18, 1967.

Notes to Chapter 6

1. "Interview with Mayor Branko Peshic," *Politika,* September 5, 1966.
2. Djilas, *The New Class,* p. 87.
3. *Komunist,* March 4, 1965; *Borba,* March 3, 1965.
4. Louis Adamic, *The Eagle and the Roots,* p. 138.
5. "Kardelj's Speech in the Federal Assembly," *Borba,* May 12, 1967.
6. *Ibid.*
7. *Ibid.*
8. *Ibid.* Our italics.
9. *Ibid.* Our italics.
10. *Ibid.*
11. *Ibid.*
12. Interview on radio and television, Belgrade, as published in *Politika,* February 28, 1965.
13. *Politika,* April 4, 1965.
14. *Borba,* October 8, 1966.
15. *Borba,* January 28, 1965.
16. Kardelj, in *Borba,* October 5, 1966.
17. *Borba,* February 23, 1965.
18. *Ibid.*
19. *Borba,* February 10, 1965.
20. *Borba,* April 2, 1965.

21. Kardelj, in *Borba,* October 9, 1966.
22. *Ibid.*
23. The *Constitution of the Federal Republic of Yugoslavia* (hereafter referred to as the Yugoslav Constitution), 1963, Articles 81, 82, 83, 92.
24. "Kardelj's Speech in the Federal Assembly," *loc. cit.*
25. The Yugoslav Constitution, Article 92, section 7.
26. *Ibid.,* Article 81, section 3; Article 82, sections 3, 4, 5; Article 83, sections 2, 3.
27. *Ibid.,* Article 220. Our italics.
28. "New generations are becoming more and more engaged in active political life and are taking over their share of responsibility," from "Kardelj's Speech in the Federal Assembly," *loc. cit.*
29. "Elections of Delegates and Representatives," *Politika,* April 23, 1967.
30. "The Elective System under the Conditions of Self-Management," *Borba,* October 8, 1966.
31. "Kardelj's Speech in the Federal Assembly," *loc. cit.*
32. *Ibid.*
33. *Ibid.*
34. *Ibid.*
35. See the speech of Milutin Baltic at the meeting of the Central Committee, *Politika,* July 3, 1966.
36. *New York Times,* March 30, 1966.
37. The Yugoslav Constitution, Chap. IX, Articles 164, 225.
38. *Ibid.,* Basic Principles, Articles 143, 144, 164.
39. "Kardelj's Speech in the Federal Assembly," *loc. cit.*
40. *Ibid.*
41. *Ibid.*
42. The Yugoslav Constitution, Article 224.
43. *Borba,* August 28, 1966.
44. *Borba,* July 29, 1962.
45. The Yugoslav Constitution, Article 178.
46. "First Meeting of the Council of the Federation," *Borba,* July 2, 1967.
47. The Yugoslav Constitution, Article 176, section 4.
48. *Ibid.,* Article 224, where specific provision is made for ". . . the members of the Council of the Federation to be elected by the Federal Chamber [all six houses in common session] upon the proposal of the President of the Republic, from among the federal officials, officials of the republics, and officials of the socio-political and other organizations."
49. *Ibid.,* Article 170.
50. See Dr. Eugen Pushic, "Recent Developments in Yugoslav Local Governments," pp. 3, 8.
51. *Ibid.*
52. This table was compiled from data published by the Yugoslav Central Statistical Institute in *Politika,* September 20, 1965; also, Milos Macura, "Basic Statistics on Yugoslav Communities," *International Social Science Journal,* XII, 1961, 3. *Jugoslovenski Statistichki Godishnyak,* 1966.
53. *Borba,* February 1 and March 13, 1966.
54. Compiled from data in *Borba,* February 2 and March 13, 1966.
55. Tito, in his speech after establishing the Presidium, October 4, 1966.
56. Miyalko Todorovic, after the establishment of the Presidium, October 4, 1966.

Notes to Chapter 7

1. Milentiye Popovic, "The Current Social Meaning of Marx's Teaching about Production," *Socialism* (a publication of the Yugoslav Communist Party on theoretical and ideological matters), May, 1965. See also *Borba,* July 7–9 and 17–20, 1965.
2. M. Popovic, *loc. cit.*
3. *Borba,* October 9, 1966.
4. Miyalko Todorovic, speaking at the Seventh Plenum of the Central Committee, *Borba,* July 3, 1967.
5. *Borba,* March 13, 1966.
6. "It is not infrequent that the rights of the working collectives, working units [enterprises], and workers themselves are reduced, as a matter of fact, to the right to divide personal incomes [wages] within the limits fixed from above. . . . *This represents, in reality, the expropriation of the working collectives and the direct producers* [workers]," Kardelj, in *Borba,* March 13, 1966. Our italics.
7. Speaking at the seminar on the Party reorganization, June 7, 1967, in *Borba,* June 8, 1967.
8. *Ibid.*
9. *Ibid.*
10. *Ibid.*
11. *Ibid.*
12. "Who is to Decide the Profit?" *Borba,* June 13, 1967.
13. M. Popovic, *loc. cit.*
14. *Borba,* March 13, 1966. Our italics.
15. *Borba,* March 20, 1967.
16. *Borba,* June 11, 1965.
17. In 1964, 0.84 passengers per million kilometers of travel were killed in West Germany; 0.77 in France; 1.05 in Italy; but in Yugoslavia the rate was 5.24. Tito evaluated the railway situation in this manner: "Our railways are excessively exploited. Their rails, carriages, all is overobsolete. Solutions were delayed until our people were killed in disasters." *Borba,* February 26, 1966.
18. Speaking at the tenth Belgrade Party Conference, in *Borba,* April 17, 1967.
19. "Director's Chair Increasingly Unwanted," editorial in *Borba,* April 6, 1967; "Director—The Most Authoritative Person in an Enterprise," *Borba,* April 11, 1967; "As a Matter of Fact—It is Desertion," *Borba,* April 12, 1967; "Disappointed Managers," *Borba,* August 6, 1967; "Why Four Managers Resigned," *Borba,* August 4, 1967.
20. "The Analysis of a Resignation," *Borba,* March 29, 1967.

Notes to Chapter 8

1. Djilas, *The New Class,* p. 122.
2. *Indeks,* No. 7, 1967.
3. *Ibid.*
4. July 13, 1965.
5. In *Borba,* March 13, 1966.

6. Speech at Morska Sobota, *Borba,* September 5, 1966.

7. *Borba,* June 11, 1965.

8. The Yugoslav press cites many examples of the confused investment situation: "Captive Machines," *Politika,* July 18, 1962; "Ruined Buildings [at Banovici, Bosnia]," *Borba,* January 23, 1964; "1.3 Billion Paid for Repairs, and Water Flows into Walls instead of Pipes [at Tuzla, Bosnia]," *Borba,* April 8, 1964; "Modern Heating Plant at Subotica Utilized Only 10%," *Borba,* September 5, 1964; "1,300 Restaurants and Hotels Abandoned in Serbia in Ten Years When Tourism Should Grow," *Borba,* October 10, 1964; "Purchase of New Tractors While No Repairs are Made on the Old," *Borba,* March 20, 1965; "Brick Plant Completed and Conserved [at Valyevo, Serbia]," *Borba,* September 8, 1964; "Beaver Farm Turns into a Rice Paddy [at Ludbreg, Croatia]," *Borba,* April 13, 1965; "Motel Construction on Buna Took Six Years, Operated for Six Days [near Mostar, Hercegovina]," *Borba,* July 9, 1965; etc.

9. According to "The Agreement about Prices," *Borba,* April 12, 1967, the 1965 ratio of shops to citizens was: France, 43; Italy, 57; . . . Yugoslavia, 419.

10. *Politika,* June 19, 1965.

11. *Politika,* June 10, 1965.

12. *Borba,* September 25, 1963; August 6, 1964.

13. *Indeks, loc. cit.*

14. *Ibid.*

15. *Borba,* May 30, 1965.

16. *Borba,* February 25, 1965.

17. *Politika,* August 20, 1962.

18. *Borba,* May 20 and 22, 1965.

19. *Borba,* February 7, 1965.

20. Based on official data in *Borba,* December 18, 1965. It is interesting to note that Tito stated the national per capita income to be $500.00, according to *Borba,* May 18, 1967.

21. Based on data in *Politika,* June 14, 1965.

22. *Borba,* May 6 and 20, 1965.

23. *Borba,* May 20 and June 23, 1965.

24. "It seems that wages are not influenced by losses. In those businesses recording a loss last year [1964], wages were increased 33 per cent in total volume and 26 per cent for each employee," *Borba,* June 23, 1965.

25. *Borba,* January 12, 1965.

26. May 30, 1965.

27. *Borba,* May 25, 1965.

28. *Borba,* June 8, 1965; Gligorov, speaking in Parliament, *Borba,* June 11, 1965; Todorovic, in *Borba,* June 18, 1965.

Notes to Chapter 9

1. Miyalko Todorovic: "It is obvious that we are now in such a situation that neither do we have a general common reserve sufficient for the economy, nor does the economy itself create the needed reserves." *Borba,* March 31, 1966.

2. All data according to *Yugoslavenski Pregled* (Survey), October, 1966, 1. 97.

3. Todorovic, *loc. cit.*

4. "As a Matter of Fact—It is Desertion," *Borba,* April 12, 1967.

5. Speaking at Prishtina, *Borba,* March 27, 1967.
6. "Report in Parliament on the Implementation of the Economic Reform," *Borba,* July 11, 1967.
7. Speaking at the Plenum of the Central Committee, *Borba,* March 13 and February 26, 1966.
8. "Increasing Number of Application for Price Raises," *Borba,* March 27, 1967. In February, 1967, requests for price increases grew by 25 per cent.
9. "Freedom as an Exception," September 24, 1966.
10. *Borba,* April 3 and 8, 1966; March 31, 1967; Boris Kraigher, *New York Times,* September 28, 1966.
11. Kiro Gligorov, "There Are No Dilemmas in the Basic Aims of the Reform," *Borba,* March 31, 1967.
12. Mika Tripalo, speaking at the seminar on the Party reorganization, *Borba,* June 9, 1967.
13. *Borba,* September 14, 1966.
14. *Borba,* February 7, 1967.
15. *Borba,* April 3, 1966.
16. *Ibid.*
17. "Sale—the Only Solution for Stocks," *Borba,* April 18, 1967.
18. *Ibid.*
19. *Ibid.*
20. *Borba,* April 21, 1967.
21. *Borba,* April 9, 1967.
22. Marin Cetinic, in *Politika,* April 27, 1967.
23. *Borba,* June 21, 1967.
24. Ranko Maksic, "Overly Optimistic Evaluations of the Economic Situation," *Borba,* July 12, 1967.
25. Tripalo, *loc. cit.*
26. "Where is the Borderline Between Stabilization and Stagnation?" *Borba,* June 9, 1967.
27. *Borba,* July 11, 1967.
28. "Without True Parliamentary Dialogue," *Borba,* July 12, 1967.
29. *Borba,* October 15, 1967.
30. *Ibid.*
31. Yanez Stanovnik, in the Economic Council of Parliament, *Borba,* April 8, 1967.
32. *Borba,* March 20, 1967. Our italics.
33. Alexander Grlichkov, speaking in Parliament, *Borba,* April 8, 1967.
34. "Theses on Cooperation Between Foreign Enterprises and Ours," *Politika,* March 16, 1967.
35. *Borba,* June 18, 1967.
36. "How to Attract Foreign Capital," *Borba,* June 7, 1967.
37. Todorovic, speaking at the Seventh Plenum of the Central Committee, *Borba,* July 3, 1967. Our italics.
38. "Technique and Security," editorial in *Borba,* June 5, 1967.
39. Tito: "When we speak of social and economic reform, the social and political aspect is always vital," *Borba,* February 26, 1966. Eduard Kardelj: "Our present orientation is not to change the sociopolitical system but to achieve its further development," *Borba,* March 13, 1966.
40. *Borba,* July 3, 1967. Our italics.
41. *Borba,* February 26, 1966.

42. Kardelj, in *Borba,* March 13, 1966.
43. *Borba,* March 13, 1966.
44. *Politika,* June 17, 1967.
45. "Agreement about Prices," April 12, 1967.
46. The Yugoslav Constitution, Article 36.
47. See *Borba,* November 12, 1965; and *New York Times,* September 28, 1966.
48. *Borba,* April 13, 1967.
49. *Borba,* January 24, 1966.
50. "To Which Countries Without a Visa," *Borba,* April 5, 1967.
51. *Borba,* August 11, 1967.
52. From the "Report of the Yugoslav State Secretariat for Labor," *Borba,* November 7, 1965.
53. "Journey into Uncertainty," *Politika,* November 7, 1965.
54. Speech at Morska Sobota, *Politika,* September 3, 1966. Our italics.
55. *Borba,* March 13, 1966.
56. *Borba,* February 26, 1966.
57. Speaking at Prishtina, *Borba,* March 28, 1967.
58. Editorial in *Borba,* April 10, 1967.
59. *Borba,* September 8, 1965.
60. Veljko Vlakhovic; "The remnants of bourgeois consciousness exist along with pressure from reactionary forces abroad," *Politika,* March 12, 1966.
61. *Borba,* February 26, 1966.
62. In 1964 the average gross product per Yugoslav worker was 1,291,000 dinars; for Slovenia alone the figure was 1,666,000 dinars. See Stane Kavcic, in *Borba,* April 1, 1966.
63. *Borba,* March 12, 1966. Our italics.
64. Krste Crvenkovski, in *Borba,* March 21, 1966.
65. Kavcic, *loc. cit.*
66. *Ibid.*
67. Crvenkovski, *loc. cit.*
68. *Borba,* March 25, 1966.
69. Theses for the Central Committee Plenum, *Borba,* February 25, 1966.
70. Kardelj, *loc. cit.*
71. *Borba,* September 16, 1966.
72. *New York Times,* January 10, 1966. This newspaper also reported that comments in the "Yugoslav press indicate that adversaries of the economic reform are to be found more in the local and district branches of the Party than in the senior ranks."
73. Crvenkovski, in *Borba,* March 25, 1966.
74. *Borba,* March 13, 1966.
75. *Ibid.*
76. "Bunkers and Dinars," editorial in *Borba,* June 12, 1967.
77. *Borba,* February 26, 1966; also, Kardelj, *loc. cit.*
78. *Borba,* April 5 and July 29, 1966.
79. Velizar Shkerovic, at the Plenum of the Central Committee of Montenegro, *Borba,* September 22, 1966.
80. *Borba,* February 26, 1966; also Kardelj, *loc. cit.*
81. *Borba,* March 13, 1966.
82. *Borba,* February 26, 1966.
83. The Plenary Meeting of Macedonia, *Borba,* March 24 and August 4, 1967.
84. "Work Stoppages," *Borba,* August 13, 1967.

85. "And at the End Collective Resignations," *Borba,* June 4, 1967; "The Resignation—A Smoke Screen," editorial in *Borba,* June 24, 1967.

86. "Proposed Disbandment of the Party Organization at the School of Philosophy of Sarajevo University," *Borba,* May 19, 1967.

87. "Enforcing Discipline," editorial in *Borba,* May 29, 1967.

Notes to Chapter 10

1. One typical Yugoslav remark: "If you think that you can feed your children only by your conscience, tell me how." *Politika,* September 9, 1966.

2. "New Issues Need New Methods of Social Communist Action," *Borba,* March 25, 1967.

3. *Politika,* September 5, 1966.

4. Danko Grlic, at the Korchula 1967 Symposium of Philosophers. "Lapsus Philosophiae," *Borba,* September 3, 1967.

5. "Derided Scoffers," *Borba,* April 9, 1967.

6. *Borba,* March 27, 1967.

7. "In a society in which the relationships of production are of a class nature, man's mind is determined by his class position." Milentiye Popovic, in *Borba,* July 20, 1965.

8. "Metamorphosis of Humanity," *Borba,* April 9, 1967.

9. Speaking at the plenary session of the Central Committee, *Politika,* March 14, 1966.

10. Zoran Glushchevic, in *Politika,* September 19, 1965.

11. *The New Leader,* August 30, 1966.

12. *Borba,* October 6, 1966. Our italics.

13. The case was opened by the State Public Prosecutor in the Belgrade District Court on the basis of Articles 52, 60, and 61 of the *Law on Press and Other Types of Information, Politika,* March 18, 1966.

14. *Politika,* April 16, 1966.

15. *Borba,* October 6, 1967.

16. According to the census of 1931, 86.1 per cent of the people of Yugoslavia were occupied with or drew their livelihood from agriculture; all others, including workers, the intelligentsia, and the urban population, comprised the other 13.9 per cent. In 1960 the ratio was 50:50, according to Radmila Stoyanovich, *Yugoslav Economists on the Problems of a Socialist Economy,* pp. 112–15.

17. Miyalko Todorovic, in *Borba,* October 5, 1966.

18. "Macedonian Plenary Meeting of the Central Committee," *Borba,* March 24, 1967.

19. "Conversations with Crvenkovski," *Borba,* May 14, 1967.

20. *Borba,* March 13, 1966. Our italics.

21. *Borba,* June 3, 1967.

22. "Apropos of the Golden Coach," *Borba,* June 14, 1967.

23. "Invitation and Response," *Borba* editorial, July 7, 1967.

24. "About the Golden Coach," *Borba,* June 14, 1967.

25. Lenin, *Collected Works,* IV, p. 392.

26. Speech to the workers of "Zheleznik" factory near Belgrade, *Borba,* December 30, 1962.

27. Veljko Korac, a professor at Belgrade University, in *Borba,* September 27, 1967.

28. *Ibid.*

29. *Borba,* February 4, 1967.

30. *Borba,* September 27, 1967.

31. "Retirement á la Yugoslav," *Borba,* April 20, 1967. One year after the beginning of the reform the number of retired persons in Yugoslavia reached 907,808 (of a population of a little less than 20 million). Among these were 333,293 retired because of injuries incurred while working, the highest percentage in Europe. Excluding those retired from work injuries, half the remainder did not actually work full time, as is required to qualify for retirement benefits. The normal rate of retirement increased by 241 per cent during the economic reform of 1965–66. During the first nine months of 1966, deficits of social insurance ran on the average of one-half billion dinars daily. All data from *Borba,* October 3 and 9, 1966. See also "Thousand Retirement Decisions in Montenegro Annulled," *Borba,* August 9, 1967.

32. *Borba,* September 19, 1966.

33. *Ibid.;* see also *New York Times,* September 29, 1966.

34. *Borba,* October 6, 1966. Our italics.

35. *Ibid.*

Bibliography

Books

Adamic, Louis. *The Eagle and the Roots.* Garden City, N.Y.: Doubleday, 1952.

Armstrong, H. F. *Tito and Goliath.* New York: Macmillan, 1951.

Clissold, S. (ed.). *A Short History of Yugoslavia.* Cambridge, England, Cambridge University Press, 1966.

Constitution of the Socialist Federal Republic of Yugoslavia. Belgrade: Federal Secretariat for Information, 1963.

Cornforth, Maurice C. *Materialism and the Dialectical Method.* New York: International Publishers, 1960.

Czeslaw, Milos. *The Captive Mind.* New York: Knopf, 1953.

Djilas, Milovan. *The New Class.* New York: Praeger, 1957.

———. *Conversations With Stalin,* New York: Harcourt, Brace & World, 1962.

Dragnich, Alex N. *Tito's Promised Land.* New Brunswick, N.J.: Rutgers University Press, 1954.

Drashkovich, M. D. (ed.). *Marxism in the Modern World.* Stanford, Calif.: Stanford University Press, 1965.

———. *Marxist Ideology in the Contemporary World: Its Appeals and Paradoxes.* New York: Praeger, *c.* 1966.

Enciklopedija Jugoslavije. Zagreb: Jugoslavenski Leksikografski Zavod, 1965, Vol. VI.

Fisher, Jack C. *Yugoslavia—A Multinational State.* San Francisco, Calif.: Chandler Publishing Co., 1966.

Halpern, Barbara. *Yugoslavia.* Garden City, N.Y.: Doubleday, 1961.

Heppel, Muriel, and Singleton, Frank B. *Yugoslavia.* New York: Praeger, 1965.

Hoffman, George W. *Balkans in Transition.* Princeton, N.J.: Van Nostrand.

Hoffman, George W., and Neal, Fred W. *Yugoslavia and the New Communism.* New York: Twentieth Century Fund, 1962.

Kolaja, J. T. *Workers' Councils: The Yugoslav Experience.* New York: Praeger, *c.* 1965.

Korbel, Josef. *Tito's Communism.* Denver, Colo.: University of Denver Press, 1951.

Lenin, Vladimir Ilyich. *Collected Works.* New York: International Publishers, 1960–67, 38 Vols.

Macesich, G. *Yugoslavia: The Theory and Practice of Development Planning.* Charlottesville, Va.: University of Virginia Press, 1964.

McVicker, Charles P. *Titoism: Pattern for International Communism.* New York: St. Martin's Press, 1957.

Marx, Karl. *Capital: An Analysis of Capitalist Production.* New York: Modern Library, 1906.

———. *The Communist Manifesto.* Chicago: H. Repnery, 1960.

———. *Criticism of the Gotha Program.* New York: International Publishers, 1938.

———. *Critique of Political Economy.* Chicago: H. Kerr & Co., *c.* 1904.

———. *Theories of Surplus Value.* New York: International Publishers, 1952.

Neal, Fred W. *Titoism in Action: Reforms in Yugoslavia, 1948–1954.* Berkeley: University of California Press, 1958.

Normand, Suzanne, and Acker, Jack. *Yugoslavia.* Fair Lawn, N.J.: Essential Books, 1956.

O'Brien, Frank. *Crisis in World Communism: Marxism in Search of Efficiency.* New York: The Free Press, 1965.

Organization for Economic Cooperation and Development (OECD). *Report on Yugoslavia.* Paris, 1964.

Plamenatz, John. *German Marxism and Russian Communism.* New York: Harper Torchbooks, 1965.

Plekhanov, G. N. *Sotsializm i politicheskaya borba* [Socialism and political struggle]. Moscow: Ogizdat, 1948.

Rubenstein, A. Z. (ed.). *Communist Political Systems.* Englewood Cliffs, N.J.: Prentice-Hall, 1966.

Savez Komunista Jugoslavije. *Yugoslavia's Way: The Program of the League of the Communists.* New York: All Nations Press, 1958.

Stalin, Joseph. *Economic Problems of Socialism in the USSR.* New York: International Publishers, *c.* 1952.

Stoyanovic, Radmila (ed.). *Yugoslav Economists on the Problems of a Socialist Economy.* New York: International Arts and Sciences Press, *c.* 1964.

Waterston, Albert. *Planning in Yugoslavia.* Baltimore, Md.: Johns Hopkins University Press, 1962.

Newspapers and Periodicals

Borba. Organ of the Socialist Alliance of the Working People of Yugoslavia; formerly the official paper of the Yugoslav Communist Party.

Campbell, John C. "Yugoslavia: Crisis and Choice," *Foreign Affairs,* January, 1963.

Indeks. Magazine of the Yugoslav Federal Statistical Institute, Belgrade.

Jugoslavenski Pregled. Monthly survey published in Belgrade.

Komunist. Weekly newspaper of the Communist Party of Yugoslavia, Belgrade.

Macura, Milos. "Basic Statistics on Yugoslav Communities," *International Social Science Journal,* XII, 1961.

Mihaylov, Mihaylo. "Why We are Silent," *The New Leader,* August, 30, 1965.

Narodna Armiya. Belgrade newspaper.

Politika. Belgrade daily newspaper with highest circulation in Yugoslavia.

Pushic, Eugen. "Recent Developments in Yugoslav Local Governments," New York: Institute of Public Administration, February, 1965.

Yugoslav Survey. Published in English by the Yugoslav Publishing House.

Index

Activists, 25, 38, 56, 190
Adamic, Louis, 114
Admission, to new class, 20, 21, 23, 24, 28
Adriatic Sea, 53, 186
Africa, 46, 98, 100
Agrarian movement, 197, reform 2
Agriculture, 161, 166, 172, 174
Aid: economic, 100, 187; mutual, 108
Albania, 134, 195
Algeria, 44, 94
Alibi, 142, 193
Alienation, 57, 58, 148, 152, 166, 207–209
Alignment, 96, 193
Amortization, 144, 171, 176
Anti-American, 109; -bureaucratism, 63; -colonialism 46, 92, 95, 106; -communism, 46, 102, 125, 185–186, 193, 196–197; -dictatorial, 198; -socialist, 119; -Semitic 98–99
Arab, 26, 96, 98–99, 105
Armed forces, 5, 7, 16, 17, 28, 48, 71, 122, 124, 132, 149, 204–205
Asia, 46, 100
Austro-Hungary, 53
Autonomy, 78, 85–86, 114, 132
Awards, 23, 30

Bakaric, Vladimir, 18, 46, 72, 80, 188, 215
Balance of payments, 161, 171
Bandoeng, 97
Bank, 83, 162, 165, 167, 173–174, 178
Bar, Montenegro, 186
Bari, Italy, 91
Belgrade, 5, 16–17, 22, 34, 39, 44, 48, 50, 52, 79, 89, 97, 101, 107, 112, 121, 128, 184, 186, 188, 200, 205, 215–217
Ben Bella, 101
Benefits, 32, 39, 148, 163, 198, 204
Bichanic, Rudolf, 71
H.M.S. *Blackmoor,* 91
Bolsheviks: 1, 94; functionaries, 15
Bosnia and Hercegovina, 26, 31, 71, 91, 121, 128, 131, 145, 165, 215
Bourgeois, 5, 6, 16, 18, 20, 55–56, 87, 111, 119, 125, 139, 186, 197
Brainwashing, 201
Brezhnev, Leonid, 124
Brioni Islands, 11, 39, 53, 38, 89
Broz, Joseph. See Tito
Budget, 38, 69, 140, 161, 170, 173
Bulatovic, Vlado "Vib," 87
Bureaucracy, 6, 8, 18, 32–33, 62, 64, 72–74, 79, 80, 85, 91, 112, 122, 124, 130, 133–134, 139, 142, 159, 166, 181, 185, 188, 196, 207, 210–211
Business, socialist, 28, 75, 83, 92, 141, 149–150, 155, 163, 166, 171, 175–176

Camouflage, 16, 18, 33–34, 38, 71, 108, 132
Candidates, 14, 83, 118–120
Capital: 2, 8, 39, 40, 55, 88, 135–142, 145–146, 154–157, 161, 171, 176, 180, 210; foreign, 178–180; formation, 146, 179
Capitalist system, 96, 100, 104, 141–142, 159, 186, 197, 207
Capitalists, 2, 8, 20, 98, 136–138, 146–147, 179
Card files (of candidates), 28, 118–119, 120, 126
Censorship, 200, 205
Central Committee, 11, 28, 32, 52, 66–

67, 72, 76, 79, 81, 89, 128, 132–133, 180–182, 187, 189, 190, 203, 214
Centralization, 41, 62, 106, 114, 188, 196, 198, 211
Ceremonies, 25, 46–47, 49
Cetinic, Marin, 215
Chauffeurs, 19, 36, 39, 40, 51
Chinese, 45–46, 48, 58, 100, 104, 109, 110, 152, 193
Church, 20, 55
Classes: social, 6, 7, 13, 20, 87, 115, 202; struggle, 35, 136, 142, 146
Classless society, 7, 87, 115
Coexistence, 94, 96–97, 212
Collective rule, 58, 70–71, 133, 213
Colonialism: 94, 96, 100, 104, 193; neo, 96, 97
Comecon, 104, 106
Comintern, 102
Communications, social, 56–57, 59, 77, 82, 189, 199
Communism: 6, 9, 19, 61, 101, 107, 110, 194, 201; international, 90
Concentration of power, 23, 129–130, 132, 185, 192
Condensation of power, 23, 71, 74, 212
Conformity, 14–15, 42, 44, 54, 78
Conservativism, 16, 20, 45, 92, 116
Consociation, 108–109
Constitution, 11, 67, 114, 119, 121–122, 125–127, 169, 178, 183
Consumption, 136, 140, 143–144, 146, 149, 151, 156–158, 161–163, 166, 170, 202, 207
Corporate state, 115, 141
Corruption, 39, 40, 166
Costs of production, 85, 136–138, 140–141, 143–146, 150, 156–158, 160–161, 167, 169, 171, 176, 180, 207
Courts, 34, 126, 128, 132, 200
Credit, 98, 100, 162, 163, 165–166, 169, 172–173, 175–176
Crime, 15, 39, 44, 125–126, 194, 201
Crisis: economic, 71, 140, 152, 159, 160–161, 164, 167, 169, 173, 176, 211; political, 65, 73, 123, 157, 198, 201, 202, 205
Criticism, 42–44, 56, 76, 84–86, 92, 166, 173, 184, 188, 200, 209
Croatia, 18, 46, 69, 71–72, 80, 121, 128, 131, 150, 165, 173, 186–188, 195, 200, 215–217
Crvenkovski, Krste, 72, 79, 215
Cult, personality, 46–47, 70. See also Tito
Currency, 40, 162, 165, 167, 172, 208
Czechoslovakia, 46, 107–108, 195, 216

Dalmatia, 199, 215
Debts, 2, 154, 163, 175, 177
Decentralization, 62–63, 114, 130, 132, 177, 193, 211
Declaration, Croatian language, 72
Decorations, 23, 49
Defectors, 20, 23
Deficit, 147, 155, 159, 162, 165, 167, 169, 173, 177, 179, 180, 203, 207
Dehumanization, 20, 152, 194, 207, 208
Delegate, 77, 83, 117–118, 124, 126
Democracy: 5, 18, 78, 80, 83, 94–95, 141, 212; direct socialist, 64, 66, 73, 117, 124–125, 141, 150, 159, 183, 185, 192, 205, 211
Democratic centralism, 11, 77–79
Democratization, 59, 68, 79, 119, 132, 153, 192
Demoralization, 68, 195
Depreciation, 144, 158, 160, 161. See also Amortization
De-professionalization, 76–77, 123, 189
De-Stalinization, 104, 307
Devaluation, 159–160, 163, 170–171, 175, 183
Development, economic, 100, 136, 137, 140, 146, 151–154, 165, 202,
Dictatorship, Communist: 3, 12, 15, 41, 62–63, 65, 71, 94, 110, 125, 204; Party, 3, 5–8, 43, 65, 71, 73, 89; police, 69; Tito's, 65, 70, 103, 122, 208
Dinar, 40, 150, 159, 163, 170–171, 183
Diplomacy, 17, 29, 67, 92, 97, 184
Discipline, Party, 14, 17, 30, 42, 78, 81, 160, 189, 191
Dissatisfaction, 43, 192, 204, 206
Djilas, Milovan, 9–12, 15–18, 24, 41, 67–68, 72, 113, 134, 201, 209, 213, 214
Dogmatism, 16, 64, 72, 92

Dugonyic, Rato, 26, 215
Dwelling communities, 51, 58

Education, 24–26, 44, 57, 73, 127, 129, 138, 144, 196, 199, 201, 208
Election: 83, 113, 118–121, 126, 147; commissions, 120–121, 125,–126, 128
Embourgeoisement, 16
Employment, 36, 42, 100, 140, 143–145, 148, 154–157, 160, 169, 171–172, 184, 200, 202
Engels, Friedrich, 7, 12, 27. See also Marx, Karl
Entrepreneur, 55, 137–138, 147
Ethics, 40, 42, 54, 57, 59, 112, 194–195, 198, 205
Europe: 93, 100, 201; East, 30, 46, 102, 197; West, 46, 183, 184
Exchange rates, 160, 167, 170–171, 176
Executive branch, 112, 123, 125
Expansion, economic, 143, 201
Exploitation, 19, 27, 30, 73, 88, 92, 146–147, 156, 181, 185, 187, 195, 198, 202, 213
Expropriation, 40, 87–88, 140, 143, 178, 180

Factions, 61, 63, 66–67, 70–71, 123, 190, 213
Family, 23–24, 57, 183, 200
Fascism, 1, 193
Federal Executive Council: 49, 121, 125, 128; structure, 2, 17, 28–29, 335, 48–49, 52, 69, 71–72, 116, 120–121, 127–123, 135, 140, 149, 170, 173, 186, 197–198
Federation, Council of, 127, 215–217
Foreign exchange: 69, 179; office, 67, 81, 92–93, 98–99, 205; policy, 66–67, 72, 91; trade, 69, 161–162, 177; capital, see Capital
France, 44, 94
Free speech, 43
Freedom, 44, 50, 88, 114, 153, 194–197, 206, 211, 212
Functions, 15, 21–22, 30, 33, 37, 40, 43, 58, 81, 121, 123–124, 129–130, 189, 205, 207, 211

de Gaulle, Charles, 44
Germany, 1, 20, 36, 46, 68, 91, 104, 108, 185
Gifts (donations), 37, 38
Gligorov, Kiro, 145, 155, 158, 167, 177, 215
Great Britain, 91
Grlichkov, Alexandar, 216

Haile Selassie, 49, 50
Hercegovina. See Bosnia
Housing, 2, 35, 51, 204, 206
Hungary, 104, 108, 134, 195

Ideology, 14–15, 19, 27, 42, 45, 61, 63, 65–66, 75, 82, 89, 124, 178, 182, 186, 190–191, 194–197
Imperialist, 92, 94, 99, 186
Incentives, 140, 177, 185, 187
Individuals, 42, 56–58, 86, 153, 186, 194, 210–214
Industrialization, 139, 153, 181, 186, 187, 193, 202
Inflation, 2, 23, 31, 100, 144, 155, 158–65, 171–172, 174, 176–177, 204
Insurance: 208–209; social, 32, 37, 144, 160, 184
Intellectuals, 25, 55–56, 184, 197–199, 200–202, 206–208, 213
International relations, 9, 13, 95–97, 102, 199, 212
Internationalism, proletarian, 102, 107
Israel, 96, 98, 99, 105
Italy, 21, 68, 91, 105, 108

Judiciary, 43, 112–113, 125, 128, 132, 212

Kadrovik, 28
Kaleb, Vyekoslav, 216
Kardelj, Eduard, 11, 13, 27, 58, 63, 66, 70, 72, 78, 96, 114, 121, 124, 127, 132, 135, 139–140, 143, 157, 167, 195, 216
Karlovy Vary, 107
Kavcic, Stane, 216
Khrushchev, Nikita, 45, 50, 98, 124, 207
Kingdom of Yugoslavia, 131
Kraigher, Boris, 216

Kremlin, 105
Krleza, Miroslav, 216

Laws, economic: 135, 137, 150, 152, 181–182, 201; political, 14, 25, 32–33, 75, 111–113, 122–127, 159, 167, 170
Lazarevic, Sava, 201
Legislature, 66, 126, 126–127, 132
Lenin, V. I., 4, 8, 27, 42, 46, 62, 91, 94, 149, 182, 197, 206–207, 211
Living standards, 136, 153, 156, 159, 164, 172, 177, 195, 202
Local authorities: 17, 28–29, 48, 74, 84–86, 89, 115, 120–121, 129, 130, 132, 140, 170, 173, 185, 188–189; leaders, 83, 87
Losses, 140, 142, 145–146, 150, 154, 156, 163–165, 167, 175, 181, 189
Lukic, Radomir, 24
Lukic, Voykan, 67
Lysenko, T. D., 199
Lyublyana, 34, 53

Macedonia, 69, 71–72, 121, 128, 131, 165, 186–188, 215–216
Manipulation of power, 14–15, 117, 125, 198, 207, 210
Mao Tse Tung, 69, 108, 139, 197, 211
Marx, Karl, 7, 8, 12, 13, 15, 18, 27, 115, 128, 135, 137, 139, 141–146, 165–166, 197, 207, 208, 211
Marxist: ideals, 7, 8, 89, 202; ideology, 15, 19, 46, 69, 211; jargon, 96; logic, 19, 41, 70, 79, 147, 159, 204, 208
Marxist-Leninist objectives, 66, 89, 96, 107
May Day, 48
Medals, 22–23, 31, 34, 69
Microphones, 67, 68
Middle East, 96, 98
Mihaylov, Mihaylo, 56, 72, 199, 200
Minorities, national, 72, 195
Mixed societies, 179
Modernization, 158, 161, 170, 179–180, 187
Molotov, 67
Monolithic structure, 15, 42, 63, 101, 181, 210, 213
Monopoly, 62–63, 71, 89, 91, 118, 124, 128, 153, 171, 178, 180–181, 194, 197
Montenegro, 36, 71, 75, 121, 128, 131, 145, 165, 186, 187–188, 190, 217
Moscow, 46, 105
Moskovlyevich, Milos, 200
Multiparty system, 141

Nasser, 98, 101
National Assembly, 26, 92, 117, 122, 125–127, 176
Nationalities, 1, 72, 86, 120, 127, 164, 181, 186–187, 189, 191, 195
Nationalization, 2, 71, 73. See also Expropriation
NATO, 96
NEP, 182, 207
Neretva battle, 68, 83
Neutralism, 94, 96–98, 101, 194
Nikezic, Marko, 216
Nonalignment, 96–100, 193

Opposition, 20, 54, 56, 57, 83, 89, 111, 122, 176, 185, 186, 191, 198, 204–205, 212–213
Ownership, 36, 116, 138, 139, 210

Parliament, 32, 36, 47–48, 113, 117, 119, 125–128, 177, 181
Partisans, 19, 21, 22, 26, 31, 46, 49, 68
Party, Communist: apparatus, 5, 7, 10, 14, 16, 28, 61, 63–64, 73–74, 77–78, 80–87, 123, 127, 130, 204, 211, 214; members, 5, 10, 19
Peasants, 2, 15, 19, 54–55, 83, 116, 155, 161, 174, 183, 186, 202, 204, 213
Personalization of power, 69, 113, 213
Personnel, 17, 27, 29, 64, 67, 113, 125, 127
Peshic, Branko, 217
Physicians, 37, 43, 57, 185
Planning, economic, 100, 111, 140, 143, 154, 176–77, 182, 207
Plekhanov, G. V., viii
Poland, 26, 46, 104, 109, 215
Police rule, 16, 28, 30, 37, 64, 68–69, 77, 129, 149, 204, 209
Polycentrism, 102, 104–107, 109
Popa, Vasco, 201

Popovic, Milentiye, 27, 80, 135–137, 139, 141, 176
Population, 10, 62, 83, 129, 131, 140, 177, 185, 201, 203, 211
Postanovka, 63, 198
Power: political, 15, 17, 20, 23–24, 193, 210; seizure, 3, 21, 25, 82, 91
Pragmatism, 44, 54, 94, 105, 113, 182, 190, 213
Presidium, 127–128, 133–135, 214–217
Prices, 3, 136, 140, 145, 147, 153, 159, 160, 162, 165–172, 174–175, 182–183, 186, 203
Prisons, 45, 64, 200, 201
Privileges, 2–4, 16–18, 22–23, 30–39, 41, 52–54, 64–65, 74, 123, 194, 200, 205, 209
Profit, 136–147, 150–151, 156, 163, 165–166, 174
Proletariat: 8, 55, 72, 204; dictatorship, 110, 113, 193; internationalism 102, 107, 195
Prosecutors, public, 113, 125
Protocol, 29, 45, 48, 50, 52, 54
Pseudo-democracy, 125, 201
Purge, 62, 64–66, 69, 70, 75, 77, 85

Radosavlyevic, Dobrivoye "Bobby," 217
Railroads, 23, 38–39, 43, 144–145, 161–162
Rank, 13, 15, 21–22, 29, 34–37, 44, 48, 50, 53, 58, 82, 111, 118, 127
Rankovic, Alexandar, 11, 41, 61, 63, 66–69, 72, 84, 123–124, 132–134, 190–191, 209, 211, 213–214, 217
Recall, 126, 128
Red Army, 102
Religion, 1, 20, 54
Rents, 3, 170, 173
Reorganizations, 9, 14–15, 65, 74, 76–77, 79, 85, 91, 109, 114, 125, 169, 194
Reproduction, simple and extended, 136
Residuum principle, 169
Resignations, 191
Retirement, 25, 31, 144, 196, 204–206, 209
Revolution: Russian, 15, 89, 94, 102; world, 92, 94, 193, 195; Yugoslav, 9, 15, 19, 20, 23, 25, 62, 113, 190, 192–196, 206, 213
Right to work, 120, 189
Roman Catholicism, 1
Rotation, 26, 33, 74, 117–118, 121–126, 129, 214
Rumania, 5, 109
Russia, 5, 15, 20, 46, 48, 49, 50, 70, 83, 100, 154–155, 200

Salaries, 17, 32, 160, 163–164, 170, 206
Schools, 25–27, 31, 56, 201
Secret police, 7, 17, 28, 30, 66–67, 69, 75, 188, 190
Security, 17, 31, 51, 53, 69, 71, 77, 162, 190, 204–205
Self-management, 33, 58, 61–66, 73–78, 80–86, 91–92, 101, 114, 116–118, 122, 126, 130–136, 140–148, 155, 169, 178–180, 194, 196, 198, 205, 209, 211
Serbia, 38, 48, 52, 69, 71–72, 74, 89, 121, 128, 130–131, 145, 165, 180, 187–189, 195, 200, 208, 216–217
Shegedin, Petar, 217
Shkoric, Edhem, 31–32
Shops, special, 16, 33–34, 37, 49, 52, 56
Slovenia, 69, 71–72, 120–121, 128, 131, 144, 165, 186–188, 195–196, 216–217
Socialist Alliance, 20–21, 47, 56, 58, 62, 119–121, 202
Solzhenitsyn, A., 200
Soviet Union, 4, 5, 15, 41, 45–46, 89, 90–91, 99, 102–104, 107–108, 110, 124, 154, 159, 182, 193, 199, 200
Sremska Mitrovica, 67
Stability, political, 91, 122, 210
Stalin, J., 4–6, 10–11, 21, 24, 41, 46, 49, 50, 64, 67, 69, 99, 101–104, 108, 152, 154, 197, 211
Stanovnik, Yanez, 217
Statism, 65, 139, 142
Stefanovic, Svetislav "Ceca," 68
Stockpiling, 165, 174–175
Strikes, 191, 203
Subsidies, 144, 160–161, 167, 171, 204

Taxes, 140, 160–163, 166, 170, 179
Technology, 27, 136, 143, 151–152, 166, 180
Telephones, 18, 38
Television, 38, 58, 199

Temelkovski, Borko, 187
Thaw of prices, 173, 175
Theory: Communist, 19; economic, 135
"Third" bloc: 97; International, 102; "Revolution," 197, 202
Tito, 4–15, 18, 20–30, 41, 50, 55, 61–68, 70–71, 79, 83, 86, 98–99, 103, 108, 122–123, 128, 132, 134, 147, 181, 193, 196–197, 206, 209, 211, 213–215
Todorovic, Miyalko, 79, 135, 167, 181, 188, 189, 209, 217
Togliatti, Palmiro, 105–106
"Topniks." See *Vrkhushka*
Traitor, 126, 185, 195, 199
Transportation, 161, 162, 170
Traykovic, Prvoslav, 201
Tripalo, Miko, 217
Tsarism, 197
Tuzla, 31

U.D.B.A. See Secret police
Unemployment, 155, 181, 183, 207, 209
Union of Yugoslav Communists. See Communist Party of Yugaslavia, i.e., Party, Communist
United Arab Republic, 98, 215, 216
UNRRA, 3
United Nations, 3, 93, 99
United Socialist Party, 103
United States of America, 3, 22, 36, 45, 48, 96, 98, 114, 154–155, 210, 216
Unity: new-class, 13–15, 42, 65, 70, 191, 195; Party, 14, 53, 61, 63, 70, 79, 81, 107, 188, 190
Uravnilovka, 164
U.S.S.R. See Soviet Union

Vested interests (rights), 29, 144, 162, 175
Vietnam, 105, 108
Vis, Island of, 91
Vlakhovic, Veljko, 96, 132, 135, 188, 190, 217
Voting, 14, 55, 118, 119, 120, 126
Voyvodina, 128
Vranye, 52
Vrkhushka, 70, 83–89, 188–189
Vukmanovic, Svetozar "Tempo," 132, 217

Wages, 17, 88, 136, 140, 155, 158–159, 160, 163–166, 169, 170, 174–175, 179, 181, 183–184, 198
Warsaw Pact, 96
Washington, D.C., 46
Waste, economic, 145–146, 150–154, 169, 176, 189, 207
Weber, Norbert, 187
White Palace, 29, 49
Wholesale prices, 165
Workers, 42, 54, 73, 80, 83, 116, 136, 139, 140, 142, 160, 164–166, 170–171, 175–177, 184, 190, 198, 202, 208
Workers': councils, 83, 86, 122, 165; Party, 103, 202–203, 207, 209
World war, 53–54, 98, 101–102, 197
Working class, 88, 181, 188, 204, 206, 213

Yeremic, Zhivoyin, 201
Yovanovic, Arsa, 5

Zadar University, 56, 199
Zagreb, 18, 34, 53, 119, 161, 186, 207, 215
Zekovic, Veljko, 28
Zenica, 175
Zvonarevic, M., 119